T0302315

Speed-Based Target Profit

Speed-Based Target Profit

Planning and Developing Synchronous Profitable Operations

Alin Posteucă

Routledge
Taylor & Francis Group

A PRODUCTIVITY PRESS BOOK

First published 2021
by Routledge
600 Broken Sound Parkway #300, Boca Raton FL, 33487

and by Routledge
2 Park Square, Milton Park, Abingdon, Oxon, OX14 4RN

Routledge is an imprint of the Taylor & Francis Group, an informa business

© 2021 Taylor & Francis

ISBN: 978-0-367-45779-2 (hbk)
ISBN: 978-1-003-02527-6 (ebk)

Typeset in Minion
by KnowledgeWorks Global Ltd.

To Emiliana, Andreea and Ștefan.

Contents

Figures

Tables

List of Abbreviations

5G	Gemba, Gembutsu, Genjitsu, Genri, Gensoku
A	Allowable Cost of Losses and Waste
ABC	Activity-Based Costing
AMCIB	Annual Manufacturing Cash Improvement Budget
AMIB	Annual Manufacturing Improvement Budget
B	Target for Net Standard Operating Time in Bottleneck Capacity Operation
BC	Basic/Initial Cost
BCM	Bottleneck Capacity Module
BM	Bottleneck Module
BO	Bottleneck Operation
BOM	Bill Of Materials
BPM	Bottleneck Profit Module
C	The Target Basic Manufacturing Cost (per period)
CapEx	Capital Expenditures
CCLW	Critical Costs of Losses and Waste
CLW	Costs of Losses and Waste
CP	Contribution (effectiveness) Productivity
DLT	Delivery Lead Time
DMAIC	Define, Measure, Analyze, Improve, and Control
E	The Target SG&A Expenses (per period)
EBIT	Earnings Before Interest and Taxes
EOQ	Economic Order Quantity
FIFO	First In, First Out
FSI	Fixed Safety Inventory
IC	Ideal Costs
L/T	Lead Time
LCC	Life Cycle Costs
MB	Management Branding
MCPD	Manufacturing Cost Policy Deployment
MDC	Methods Design Concept
MLT	Manufacturing Lead Time
MRP	Material Requirements Planning

MTBF	Mean Time Between Failures
MTM	Methods-Time Measurement
MTTR	Mean Time to Repair
NWH	Number of Working Hours
OEE	Overall Equipment Effectiveness
OLE	Overall Line Effectiveness
OMI	Overall Management Indicators
OPF	One-Piece Flow
OTIF	On Time In Full
P	The Target Sales Price (per period)
PDCA	Plan-Do-Check-Act
PF	Performance Forecast
PLF	Production Load Factor
PLT	Plant Lead Time
PLW	Physical Losses and Waste
PTT	Production Takt Time
QFD	Quality Function Deployment
RC	Running Costs
ROI	Return On Investment
RT	Reduction Target (for CLW) or KAIZENSHIRO
SLT	Supply Lead Time
SOP	Standard Operating Procedure
TMC	Total Manufacturing Cost
TP	Throughput (efficiency) Productivity
TPL	Total Production Loaded
TPLT	Total Plant Lead Time
TRLW	Time-Related Losses and Waste
V	The Target Volume of Quality Products (per period)
VSI	Variable Safety Inventory

Preface

Profitable production planning is and will remain an eternal challenge to ensure the prosperity and dignity of companies in a global market. Even though there are different approaches to achieving the target profitability through productivity, these approaches do not guarantee consistent planning, creation, and sustenance of synchronous profitable operations for annual and multiannual target profit.

Today's managers in companies around the world have studied and adopted the concept of synchronization to have the right things in the right place at the right time and in the right quantities, reducing waste and ensuring the level of flexibility, change and innovation needed. Simplifying processes, shortening information flows, extending the state of one-piece flow along the entire manufacturing flow, increasing flexibility by reducing the lot size values, and decreasing material transportation by determining and analyzing the movements of materials are the basic concerns of today's managers in their ongoing struggle to meet business expectations. Managers often try to apply sophisticated technologies, methods, and tools to solve with dignity their eternal problem: achieving the annual, and especially the multiannual, profitability target – the one promised to shareholders. But is synchronization really the best production system to meet all business expectations for any manufacturing company? This was the question that arose from my participation in a detailed presentation of a production system at a renowned car assembly company. During my participation in an individual workshop in that plant, they presented the importance of designing the total lead time for each order, from each customer, in order to be able to promise and fulfill their promise regarding the delivery time. They tried to take into account absolutely everything that could happen at that time of the year in their plant but especially in each of their suppliers (e.g., a legal holiday in a certain country in the time frame that affects production volumes of the supplier). They tried to ensure a synchronization of the information and material flow on the whole manufacturing flow and beyond in order to eliminate the occurrence of waste as much as possible. In fact, much of their success was ensured by their management with suppliers of components and materials, in other words, by putting pressure on suppliers and moving any non-performance toward suppliers – this non-performance being visible in the decrease of suppliers' profitability.

In feedback to this predicament, even though synchronization is very important, a new management and manufacturing improvement system called *speed-based target profit (SBTP)* has been successfully developed and applied over the years to address the multitude of problems that can arise at the level of profitability, both for assembly companies and for their supplier companies in their synchronization practices. The SBTP is the profitable production management targeted for achieving synchronous profitable operations based on reaching the target profit per minute in the bottleneck operation by planning and improving both the capacity of the bottleneck operation and the costs of losses and waste (CLWs) for all operations.

The usefulness of any new management theory is up to practical application rather than logical matters. An effective management methodology should be theory of practices. That is to say practice them first. Therefore, this SBTP book is not just a book of a new managerial theory, but a book of action. SBTP was created and developed on the basis of knowledge gained following successive observations of manufacturing companies and the profound discussions with the people in these companies at all levels and not just gained in academic education and topped up from topical research published in books and academic and practitioner-based journals.

The managers and practitioners within manufacturing companies will discover a practical approach to the need for cost down and cash up by applying a powerful operational profitable production planning formula to meet profitability expectations through productivity based on strong leadership and with the help of a specific control system called *control trilogy for KAIZENSHIRO* – feedforward-driven control, concurrent-driven control, and feedback-driven control. (KAIZENSHIRO is the necessary, localized, and feasible target of reducing annual and multiannual manufacturing costs by reducing critical cost of losses and waste – CCLWs.) Therefore, the SBTP system in this book presents a holistic approach to the profitability of target products and the development of its own mechanism since the acceptance of each order from customers in order to achieve continuous synchronization of all manufacturing modules to market requirements, profitability management, and profitable production planning.

The uniqueness of the book is reinforced by the detailed presentation of the successful application of the SBTP system in two case studies, as a way of life and a unit speed of target profit improvement ethos at all hierarchical levels, in two multinational manufacturing companies operating in highly competitive markets in order to address the synchronous profitable operations for both the sales increase scenario and the sales decrease scenario.

Therefore, the author's hope is that the SBTP system will provide a way to successfully approach *planning and developing synchronous profitable operations* by constantly and continuously discovering hidden profit reserves from manufacturing directly from the manufacturing process. By adopting the SBTP system, your company will be able to consistently achieve unit speed of target profit for fulfilling multiannual and annual target profit as a unique and effective way through a new profitable production planning paradigm that operates according to its own production system.

About the Author

 **Alin Posteucă, PhD,** is a consultant in productivity and profitability and the CEO of Exegens® (Romania). Prior to this position, he held top management positions in manufacturing and services companies.

His major research areas include manufacturing policy deployment, manufacturing cost improvement, and visible profitability of operational excellence by improving productivity. His recent research includes the impact of Industry 4.0 on planning and developing synchronous profitable operations and on information systems of cost and budget in order to substantially improve the manufacturing unit costs.

He received his PhD in industrial engineering from the Polytechnic University of Bucharest (Romania) and PhD in managerial accounting from the Bucharest University of Economic Studies (Romania). He received his MBA from the Alexandru Ioan Cuza University of Iaşi, Romania. Also, he is certified public accountant in Romania.

He has been actively involved in various industrial consulting and training projects for more than 20 years in Romania and has been published in various research journals and presented papers at numerous conferences regarding productivity, profitability, and quality.

Books written by Alin:

- Posteucă, A. and Sakamoto S., 2017. *Manufacturing Cost Policy Deployment (MCPD) and Methods Design Concept (MDC): The Path to Competitiveness.* New York, NY: Productivity Press/CRC Press.
- Posteucă, A., 2018. *Manufacturing Cost Policy Deployment (MCPD) Transformation: Uncovering Hidden Reserves of Profitability.* New York, NY: Productivity Press/CRC Press.
- Posteucă, A., 2019. *Manufacturing Cost Policy Deployment (MCPD) Profitability Scenarios: Systematic and Systemic Improvement of Manufacturing Costs.* New York, NY: Productivity Press/Routledge.

He continues to investigate the extensions of the MCPD and SBTP systems in order to meet the reduction of costs beyond the manufacturing area to achieve total cost reduction (across the supply chain) and apply MCPD and SBTP adjusted to other industries (health, public institutions, banks, etc.).

Introduction

My previous books on MCPD – *Manufacturing Cost Policy Deployment (MCPD) and Methods Design Concept (MDC): The Path to Competitiveness* (written with Dr. Shigeyasu Sakamoto, Productivity Press/CRC Press, 2017), *Manufacturing Cost Policy Deployment (MCPD) Transformation: Uncovering Hidden Reserves of Profitability* (Productivity Press/CRC Press, 2018), and *Manufacturing Cost Policy Deployment (MCPD) Profitability Scenarios: Systematic and Systemic Improvement of Manufacturing Costs* (Productivity Press/Routledge, 2019) – explained the major components of the cost of losses and waste (CLW) approach for annual and multiannual planning of manufacturing profitability, more exactly continuously increasing productivity at the policy deployment level. The principles and concepts necessary for a harmonious transformation through productivity for the profitability of manufacturing companies were presented.

In recent years, especially since the publication of my MCPD trilogy, I have received many questions from the top managers, middle management, and professional support staff about how to plan and develop synchronous and profitable operations in same at the same time. The discussions focused on the fact that the synchronization of operations alone is no longer enough, especially for supply companies. There is a need to ensure a level of profit that ensures the continuity with dignity of companies. So I decided to detail the MCPD approach with this new book and present the development on how to achieve a profitable synchronization of operations from the production planning and scheduling phase; what mechanism can be developed to ensure *takt profit* and *takt time* at the same time; how to address inefficiency that strictly takes into account customer needs; how to plan and carry out systematic (*kaizen*) and systemic (*kaikaku*) improvements to achieve synchronous profitable operations; and last, but not the least, how to develop and apply daily management for synchronous profitable operations based on strong leadership and a culture truly geared toward improving the productivity mind. The idea of the new speed-based target profit (SBTP) concept was born from the careful observation of the challenges, principles and phenomena of the manufacturing companies and from the deep discussions with the people from these companies at all levels. The aim is to provide a practical answer to achieving the expected and necessary results of profitability through productivity.

THE SYNCHRONOUS PROFITABLE OPERATIONS, SBTP MECHANISM

By implementing SBTP, the production planning methods used in manufacturing companies will concurrently support only profitable products needed to meet annual and especially multiannual profit needs, and only products needed to fully satisfy the clients' requirements.

SBTP is the profitable production management aimed at achieving synchronous profitable operations based on reaching the target profit per minute in the bottleneck operation. This is done by planning and improving both the capacity of the bottleneck operation and the costs of losses and waste for all operations, in order to:

- deeply understand all the restrictions of the operations that are in the way of the target operational profitability;
- establish the profitable production framework and the production parameters;
- address fluctuating elements in order to reach the targeted profitability;
- plan and implement effective and efficient improvements;
- accurately control the quantitative efficiency and strengthen the rules;
- reduce stocks and reach target profit; and
- promote an ethos needed to implement and sustain a culture of profitable synchronous operations as a way of life at all hierarchical levels.

SBTP enables manufacturing companies to meet the *takt profit* (the rate required to achieve the unit profit in the bottleneck operation) and, implicitly, the annual and multiannual manufacturing target profit per period, regardless of future sales scenarios, increasing or decreasing, while their own production activities become maximally effective and efficient at the same time.

The continuous and harmonious transformation of the manufacturing flow to the state of synchronous profitable operations is done with the help of the SBTP mechanism passing from:

- *deep understanding of the current state:* takt profit and takt time (through determining the theoretical target of improvements; actual costs of losses and waste and actual net processing production, future costs of losses and waste and future net processing production, profitability reform through productivity reforms); to
- *fulfillment of the needs of future state:* takt profit and takt time (through planning and developing synchronization of profit and customer demands).

The SBTP mechanism is a complement to the production management function in accordance with the specificity and individual needs of each company and their own production system, in particular a complement of the function of planning and scheduling the profitable production ensuring at the same time the synchronization (or the capacity required to be provided by the bottleneck operation for all operations that have the same takt time) and the required level of manufacturing cost associated with the processes in question (the allowable cost level through the improvement of the costs of losses and waste – CLWs).

Once the SBTP mechanism is developed, it becomes a way of life for the entire company. The SBTP mechanism deals with the roles of managers to sustain a true culture aimed at improving the productivity mind as the basis of a true learning organization.

CONTROL TRILOGY FOR *KAIZENSHIRO*: FEEDFORWARD, CONCURRENT, AND FEEDBACK CONTROLS

Once the SBTP mechanism is established, it must put into practice using the control trilogy for KAIZENSHIRO.

The KAIZENSHIRO concept was introduced into the literature and practice by Dr. Shigeyasu Sakamoto (co-author of my first book) to define improvable value as a target for the design of new working methods (methods design concept – MDC – a great technology for improving innovative and non-investing productivity for profitability). Fully respecting the MDC, this approach is one at the level of micro-productivity (at the level of cycle time).

The KAIZENSHIRO approach in this book is an extended one in terms of all costs of losses and waste from the entire manufacturing system of a company (improvable value as a critical costs of losses and waste target; CCLW target; or CLWs that are the root cause of other CLWs along a manufacturing flow). It is an approach both at the level of macro-productivity and at the level of micro-productivity, because in addition to losses at the cycle time level, the approach in this book plans and develops improvements for a much greater number of losses and waste, presents a control trilogy for KAIZENSHIRO, presents a budgeting system for KAIZENSHIRO, presents how to define KAIZENSHIRO at the level of all manufacturing flow modules in order to meet takt profit and takt time, presents a type of leadership specific to annual and multiannual KAIZENSHIRO, presents a cultural approach for KAIZENSHIRO, presents examples of practical implementations for the annual and multiannual fulfillment of KAIZENSHIRO through kaizen and kaikaku projects.

So, everyone in the company must work to fulfill the future state of SBTP by practicing the three types of controls in order to fulfill annual and multiannual KAIZENSHIRO:

1. feedforward-driven control;
2. concurrent-driven control; and
3. feedback-driven control.

The feedforward-driven control is an indispensable ingredient of a good management of the production planning at the same time as the planning of systematic (kaizen) and systemic (kaikaku) improvements. In the production planning phase, it is essential to decide on effective and efficient improvement projects that will contribute to the annual fulfillment of KAIZENSHIRO – before the start of the next physical production. Based on awareness of the level of costs of losses and waste (CLWs), planning to reduce or eliminate critical costs of losses and waste (CCLWs) that are probable and preventable is the purpose of the feedforward-driven control. The development of the KAIZENSHIRO budgeting framework is essential to sustain the consistency of the anticipatory-driven control.

The concurrent-driven control is the continuation of the feedforward-driven control at the level of CLW's daily management. The review of the role of manufacturing operators, supervisors, and managers, and of the control of the CLW level has become necessary. The workshop staff needs to be aware of the types, level, and trend of each CLW category in their area in order to approach them continuously and consistently. For example, it is nothing spectacular if an operator knows and continuously addresses together with his colleagues the top five types of losses and waste in his area (managers setting this top by knowing the level of costs associated with each type of losses and waste in each area covered). From the SBTP perspective, statements such as: "the high level of costs is the fault of managers and those in offices or this high cost is caused by … (someone else, from another department)" must be corrected. Many of the CLWs can be addressed at the time of production (concurrent controls) and many can be prevented (from feedback controls to feedforward controls) if the workshop staff has performed timely problem-solving activities related to production planning and sales plan.

The feedback control of CLW aims to monitor the control of CLW performance at the level of the effect (outputs) of the production system. The aim is to monitor the performance of production outputs on the level of CLWs (especially those necessary to support KAIZENSHIRO) and compare the parameters of CLWs to achieve total synchronous profitable operations control in order to provide the new level of control and robust restrictive conditions based on lessons learned. The basic purpose of the feedback control of CLWs is to verify that the production has achieved only what is necessary for the customers and profitable for the company.

In this way, the control trilogy for KAIZENSHIRO provides the scientific route to support a culture of endless improvements. When managers in manufacturing companies concurrently combine synchronous operations (*for fulfilling takt time*) with their profitability (*for fulfilling takt profit*), their companies will be much more competitive.

HOW THIS BOOK IS ORGANIZED

In order to concurrently address the two main directions of the SBTP approach in this book, (1) the planning of synchronous profitable operations; and (2) the development of synchronous profitable operations, the book is structured in three parts and six chapters, which are described in the following sections.

PART I: UNDERSTANDING SPEED-BASED TARGET PROFIT

The first part of the book presents the role of the SBTP system from the perspective of the new role of production panning for striving the target profit. It shows that often the expectations for complete synchronization and annual and multiannual target profitability are not fully met at the same time. Specifically, Peter F. Druker's concept of "doing the right things" (the right time, the right place of delivery, the right quantity, the right combination, the right quality, the right price) is not completely fulfilled and it does not extend automatically and safely to the concept of *doing the right profit*.

At the same time, the first part of the book presents how to analyze the current conditions, such as (Chapter 2):

- setting the main operational parameters (target products, bottleneck operation, and buffer size);
- defining actual manufacturing costs structures (actual cost of goods manufactured vs. actual costs of losses and waste);
- defining future manufacturing costs structures (determining the theoretical target of cost reduction and detailed targets and means design);
- SBTP steering committee;
- introductory education on SBTP – managers, supervisors, and operators; and
- structural reform of profitability through productivity reform (profitability scenarios through productivity).

CHAPTER 1: CHANGING THE PRODUCTION PLANNING PARADIGM

In this chapter, we will present the new concept of speed-based target profit (SBTP) which aims to achieve synchronous profitable operations or, in other words, the satisfaction of both customers, by synchronizing the entire production flow to the customers' requirements, as well as satisfying the expected level of profit through the synchronization of the entire flow to the requirements of annual and multiannual profit. The answer to the following question is presented: Why are just synchronous operations no longer enough? Then a board meeting story on insufficiently profitable synchronization and the new role of production planning for striving the target profit are given briefly by presenting the new concept of SBTP and implicitly the one of takt profit in tandem with takt time. At the end, the types of main results expected of the implementation of the SBTP system are presented and the following conclusion: synchronous profitable operations must be approached from the production planning stage.

CHAPTER 2: DEVELOP YOUR SPEED-BASED TARGET PROFIT MECHANISM AND START TO LIVE IT

Often the top managers make statements, such as: "We tried everything we could, but we feel that we have reached the limit for further improving both value-adding operating time in bottleneck operation, in order to increase production volume and the necessary reductions of unit costs. Or We are not sure that we will be able to maintain or increase enough the current favorable profit in the future".

In this chapter, starting from the presentation of the approach to managerial commitment in SBTP, we present the SBTP mechanism, respectively, the determination of profit demand and customer demand, how to establish the main operational parameters, simple determination of current costs of losses and waste and their effects, establishing future manufacturing costs structures to meet SBTP expectations and not least, how to approach structural profitability reform through productivity reform.

Therefore, this chapter presents the basic ingredients of the SBTP mechanism, ingredients that are also planted in the production planning stage.

PART II: PLANNING SYNCHRONOUS PROFITABLE OPERATIONS

In the second part of the book, we present the way of planning synchronous profitable operations:

1. by approaching the measurement of the ingredients of the SBTP mechanism and setting the targets of the expected and necessary future state, more precisely the presentation of the following aspects (Chapter 3):
   - predicting the possibility of improving productivity;
   - current losses and waste structures and maps;
   - methods for setting annual cost of losses and waste (the unique rate; the modules rates and the causality);
   - annual costs of losses and waste deployment maps;
   - setting profitable production formula;
   - improvement budgets: KAIZENSHIRO's financial visibility; and
   - the KAIZENSHIRO budgeting framework, and
2. by planning and scheduling production profitably and synchronously, more exactly (Chapter 4):
   - from method and performance to production planning and scheduling;
   - the main factors for production planning improvement;
   - control trilogy for KAIZENSHIRO – the basis for planning and developing the SBTP mechanism; and
   - feedforward control: production planning and scheduling and project planning for manufacturing costs improvement (MCI).

CHAPTER 3: SUPPORT STRIVING FOR SPEED-BASED TARGET PROFIT

Sometimes such CEO statements are heard in companies: "We are aware that our company has a high cost structure compared to other companies and that profitability can be improved, but we do not know now what the possible level of improvement in costs and profitability is because we do not continuously know the level of non-productivity in detail". Therefore, an important step in addressing the SBTP is to establish the quantitative potential to prevent the non-productivity and to establish the potential feasible improvements. The aim is to scientifically identify the maximum potential for feasible prevention of non-productivity by continuously measuring the level of losses and waste and by transforming them into costs; then by establishing the annual costs of losses and waste deployment maps, by establishing a profitable production formula, and by developing the improvement budgets to provide guidance on how to address the most feasible productivity improvements to support the profitable production planning. All these topics will be addressed in turn in this chapter. In conclusion, this third chapter provides an effective approach to planning operations that should no longer be strictly tailored to customer needs, as the premises for systemic inefficiency are often created.

CHAPTER 4: FEEDFORWARD CONTROL FOR PRODUCTION PLANNING AND SCHEDULING

As presented in previous chapters, speed-based target profit (SBTP) allows profitable production management to achieve synchronous profitable operations based on reaching the target profit per minute in the bottleneck module by planning and improving both the capacity of the bottleneck module and the costs of losses and waste for all operations, especially in the bottleneck profit module.

Starting from the need to improve productivity from the production planning and scheduling phase, in this chapter we present a global image of the feedforward control architecture for production planning and scheduling of SBTP. To establish a SBTP profitable production management, a company has to build up the following key elements from the feedforward control perspective: production planning, production scheduling and planning for manufacturing costs improvement by setting targets, and means for improvement depending on the probable sales scenario from next period (increasing or decreasing). An important feature of SBTP is that manufacturing costs improvement is done concurrently with the planning and scheduling of the profitable production system. Synchronized and profitable scheduling involves scheduling of manufacturing cost improvement in the modules that cause drifting and unprofitable production schedule.

The conclusion of this chapter, as an introduction to the concept of control trilogy for KAIZENSHIRO (feedforward-driven control) is that production planning is useless if it doesn't take into account the necessary improvements and the necessary takt profit.

PART III: DEVELOPING SYNCHRONOUS PROFITABLE OPERATIONS

In the third part of the book, we present the way of developing synchronous profitable operations:

1. by designing and developing concurrent and feedback controls (as the last two ingredients of the new control concept trilogy for KAIZENSHIRO) and presenting specific leadership and culture of SBTP, more precisely the presentation of the following aspects (Chapter 5):
   - concurrent control: CLW's daily management (roles, tools, and implementation);
   - feedback control: total manufacturing flow control based on 5 PULL;
   - feedback control: production volumes and profitability;
   - feedback control: results report; robust restrictive conditions, and next feedforward controls for next KAIZENSHIRO;
   - synchronous profitable operations leadership: tasks, instruments, and behaviors;
   - implementation of SBTP and critical success factors of SBTP implementation;
   - running strategic and daily improvements and verifying implementing solutions for fulfilling KAIZENSHIRO; and
   - SBTP culture: creating and sustaining the culture for SBTP as a way of life, and
2. by presenting two real case studies of SBTP implementation (Chapter 6):
   - Case study 1 from "AA Plant": speed-based target profit for sales increase scenario (company in the automotive components

industry; manufacturing and assembly manufacturing regime); and

- Case study 2 from "BB Plant": speed-based target profit for sales decrease scenario (food industry company; process industry manufacturing regime).

CHAPTER 5: CONCURRENT AND FEEDBACK CONTROLS

The first part of this chapter, starting from the presentation of the objectives and needs of effective concurrent control by using CLW's daily management, describes the roles of concurrent control for supporting synchronous profitable operations, the basic tools of concurrent control and the main steps of implementing concurrent control. The second part of this chapter, starting from the need for a feedback control for the fulfillment of KAIZENSHIRO, presents the approach of total synchronous profitable operations control, respectively the total manufacturing flow control based on five pull, a control of production volumes and profitability, a results reports of synchronous profitable operations, a robust restrictive conditions and finally the substantiation of the future feedforward control to resume the endless control trilogy for KAIZENSHIRO. The chapter continues with the presentation of synchronous profitable operations leadership, with the presentation of the phases and main steps of implementation of SBTP, with the presentation of critical success factors of SBTP program and finally with the presentation of the main ingredients of KAIZENSHIRO culture. The conclusion of this chapter is that production management must lead the synchronous profitable operations continuously.

CHAPTER 6: SPEED-BASED TARGET PROFIT CASE STUDIES

This last chapter presents the practical application of SBTP. As I said before, this book about SBTP is not just a book of a new managerial theory, but a book of action, a practical book whose information can be applied to any manufacturing company.

The first part of the chapter presents an implementation of SBTP at "AA Plant" against the background of a sales increase scenario that aimed to focus on fulfilling the multiannual and annual manufacturing target profit, especially through external manufacturing profit through maximizing outputs – the predominant need for productivity growth by improving effectiveness (reducing losses – not effectively used input). The description of the SBTP implementation at AA Plant is aimed at describing the initial and expected conditions of the manufacturing flow and the presentation of four improvement projects. At the same time, the main challenges of implementing SBTP mechanism at AA Plant are presented. The second part of this last chapter presents an implementation of SBTP at BB Plant against the background of the economic crisis, amid the sharp decline in sales that aimed to focus on multiannual and annual manufacturing target profit fulfillment, particularly through internal manufacturing profit through minimizing inputs – the predominant need for productivity increase through improving efficiency (waste reduction – excess amount of input). The description of the SBTP implementation at BB Plant is aimed again at the background description to developing SBTP, establishing the continuous measurement indicators for CLWs and KAIZENSHIRO design, presentation of the approach of promotional organization for introducing SBTP, presentation of four improvement projects. At the same time, the tangible and intangible results of SBTP at BB Plant and obstacles encountered while implementing SBTP at BB Plant are presented. The two case studies were successful and plant managers made statements such as: "Through SBTP we have built a more profitable production management system that facilitates directing our improvements to a goal clearly defined and understood by all of us: KAIZENSHIRO. Now we will be able to better respond to our customers' orders and we will be able to better plan the annual profit and especially the multiannual one".

In conclusion, I am confident that the SBTP system will help your company to meet multiannual and annual profit plans through the successful planning and development of synchronous profitable operations based on a continuous and consistent increase in productivity, regardless of whether sales are increasing or decreasing.

Section I

Understanding Speed-Based Target Profit

1

Changing The Production Planning Paradigm

It is hard to imagine a CEO saying that "the primary goal of our business is customer satisfaction". Even if customer satisfaction is important, any company must continually earn a reasonable profit in order to survive and prosper with dignity in an increasingly challenging business environment. Therefore, in manufacturing plants, production planning must ensure the right things at the beginning, respectively the satisfaction of both customers and those interested in the consistent profitability level of the company. Even if profitability is vital to companies, especially against the downward trend of sales, it is not sufficiently promoted and scientifically supported within companies, at least at the managerial level. Moreover, often the production planning is mainly focused on ensuring the delivery of production quantities on time and on an acceptable stock level.

In this chapter, we will present the new concept of speed-based target profit (SBTP) that aims to achieve synchronous profitable operations (SPO) or, in other words, the satisfaction of customers, by synchronizing the entire production flow to the customers' requirements, as well as the expected level of profit through the synchronization of the entire flow to the requirements of annual and multiannual profit.

1.1 WHY JUST SYNCHRONOUS OPERATIONS ARE NO LONGER ENOUGH

The concept of synchronization of the company's operations (synchronous coordination of all resources and processes in the company and beyond to achieve the best possible results) has gained worldwide recognition and appreciation.

Looking for the best ways to maximize results, in particular, meeting target sales volumes, annual and multiannual target of profit margin percentage (operating income ÷ revenues), and increasing cash-in and minimizing cash-out are often the big challenges for manufacturing companies, even if they seek to synchronize their volume operations to the market by: (1) the continuous reduction of materials lead time, production lead time, and delivery lead time; (2) the successful implementation of solutions for good management of bottleneck processes; (3) identifying solutions to continuously reduce the replacement period for material, work-in-progress (WIP), and finished product stocks; (4) reducing and/or eliminating overtime; (5) reducing and/or eliminating handling; (6) the continuous improvement and simplification of the standard operating procedure (SOP), including set-up time; (7) the increase of overall equipment effectiveness (OEE) and its synchronization at takt time, etc.

Even though some manufacturing companies, including final producers (those who process and assemble finished products and provide them to customers), can often achieve a high level of synchronization with an increasingly shorter replacement time for raw material and finished products stocks, and even though some companies have adopted different Industry 4.0 specific solutions, they may still have deficiencies in operations regarding the volumes of target products, annual and multiannual target profit margin percentage, and cash flow against an increased level of *losses* (not effectively used input; with particular impact on effectiveness) and *waste* (excess amount of input; with particular impact on efficiency) and against the background of a deficient level of innovation (products, processes, technologies, materials, or ideas that can be easily and feasibly implemented).

At the same time, the top managers of manufacturing companies often ask themselves the following question: *What really determines the concurrent performance of both synchronous and profitable operations within the company I work for?* They are fully aware that they must only produce and sell products that are both:

- *necessary on the market* (not to make excess products without having a firm order from a customer or a storage policy for additional orders from customers and/or mitigating the lack of temporary

production capacity or making products too fast for a firm order but well in advance of the delivery time specified by the customer); and especially
• *profitable* (not to produce products that do not reach their target of unitary profitability).

At the same time, often top managers find that they actually have more concerns and achievements in terms of manufacturing flow synchronization, its efficiency or "doing the right things" (Drucker, 1963), which is not automatically a profitable enough, efficient enough manufacturing flow or "doing things right" to ensure the maximization of the profit margin percentage and its inclusion in the annual, and especially, the multiannual expected targets of the profit margin percentage.

Even if companies seek to develop strategic goals that are intelligible to all employees and creatively integrate these goals from top to bottom and bottom up, the expectations for complete synchronization and annual and multiannual target profitability are not fully met at the same time. Specifically, Peter F. Drucker's concept of "doing the right things" (the right time, the right place of delivery, the right quantity, the right combination, the right quality, the right price) is not completely fulfilled and it does not extend automatically and safely to the concept of *doing the right profit*.

Going beyond doing the right synchronization, ensuring a level of synchronization as complete as possible to fully satisfy the customers' requirements (the complete/ideal synchronization is not available to any manufacturing company; especially to the supplier manufacturing companies), doing the right profit (the right annual and multiannual target profit margin percentage) is the subject of this book or planning and developing SPO, through the continuous use of all the resources available in a company (equipment, people, materials, utilities, methods, and information) to the maximum capacity limit by reducing/eliminating all losses and waste feasibly approached to ensure profitable and worthy business continuity. Specifically, the presentation of how to develop and use a mechanism to produce only the necessary and profitable products by understanding and addressing the main internal (within the reach of the company) and external restrictions in depth, and continuously seeking to plan and control them as accurately as possible through their standardization and continuous improvement.

There have been no papers and books that have directly addressed the methodology of planning and developing SPO. In this context, the purpose of this book is to develop a good methodology that scientifically and systematically establishes a program for planning and developing SPO. The following issues will be solved in this book:

- Investigating the relationships between synchronization (fulfilling the pace of customer demand) and profitability (fulfilling the pace of profit demand) of manufacturing operations based on the continuous need for productivity growth, regardless of the evolution of sales, increasing or decreasing.
- Presenting a mechanism for production planning and control that will ensure continuous planning and developing SPO, both for the companies that assemble the final finished products and for their suppliers.
- Presenting the way of choosing and implementing the most effective and efficient improvements, beyond the conventional priorities based, in particular, on improving time and quality, looking for a relationship among bottleneck operation and cost of losses and waste (CLW), and finding the connection between the feasibility of the improvements and the attainment of the one-piece flow (OPF) status based on takt time.
- Achieving and sustaining SPO through leadership to implement the scientifically estimated improvements for the continuous achievement of the annual and especially multiannual target profitability.

This methodology was invented to achieve the status of SPO for a production system that consists of several operations. After the production system is understood in detail and defined, the mechanism for SPO is developed and supported.

Therefore, a conventional approach, i.e. synchronization of bottleneck operation at takt time, is not so effective and especially efficient enough, as it really could be and as it will be presented in the subsequent section.

1.2 A BOARD MEETING STORY ON INSUFFICIENTLY PROFITABLE SYNCHRONIZATION

During a year-end board meeting at a manufacturing company ("AA Plant", with a production regime of the manufacturing and assembly type, automotive components; with the focus on synchronizing bottleneck at takt time), the tangible, and also the intangible, effects of the application of systematic (kaizen) and systemic (kaikaku) improvements with impact on productivity and profitability were presented.

For several years, the company has been keen to increase the level of synchronization of current and future production capacities to the market needs in order to fulfill its productivity vision and mission (sales factory turnover is manufacturing profit). To increase the current production capabilities, the company used a mix of world-famous productivity measurement and enhancement methodologies and tools, such as the theory of constraints (ToC), lean manufacturing, Six Sigma, kaizen and kaikaku, OEE, etc.

At the same time, a tour of the factory was planned that day to present the concrete effects of the strategic improvement projects of the almost completed year. The middle management and support staff were excited and proud that all the improvement projects had reached their operational targets and could show some of the measurable results of their work at the key performance indicator (KPI) level (at the level of information boards: plant level, production level, improvements level, problem-solving level, and lines level). The atmosphere was cheerful and comfortable, especially as the winter holidays approached. I participated in discussions from the position of external consultant in productivity and profitability, carrying out different improvement projects in that company over the years. We all went through the entire production flow step by step and finally reached the main final assembly line. Three projects of strategic systematic improvement (kaizen) were presented.

At the end of the presentation of the three kaizen projects, in which the way of obtaining tangible and intangible results was presented, the chief financial officer (CFO) presented his observations approximately as follows:

> I have understood and respect the work done by all our colleagues involved in all improvement projects, as you know, we did everything was necessary to make all the money resources needed for improvement projects always available on time, but as we know, we often have gaps between the target cost established annually at the level of products and divisions and the achieved level of cost reduction. This gap tends to increase and significantly affect the level of multiannual operating target profit. The value of cost improvement at the operational level seems to be high, but this improvement is not so visible in the business results and especially in the financial results of our company. Moreover, our cash flow often has problems for different reasons. The level of stocks is still insufficiently controlled, our unit

costs being higher by 8.5% based on the WIP ratio of 55% of total stocks, the planned man × hour is often not respected, which requires overtime, and often special orders force us to make expensive purchases. I will limit myself only to these stringent aspects. Therefore, I believe that the improvement projects carried out should show quite clear results in terms of reducing the costs of individual products and at the level of profitability (in the budget and in the profit and loss statement) in order to be truly credible and to ensure all the financial resources needed exactly when needed, even if these financial resources do not represent large amounts of money.

Gradually, the state of joviality disappeared and people began to discuss the differences in the perception of the improvements between those involved in operations and those in the financial sector, especially as the need for a visible increase in productivity, both at the level of output and at the level of cost improvement was a very acute one, especially for the years to come.

Meanwhile, the plant manager expressed his intention to speak. We all went to a training room near the production area, quieted for several tens of seconds in the room; he turned his eyes several times on those in the room, then he began to express his real concerns about the future level of profitability briefly described by the CFO, as follows:

- The decrease in the prices of finished products on the market has become stronger than expected and tends to put increasing pressure.
- The cost reductions of the company cannot keep up with those practiced by some competitors for some strategic products of the company.
- The profitability of the new products does not contribute to the operational profit according to the initial plans.
- Certain categories of costs tend to continuously increase objectively (especially raw materials, components, and utilities).
- The volumes of products made and sold tend to decrease further in the future.

In the end, he said this about it:

So far, we have given high priority to the terms of production with the necessary quality, the products have been diversified, which has led to increased sales, but also stocks, in particular stocks of components, materials, and raw materials, the level of profit has been acceptable so far, we always have had concerns about reducing costs, but we do not know now if we can continue to visibly reduce costs to an acceptable level of competitiveness and profitability, how much the costs of each process and for each product can be reduced, and if our way of selecting priority improvements ensures the choice of the most feasible improvements for the problems considered most stringent in operations. At the same time, now the production planning here does not take immediate account of the capacity increases achieved by unblocking the bottleneck processes through kaizen projects and implicitly neither the possible increases in the number of products made and sold, nor the increases in profitability obtained by manufacturing costs improvement based on the results of kaizen projects. In conclusion, in order to continuously and simultaneously achieve the necessary and profitable target products, I believe that we need a new system of accentuated and visible reduction of the operational costs, of a new way of planning and controlling the production to support the operational profitability regardless of the evolution of sales, increasing or decreasing.

After the presentations of the plant manager and CFO, all participants understood that a new approach to cost reduction and production planning and control is needed to make the necessary and profitable products.

Returning to the office, they briefly reviewed the current way of work for standardization and improvement [ToC, drum buffer rope (DBR), lean, kaizen, kaikaku, OEE, Kaizen Teian, etc.]. They concluded that a cost-savings and cost-avoidance system is practiced at the end of the improvement projects. The improvement projects are proposed by the employees to meet the cost reduction targets at the division level and at the product level, but they did not have a system to validate the scientific feasibility of the improvements before they were approved to be carried out, nor could they prioritize the improvement planning so as to achieve the congruence of the objectives of those involved in the synchronization of the operations who argued that meeting customer delivery deadlines is essential and of those in the financial sector, who fully agreed that the terms of delivery to customers are very important, but only if the annual and especially multiannual marginal profit targets are reached. Once a product was considered profitable based on the standard costs incurred, the production planning only considered the delivery time to the customer and not the possible profitability actually obtained under the current conditions of the respective period of the year.

After a few weeks, as a countermeasure, the plant manager made the decision to contract the consulting for the implementation of SBTP (briefly described in Section 1.4, "What Is Speed-Based Target Profit?"; then in detail in the rest of the chapters of this book) for the concomitant and scientific achievement of the productivity and profitability targets of the entire manufacturing flow, as a result of planning and controlling the bottleneck processes and as a result of choosing the most effective and efficient improvements. From the perspective of SBTP, there is no point in planning the production and delivery of finished products to the customer beyond the profitable capacity decided in the bottleneck operations. The basic question to which SBTP answers is: *Why reducing unnecessary stocks and unnecessary costs become goals?* The purpose of the companies is actually to prevent their occurrence.

SBTP is an extension of the concept of manufacturing cost policy deployment (MCPD), already applied by "AA Plant" for several years now. The intermediate discussions that convinced the team of top managers to join the SBTP, based on a feasibility study, aimed at:

- three practical simulations of profitable production planning for the target products of the next period in the bottleneck process and the definition of the opportunity to increase the capacity up to at least 85%;
- the development of reduction scenarios for inventory and WIP;
- the development of three profitable scenarios for the evolution of sales volumes and prices;
- determining the ideal cost level of the target products (obtaining in a feasible way the *zero CLW* status from the current unit cost structure; or in other words, attacking the hidden reserves to reduce current operating costs and with future projections without affecting the quality level and the delivery times; or, more precisely, determining the productivity stake for profitability at the product level); manufacturing cost reductions up to 40–45%, especially on the basis of the CLW reduction; and
- the development of simulations of innovative and profitable redesign of production processes to achieve a reduced cycle time for bottleneck processes (with the full support of industrial engineering science); the reduction mode with 25% of raw materials and components inventory was justified by reducing cycle time for bottleneck processes.

Like any new approach, the discussions had multiple challenges. One of the challenges was that managers understand that even if all the conditions of the clients are fulfilled and their full satisfaction is ensured, the continuation and growth of the business with them and the expected profitability are not obtained automatically. Or in other words, full and continuous customer satisfaction is often inefficient for the company. Managers understood that no matter who the customers are, the company must continue:

- to make a reasonable profit to survive and prosper with dignity;
- to see the effects of productivity improvements at financial level;
- to allocate on time all the resources needed to make improvements; and
- especially, to plan the visible productivity improvements in profitability at the time of production planning (to support target profit in the bottleneck operation).

Even if SBTP does not involve changing the current production system, but only completes the weaknesses of achieving productivity concomitantly with profitability, the continuous measurement of losses and waste at the level of operations, quantification of losses and waste in costs, and reaching the target of improving bottleneck were relatively easy to be achieved. One of the biggest challenges was changing people's attitudes and behaviors toward profitable production planning and directing and making improvements to support profitable operations in the bottleneck operation. Practitioners in production planning, beyond what they were currently doing (ensuring timely deliveries to customers and optimum loading capacity), learned and applied profitable order planning and control based on the actual capacity of the bottleneck process and on the improved level of CLW after all planned improvements are implemented effectively and efficiently.

After the implementation of SBTP for the products and pilot areas, the results have started to be seen just after the first 10–12 months, more precisely the fulfillment of the annual profit target and the delivery deadlines, through the visible reduction of costs, cash flow stabilization, stock reduction, lead time reduction, and planned man × hours and OEE compliance.

The greater effects of SBTP have become more evident after the first three years of hard work.

By implementing SBTP, operations managers and practitioners understand that the goal of synchronizing processes with customer needs is not enough. A flow may be sufficiently synchronous at a certain level of customer demand (framed in takt time), but that flow may still conceal many CLWs that can be reduced/eliminated to ensure the required target profitability. The CFO and the financial accounting department have understood that they need to be much more involved in the operations to support the achievement of SPO. Eliminating autocratic barriers and involving everyone in the company and beyond in profitable business planning, especially the real involvement of top managers, are just some intangible results of using SBTP. For companies applying it, SBTP is a way of life and profitable planning of synchronous operations ethos at all hierarchical levels.

1.3 THE NEW ROLE OF PRODUCTION PLANNING FOR STRIVING THE TARGET PROFIT

Regardless of industry, production planning activity is one of the most important activities in a manufacturing company. The ultimate goal of production planning is to contribute to the company's profit. With the help of production planning, each and every material and component required at the shop floor level is ensured at the right time, at the right place, at the right quantity, at the right quality, and in the right combination, to ensure smooth flow, to allow the progress of all operations in accordance with predetermined schedules (especially ensuring the right effectiveness), and to allow the achievement of a minimum acceptable cost (especially ensuring the right efficiency).

Production planning practiced in many companies in the past (but still found in some of them, at least partially) is the one that focuses on the realization of goods that can be made. As you can see in Figure 1.1, even if they are PUSH-type areas, at first glance, what is going on is largely indicated; the flow provides the output requested by the customers, the operations are orderly and quite performant, but, often, the inventory and the number of people are in excess, the level of scrap and rework is high, and the time between sending work instructions and delivery to the customer is long (manufacturing lead time). The

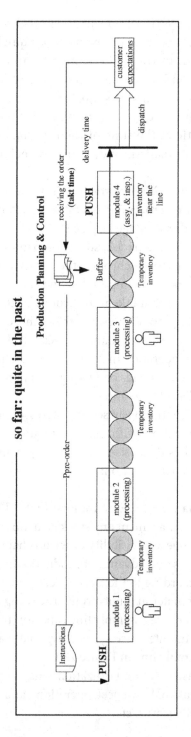

FIGURE 1.1
Production planning and control according to what can be produced. PUSH production.

main goals are to reduce WIP (often the excess is thrown away at the end of the year because it occurs too much or too quickly) and manufacturing lead time [just-in-time (JIT) concerns are only in production areas] by focusing on improving operations and layout locations. In fact, delivery time is what matters most in this logic of production planning. From a cost perspective, accepting orders must fall within a standard unit cost (static at the time of their establishment and with high chances of having unrealistic budget and financial results that are difficult to master).

In the example in Figure 1.2, the bottleneck is at the assembly. It could be in any of the other three processing operations (1, 2, or 3). Over time, bottleneck operation tends to change its place.

Further, as can be seen in Figure 1.2, some companies carry out a production planning that seeks to synchronize the capacity of the bottleneck operation at the level of takt time imposed by the customers. These companies seek to accept orders that take into account, at the same time, the takt time level (with many possible events that can occur from accepting the order to the actual execution and delivery of the order) and the capacity of the bottleneck operation that dictates the capacity of the entire manufacturing flow (which depends on any significant fluctuations in the effectiveness of the bottleneck operation).

These companies that continuously seek to increase the level of bottleneck capacity synchronization with market requirements (takt time; PULL production), which is the basis for the development of the standard production plan, focus in particular on:

- continuous compliance with First In, First Out (FIFO) as a method of removing from management any stock structure;
- continuous knowledge and visibility of what is happening in manufacturing flow (delays and advance of production);
- planning orders according to their priorities;
- synchronization of material inputs from processing operation 1 (and 2 and 3) at the level of the assembly line capacity (bottleneck);
- strengthening the maintenance system, especially at the bottleneck operation (the assembly line in Figure 1.2);
- continuous increase of standardization and improvement level (especially in the case of bottleneck operation); and
- maximizing the OPF status, etc.

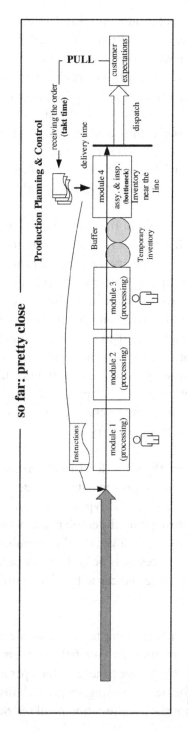

FIGURE 1.2

Synchronous production planning and control according to the continuous matching of the capacity of the bottleneck operation with takt time.

The main goals of this type of production planning are to produce what is needed (to reduce all types of stock), when it is needed, and to respect the delivery time. The buffer level is stable taking into account the capacity of the bottleneck operation to establish the synchronization between delivery lead time and manufacturing lead time. As shown in Figure 1.2, total lead time and especially manufacturing lead time fall significantly compared to PUSH production planning (see Figure 1.1). However, even if the delivery time, the level of stocks (between the minimum and maximum), and the lead time are often fulfilled, etc., this state does not guarantee the continuous fulfillment of the need of making the right annual and multi-annual profit.

For the continuous fulfillment of the need of doing the right profit, as can be seen in Figure 1.3, it is necessary to move from the synchronization state between the bottleneck capacity with the takt time, to the synchronization of the bottleneck capacity with the takt profit and the takt time (a manufacturing flow can have the same bottleneck process, from both the takt profit perspective and the takt time perspective; at the same time, a manufacturing flow can have two distinct bottleneck processes, one from the perspective of takt profit in which the CLW level is the highest in a certain process, especially against the background of a high level of costs in that process, and another bottleneck process from the perspective of takt time, in which the level of manufacturing flow capacity is the lowest).

To fully understand this, it is necessary to:

- continuously measure the CLW level in all processes and improve CLW by addressing the improvements associated to critical cost of losses and waste (CCLW) or the type of CLW in the operation that causes other CLWs throughout the entire manufacturing process flow and beyond (in Figure 1.3 CCLW is in the assembly which is bottleneck; CCLW may not necessarily be in the bottleneck operation); and
- continuously synchronize the capacity of the bottleneck operation at takt time.

As can be seen in Figure 1.3, in order to continuously and concurrently achieve the target level of productivity (effectiveness × efficiency; to achieve *maximum productivity* over time) and the operating target profit, companies set their priorities according to profitability, analyzing and defining the conditions for the manifestation of all restrictions (especially

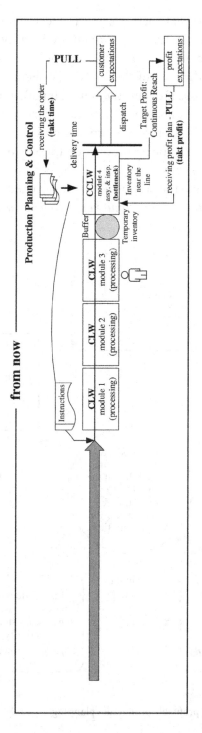

FIGURE 1.3

Synchronous and profitable production planning and control according to the continuous matching of the capacity of the bottleneck operation with takt profit and takt time.

in bottleneck operations) and then observing and improving the rules for these restrictions. In fact, the capacity and profitability of processing operations mean the capacity and profitability of the bottleneck operation, and the increase of the capacity of the bottleneck operations means the visible reduction of all losses (not effectively used input) and waste (excess amount of input) that determines and affects the occurrence of bottleneck. The main characteristic of a profitable production planning is the continuous achievement of cost down and cash up (*maximum efficient*) and then the fulfillment of the delivery time, the control of the stock level, the shortening of lead time, and the observance of the planned man × hour by observing the production rules (*maximum effectiveness*) (see Figure 1.4).

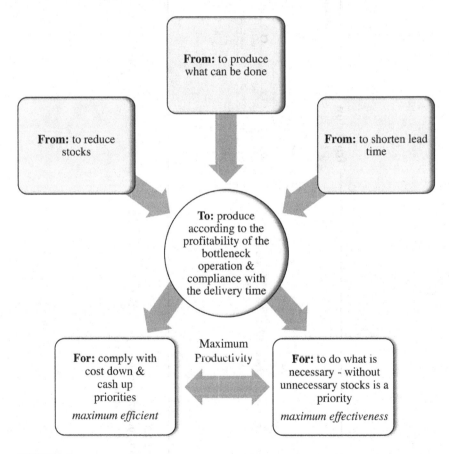

FIGURE 1.4

Maximizing productivity for profitable production planning.

Therefore, profitable production planning must focus on:

- achieving a continuous synchronization of all current and/or future processes and resources at takt time, taking into account continuously the actual capacity of the bottleneck operations (especially the cycle time and the set-up time); and
- the continuous connection with cost management and the need for annual and multiannual targets profit by continuously exploiting the cost level of losses and waste (CLW) through systematic (kaizen) and systemic (kaikaku) improvements.

In fact, as shown in Figure 1.5, the production planning must go from a planning based only on takt time and bottleneck to a planning based on the required profitability or takt profit (the rate required to achieve the unit profit in the bottleneck operation), without neglecting in any way the respect of takt time and fitting in the bottleneck capacity. This way, the output required to be ensured by the production planning must focus concurrently on bottleneck operation, takt profit, takt time, and especially on target profit margin percentage.

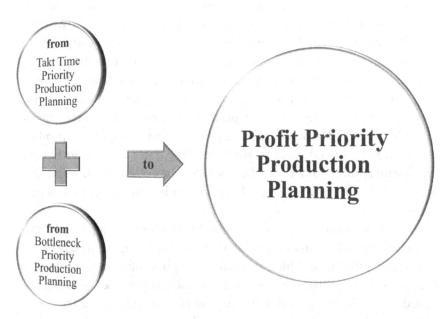

FIGURE 1.5
Profit priority production planning.

In conclusion, planning operations strictly for the needs of customers is often inefficient, impedes the freedom of profitable production planning, and often leads to unnecessary stocks of all types. The production planners should give up the arguments (excuses) of the following kind: "We only exceeded by x% the finished product stocks on this order, but we made the deliveries on time" or "the total profitability of the order was not so affected of y% of the supplementary stocks of finished products and of z% of raw materials; we have fulfilled all the customer's requirements on time and have optimally loaded the equipment and lines".

Therefore, profitable planning of operations focused on *innovation of bottleneck operations* and *continuous improvement of CLW* is the goal of this book, because the age when "we can profitably sell almost anything we produce" is long gone.

1.4 WHAT IS SPEED-BASED TARGET PROFIT?

The production planning methods used in companies should be useful for supporting the concomitant production only of the profitable products necessary to satisfy the needs of annual and especially multiannual profit and only of the products necessary to fully satisfy the clients' requirements. As mentioned before, product planning that mainly involves only full customer satisfaction can often be inefficient. To avoid this, companies need a planning control to provide a quick and correct answer on the deviations of profitability and unnecessary stocks, to facilitate a good problem-solving process, and to support a production with SPO. As indicated by the title of the book, besides bottleneck synchronization at takt time, the book consists of addressing the new concept of SBTP (establishing *takt profit* and how to achieve it) to perform SPO.

In order to ensure SPO, it is necessary to continuously apply a production planning and control mechanism to avoid accepting seemingly profitable orders initially, but which prove ultimately unprofitable, a mechanism focused on both bottleneck operation, as much as possible, and on CLW, in order to provide freedom of production planners regarding the profitable acceptability of orders; in other words, freedom to choose the necessary profitability by maximizing productivity. This requires a better collaboration between the production planning department, production, and support departments – especially maintenance, cost management, and improvement departments.

1.4.1 Speed-Based Target Profit Concept

SBTP is the profitable production management targeted for achieving SPO based on reaching the target profit per minute in the bottleneck operation by planning and improving both the capacity of the bottleneck operation and the CLW for all operations, in order to:

1. have deep understanding of all the restrictions of the operations that are in the way of the target operational profitability;
2. establishing the profitable production framework and the production parameters;
3. addressing fluctuating elements in order to reach the targeted profitability;
4. planning and implementing effective and efficient improvements;
5. having accurate control of quantitative efficiency and strengthening the rules;
6. reducing stocks and reaching target profit; and
7. promoting an ethos needed to implement and sustain a culture of profitable synchronous operations as a way of life at all hierarchical levels.

SBTP enables manufacturing companies to meet the *takt profit* and implicitly the annual and multiannual manufacturing target profit per period, regardless of future sales scenarios, increasing or decreasing, while their own production activities become maximum effective and efficient at the same time. SBTP is a complement to the production management function in accordance with the specificity and individual needs of each company and their own production system, in particular, a complement of the function of planning and scheduling the profitable production ensuring, at the same time, the synchronization (or the capacity required to be provided by the bottleneck operation for all operations that have the same takt time) and the required level of manufacturing cost associated with the processes in question (the allowable cost level through improve the CLW).

1.4.2 The Main Goal: Takt Profit

If sales are talking about a unit price, if productivity is tracked at the product cycle time level in the bottleneck operation or man × hour per product, if any company has a unit cost of products, then a question arises: *Why not a unit profit per minute scientifically obtained?*

The takt profit is the rate at which the unitary target profit of the period must be met or in other words, the flow rate to satisfy the need for unitary profit of the company for a period, or the contribution of the unitary profit as cash at the pace sold based on bottleneck operation capacity (per minute).

The formula for determining the takt profit is as follows:

$$\text{Takt profit} = \frac{\text{Contribution profit per unit (\$)}}{\substack{\text{Net standard operating time per unit in} \\ \text{bottleneck operation (minutes)}}} \quad (1.1)$$

In Figure 1.6, there is an example of the calculation of the takt profit and its interpretation.

The calculation of the takt profit can be done for any period of time and for any number of products to satisfy the target contribution profit for all the products made (but especially for the target products). Takt profit is different from throughput costing (throughput costing is the contribution margin left after the price of a product is reduced by the amount of its totally variable costs). The takt profit refers to how quickly the unit profit is generated by the bottleneck operation. Takt profit is different from contribution profit in $ per minute by product because even if more quantities of stock released in production are recorded (increasing variable costs), the increase of the profit flow is not obtained because it is limited to the level of net capacity of the bottleneck operation. The increase of contribution profit per unit can be achieved, in particular, by reducing variable costs, especially the indirect variable (in the absorption costing logic). The ultimate goal is to reach *net target operating income* (sales – variable expenses – traceable fixed expenses) or *earnings before interest and taxes (EBIT)* as an element of *return on investment (ROI)* (net operating income/average operating assets).

In other words, the takt profit is the demand for profit from the shareholder (treated as profit making speed). Moreover, takt profit is evaluated by the cash at the pace sold. From this perspective, reducing the cash-to-cash cycle is essential (for estimating and limiting financing requirements), if sales tend to increase and especially if they tend to decrease

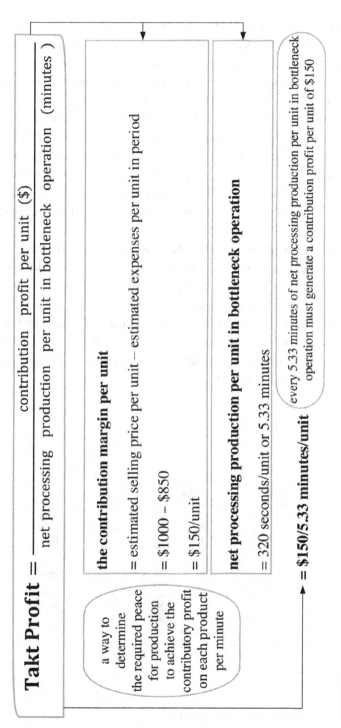

Takt Profit = $\dfrac{\text{contribution profit per unit (\$)}}{\text{net processing production per unit in bottleneck operation (minutes)}}$

a way to determine the required peace for production to achieve the contributory profit on each product per minute

the contribution margin per unit

= estimated selling price per unit − estimated expenses per unit in period

= $1000 − $850

= $150/unit

net processing production per unit in bottleneck operation

= 320 seconds/unit or 5.33 minutes

every 5.33 minutes of net processing production per unit in bottleneck operation must generate a contribution profit per unit of $150

= **$150/5.33 minutes/unit**

FIGURE 1.6
Takt profit example.

(adjusting the entire system to the level of sales volumes required by the market at the level of bottleneck operation and eliminating/reducing all unnecessary costs is essential to meet the takt profit).

Net standard operating time per unit in bottleneck operation must generate volumes of quality products that satisfy the takt profit, regardless of the level and/or fluctuation of availability, performance (speed), and quality of the bottleneck operation, but fully respecting the takt time. In the example above, the OEE expected in the bottleneck operation is 80%, the number of seconds available per hour is 2.880 seconds (60 minutes × 60 seconds × 80%), and standard cycle time of 320 seconds (5.33 minutes) or nine products per hour to meet the level of takt time required by customer requests (see Figure 1.7).

The contribution profit per unit has to generate the contributing profit per unit (in our example of $150) that will satisfy the profit takt regardless of the evolution of the sale prices (in our example being of $1,000) – decreasing or increasing, and regardless of the variable level of the variable costs. In this case, the contribution approach (costs organized by behavior; used primarily by management), *contribution profit per unit* is of $150 (sales – variable expenses – traceable fixed expenses – common fixed expenses: $1,000–$648–$100–$102).

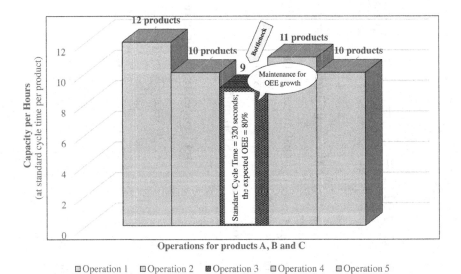

FIGURE 1.7
Working time in bottleneck operations – Example.

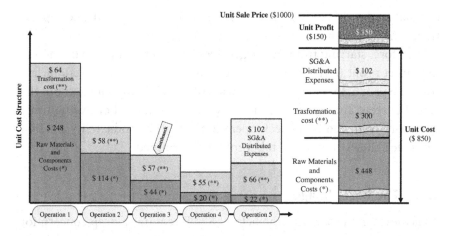

FIGURE 1.8
Contributing profit per product – Example.

In the case of the traditional approach (absorption costing; costs organized by function; used primarily for external reporting), *contribution
profit per unit* is also of $150 [sales – unit manufacturing costs – selling,
general, and administrative expenses (SG&A): $1,000 – $748 – $102]. The
unit manufacturing costs (unit cost of goods sold) are formed from raw
materials and components costs in addition to transformation cost. SG&A
are distributed expenses in the last operation – operation 5 (see Figure 1.8).

Ideal takt profit represents the state of maximum SPO by concurrently
ensuring the maximum effectiveness (by maximizing the effectiveness of
the bottleneck operation) and the maximum efficiency (by minimizing
the costs to the maximum). Usually the ideal takt profit is considered as
having a 100% index. Based on this index, the current status is measured,
for example, the actual takt profit of 78%. An 82% takt profit rate is a target
compared to the current state of 78%. The companies develop robust plans
for achieving the ideal takt profit status with targets, means, and results
run in KPIs, often by clearly defining "dream digitalization factories".

Therefore, in order to meet the takt profit, production planning is
required based on the speed of the unit profit per minute. Production
planning orders the products daily according to the production speed
of the products to meet the takt profit. Specifically, the products with
reduced cycle time in bottleneck operations, which ensure the required
quality level and with a high contribution of unit profit, will have priority
in production planning. Then the production planners strive to ensure

optimal loading of equipment and assembly lines in the bottleneck operation, considering the set-up times.

Therefore, starting from the target sales turnover and the manufacturing target profit (estimated at the multiannual and annual level), in fact from the productivity vision (Posteucă, 2019) and taking into account the actual current and future production capacity (standard operating time) obviously from the bottleneck operation, and the productivity mission (Posteucă, 2019), the annual takt profit is determined.

1.4.3 The Basic Image

To achieve takt profit with the help of SBTP requires a deep concern for real and permanent productivity, it shouldn't just be a temporary idea, a sudden promotion or a fashion. For planning and developing SBTP, it is important to systematically develop it and forecast the potential for profitability by continuously defining the potential for increased productivity.

The aims of the basic image of SBTP are presented in Figure 1.9.

1.4.4 Deep Understanding of the Actual State of Takt Profit and Actual Productivity Level

A deep understanding of the current state of the takt profit requires focusing on understanding the production management system (especially the bottleneck operation) and beyond, and understanding the way operations

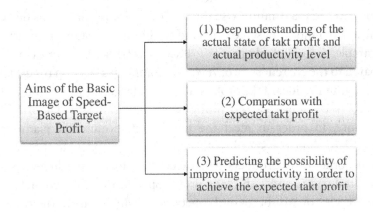

FIGURE 1.9
Aims of the basic image of speed-based target profit.

are run for business execution. The productivity level represents the number of parts made in a period of time by a distinct production flow in order to fulfill the synchronization required to complete the takt time, and the profitability level represents the rate at which the target profit expected in a period or takt profit must be met (see Figure 1.10). The actual state of takt profit is $138/394 seconds/unit, OEE of the bottleneck operation = 74% (operation 3), and actual cycle time of the bottleneck operation is 394 seconds.

1.4.5 Comparison with Expected Takt Profit

To achieve the expected takt profit with the help of SBTP, the expected image of the entire production flow is required. Scheduling the monthly production (or setting the production framework) based on the capacity of the bottleneck operations and fitting this capacity in takt profit and implicitly in takt time requires:

- ordering orders from shareholders and their need for target operational profitability directed back to the bottleneck operation (*respecting the takt profit*); as well as
- ordering orders starting from the dispatch and from the assembly term or the last operations of the flow directed back to the bottleneck operation (*respecting the takt time*).

The compliance with the two coordinates above regarding the ordering of the orders helps to alleviate the many dysfunctions of cooperation between the personnel in charge of receiving orders (control of sales, sales that often have large fluctuations) and the personnel who fulfill the daily plan of assembly and/or processing, because the main purpose in SBTP thinking logic is to achieve takt profit. Cost down, cash up, the compliance with the delivery time, lead time, planned man × hour per product, and stock levels are the ingredients of the takt profit.

Figure 1.10 shows the basic thinking mode of SBTP to perform SPO through production planning based on bottleneck operation and implicitly achieving the expected takt profit. It is the continuation of the example of takt profit from the previous section. As can be seen in Figure 1.10, the takt time to fulfill customer orders of 9 pieces/hour is synchronized with the capacity of operation 3, which is also of 9 pieces/

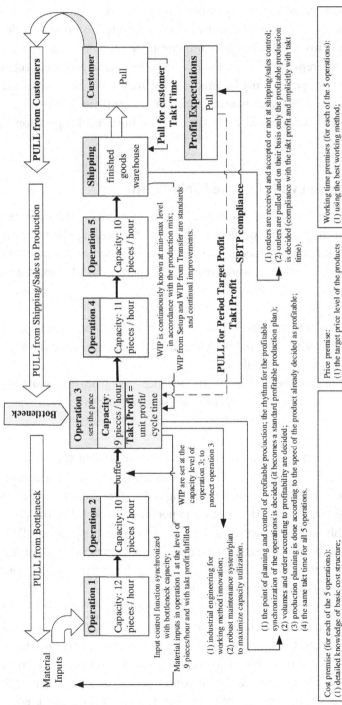

FIGURE 1.10

The basic image of synchronous profitable operations.

hour, to ensure a profit rate of $150 every 320 seconds (standard cycle time per piece in operation 3; with an OEE level of 80% in operation 3) or in other words, pieces must be produced to fulfill operational profit expectations. In this way, the calculation of the takt profit becomes the key for the daily profitable production schedule. Takt profit is achieved with SBTP.

1.4.6 Predicting the Possibility of Improving Productivity in Order to Achieve the Expected Takt Profit

Improving productivity is an eternal theme. The desired level of productivity can be far from reality unless a measurable and visible target is defined. It is necessary to make a continuous comparison between the current state, the target state, and the ideal state ("dream factories" or "dream digitalization factories"; with results in meeting the KPI targets). To achieve the takt profit, it is not enough just to have a deep understanding of the current state of productivity and profitability to capture the current state of productivity, for example, loss and to search for weak points. It is necessary to understand the deviations between the current and the necessary state. Awareness of these differences helps not only in the exact location of phenomena and problems, but also in choosing the management technology that needs to be introduced. In order for the improvement activities to be effective and efficient, it is necessary to realize the need for productivity improvement for each target and these should be in line with the profit plan. In this regard, it is important to compare with the annual and especially the multiannual level of target productivity in order to achieve the target profitability.

Therefore, in order to perform SPO, it is necessary to have the ability to predict and fulfill the possibility of improving productivity in order to obtain the expected profit, namely:

- detailing how to increase not only the production capacity of the equipment from the bottleneck operation to support the increase of the volumes, but also of the capacities of the other operations such as:
  - increase OEE;
  - reduce breakdown time and minor stoppages;
  - reduce cycle time of the equipment/line;

- decrease set-up time;
- decrease WIP; and
- decrease lead time;
- elimination of losses and waste for each operation along the entire flow with impact on CLW to support the visible reduction of costs:
  - decrease cost of transformation losses (time related losses);
  - decrease cost of non-quality losses (physical losses);
  - decrease cost of finished product waste (physical losses);
  - decrease cost of material losses (physical losses);
  - increase employee productivity (time-related losses and physical losses).

Therefore, SBTP is a way of understanding the actual losses and waste, the costs of actual losses and waste, and the restrictions of the bottleneck operation, and comparing them with their expected level to achieve the expected profit (takt profit). Then you can make a scientific, robust, and objective diagnosis, and last but not least to achieve the expected and consistent results. Predicting the possibility of improving productivity and profitability, as a percentage and their fulfillment is the purpose of SBTP. It is important to consider how to reflect the results of the activity of improvement in the visibility of productivity and profitability, generally in the whole performance of the business.

1.4.7 Computation of Speed-Based Target Profit

Establishing SBTP is based on reconciliation between (see Figure 1.11):

1. *target profit planning*: harmonized with corporate planning (long- and medium-term profit plans); through a top-down approach (takt profit);
2. *target bottleneck planning*: the estimation of the possible profit to be obtained by improving the capacity of the bottleneck operation (the contribution of improving the real working time in minutes in the bottleneck operation for the planned period or utilization for quality products); sustaining external profit from sales through increasing production volumes; through a bottom-up approach;
3. *target of CLW planning*: estimating the profit obtained by improving the CLW throughout the entire manufacturing flow, in particular, by

FIGURE 1.11
Establishing the basic mechanism of SBTP through successive reconciliations.

addressing the CCLW or processes that are responsible for contamination with losses and/or waste of other processes along the flow; supporting internal profit through manufacturing cost improvement; a bottom-up approach.

Usually, the companies balance the external and the internal profit (50%/50%) to achieve the annual profit plan. However,:

- if sales tend to increase in the planned period, then it is normal to look for increasing the production capacity of bottleneck (emphasis on effectiveness) to support the volumes of products delivered and paid, that is to say, a higher percentage is allocated to be obtained from the external profit, considered more handy to be obtained; and
- if the sales tend to decrease during the planned period, then the task allocated to the CLW is higher (emphasis on efficiency), in other words a higher percentage is allocated to be obtained from the internal profit, considered more handy to be obtained.

Productivity (effectiveness × efficiency) is the means of achieving SBTP goals. For this, a special role is played by industrial engineering (IE) – engineering to improve productivity. Meeting the annual and especially multiannual targets of ROI is the visible face of SBTP. This is achieved by increasing the volumes of products requested by customers (in the case of external profit; less or not at all on the price increase) and by reducing unnecessary costs or CLW (in the case of internal profit; excluding the reduction of the quality level of products and services).

Therefore, achieving takt profit and moving to the *ideal takt profit* status is the basic purpose of production planning using SBTP for the next period (usually one year and several years; but it is also practiced for shorter periods – a month, a week, a day, or a shift).

The calculation formula of the SBTP is:

$$\text{SBTP} = \frac{V \times [P-(E+C+A+RT)] \ (\$ / \text{period})}{B \ (\text{minutes} / \text{period})} \tag{1.2}$$

where:

V is the target volume of quality products (per period),
P is the target sales price (per period),
E is the target SG&A expenses (per period),
C is the target basic manufacturing cost (per period),
A is allowable CLW (per period),
RT is reduction target for CLW (per period), and
B is target for net standard operating time (minutes) in bottleneck operation (per period).

The purpose of SBTP (profit offer) is to support takt profit (profit demand) starting from the current state of takt profit and SBTP and projecting a future status obtained through a profitable production planning and by implementing the successful solutions discovered following the development of systematic and systemic improvement projects, both effective and efficient improvements. In order to reach an acceptable future state of the SBTP, successive scenarios are made to achieve consistent reconciliation of the future level of the SBTP to meet the future level of the takt time. In fact, the company seeks to reach an acceptable level of profitable synchronization of operations.

Below is a simple SBTP calculation to meet the takt profit of (continuation of the example in Figure 1.6; every 320 seconds of standard cycle time from the bottleneck operation, net standard operating time per unit, must generate a contribution profit per unit of $150, see Figure 1.10 – developed to support this level of takt profit).

$$SBTP = \frac{2,190 \text{ units} \times [\$1,000/\text{unit} - (\$110/\text{unit} + \$484/\text{unit} + \$211/\text{unit} + \$45/\text{unit})]}{11,673 \text{ minutes per shift/month}}$$

$$SBTP = \frac{2,190 \text{ units} \times \$150}{11,673 \text{ minutes per shift/month}}$$

$$= \frac{\$328,500}{11,673 \text{ minutes per shift/month}} = \frac{\$28.14}{\text{minute}} \tag{1.3}$$

Interpretation: In order to achieve the annual and multiannual profitability plan, based on the takt profit and takt time fulfillment, an average SBTP of $328,500 per shift/month, $28.14/minute, and an annual profit of $11,826,000 ($328,500 per shift/month × 3 shifts/day × 12 months) – profit reconciled through a top-down and bottom-up approach. Therefore, if a unit profit generated by the system of $28.14/minute is reached, then the takt time is met ($150/5.33 minutes/unit) and implicitly the annual profit plan. To reach the final version of SBTP, several simulations are performed based on productivity and profitability scenarios. The SBTP process ends when the profit target is acceptable (convergent with the annual and multiannual plan of operational profitability) and the chosen improvements are effective and efficient within the preset time intervals.

Figure 1.12 shows the results of the application of the production planning with the help of SBTP through the structural reform of the profitability based on the productivity (it is the continuation of the example in Figures 1.6–1.8 and 1.10).

As can be seen in Figure 1.12, the production planning in the SBTP logic, for the period in question, starts from the initial state, which can be the first year of the SBTP implementation or the previous year and is guided according to the ideal state of the takt profit. Therefore, even if the orders are fluctuating, even decreasing, SBTP is the basis of the development of the general production plan, the periodic (or 3 months)

Planning and Development of SBTP:
Example of the Structural Profitability Reform Results by SBTP thinking
Target reached after 3 years for "AA" Product-Family Cost (PFC)

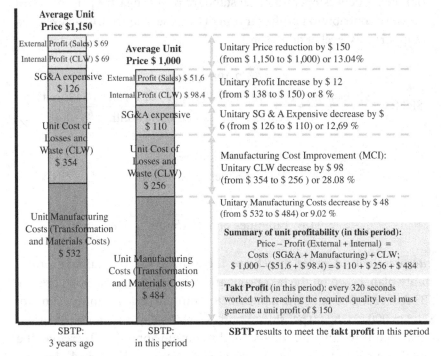

SBTP: SBTP: SBTP results to meet the **takt profit** in this period
3 years ago   in this period

Annual SBTP (based on working time in bottleneck and fulfilled takt profit):
- SBTP (3 years ago) = Annual Volume * Unitary Profit = 59,130 units * $ 138 = $ 8,159,940
- (OEE of the bottleneck operation = 69%; Cycle Time of the bottleneck operation = 370 seconds; Takt Profit = $138/370seconds/unit)
- SBTP (in this period) = Annual Volume * Unitary Profit = 78,840 units * % 150 = $ 11,826,000
- (OEE of the bottleneck operation = 80%; Cycle Time of the bottleneck operation = 320 seconds; Takt Profit = $150/320seconds/unit)
- Results of the profitability reform:about 30% profitability growth over 3 years; reaching the annual strategic target profit of 10%.

FIGURE 1.12
Example of the structural profitability reform results by SBTP thinking.

production plan, the production framework (weekly and daily), and a realistic budget, etc.

1.4.8 Features and the Basic Mechanism

Therefore, according to the SBTP definition, the annual production planning stage to meet the needs of profitability and synchronization is included in the SBTP process. A narrower interpretation of SBTP is that in order to fulfill the status of SPO continuously two processes are required as a basic mechanism and these are roughly classified as follows:

1. *The planning process:* For an annual production that concurrently meets the targets of profitability (stakeholder satisfaction takt profit) and synchronization (customer satisfaction – takt time) and establishes the annual target profit based on the contributory profit of each product taking into account the opportunity for improvement/ elimination of the CLW and taking into account the opportunity to optimize the use of the value capacity of the bottleneck operation.
2. *The developing process:* To achieve the annual target profit through profitable production planning and through the development of improvement projects to meet the targets of improving the CLW and of the need to optimize the capacity utilization of the bottleneck operation, based on leadership and on a pro-SPO culture as a way of life and as a continuous comparison between the annual target profit and the obtained one.

All improvement projects targeting the CLW (especially maximizing efficiency) and optimizing the utilization of bottleneck operations (especially maximizing effectiveness) are converging to annual and multiannual profitability targets. These projects aim at both systematic and systemic improvements and are, therefore, both effective and efficient. Figure 1.13 presents the characteristics of SBTP.

Other reasons why SBTP has become important in companies that use it alongside MCPD is that the ratio of CLW to total manufacturing costs is up to 40–45%; variable indirect costs tend to increase in most companies; companies tend to be forced to go through periods with significant and unpredictable changes in sales volumes requested by customers. Continuous measurement, mastery, and improvement of the CLW and bottleneck operations are becoming increasingly important against the backdrop of a need for profitability that will ensure the continuity and development of the companies. As the ratio of direct labor costs to total manufacturing costs tends to drop sharply, sometimes below 3%, due to adherence to various Industry 4.0 specific digitization solutions, direct cost management with materials/components/consumables by cost of waste associated with all types of stocks has become more important than managing direct labor costs and the cost of waste associated with human labor; continuous knowledge of WIP according to the production mix

✓ It applies in the production planning phase and differs from the conventional production planning system in that it takes into account that processing operations actually mean the bottleneck operation and achieves the simultaneous acquisition of takt profit and takt time;

✓ Although the main purpose is to achieve the annual target profit with projections toward the multiannual target profit fulfillment, it is not a method of profit planning in the conventional sense because it covers all aspects of production planning;

✓ The SBTP process has an impact on all dimensions of company performance and requires continuous cooperation between the production planning department and all other departments in order to achieve continuous and consistent productivity improvement;

✓ SBTP is suitable for both sales increase scenario and sales decrease scenarios and should be closely linked to annual and especially multiannual profit planning;

✓ Involves takt time follow up by all the operations and new processes and takt profit follow up by bottleneck operation;

✓ Makes the link between the production lead time and the material and factory lead time and identifies the non value added activities/auxiliary function and minimizes them;

✓ To support takt profit in time it focuses on the reduction of the operations takt time for the man*hour reduction, by percentage of OEE increase at least for equipment in bottleneck operations and decrease of set-up minutes considered strategic.

FIGURE 1.13
Features of SBTP.

is essential, as is establishing the WIP requirements and following the min-max levels. At the same time, dealing with the quality constraints that generate frequent changes in production planning is becoming more and more important. Mastering WIP is a priority for SBTP. Moreover, the SG&A ratio of total unit cost often tends to increase as a result of poor timing between production takt time and customer demands, and between suppliers and production takt time that causes concern about the CLW associated to SG&A expense. From the quality perspective, it must be said that managing the bottlenecks is actually quality control. To achieve this, companies that use SBTP develop a mechanism for SPO planning and development processes to meet takt profit concurrently with takt time.

1.5 THE SYSTEM: TAKING PROFITABILITY FUTURE ACROSS BOUNDARIES

To meet the above characteristics, we will detail the two major basic processes of the SBTP (planning and developing) mechanism in the following five steps: (1) full understanding of the current condition; (2) measuring and targeting; (3) planning and scheduling; (4) deployment; and (5) leadership and culture. Figure 1.14 shows the SBTP steps.

In step 1, corporate planning is harmonized with the situation of the current basic conditions. Specifically, based on the company's long-term and medium-term profit plans, the annual target profit for the company and for each product is determined by determining the takt profit. The medium-term profit plan projects the takt profit to achieve the margin contribution (in particular) and net operating income for the average turnover expected for the target products from the following period, depending on the sales scenarios (increasing or decreasing). At the base of these calculations is the deep understanding of the basic conditions of the company, especially for the target products, for each particular area (equipment, assembly line, storage area, etc.); these areas are as follows:

- *Delivery:* possibilities to reduce the manufacturing lead time (number of operations, distances, transfer times, set-up, OEE); WIP structure (ordering system, maps, set-up time synchronization,

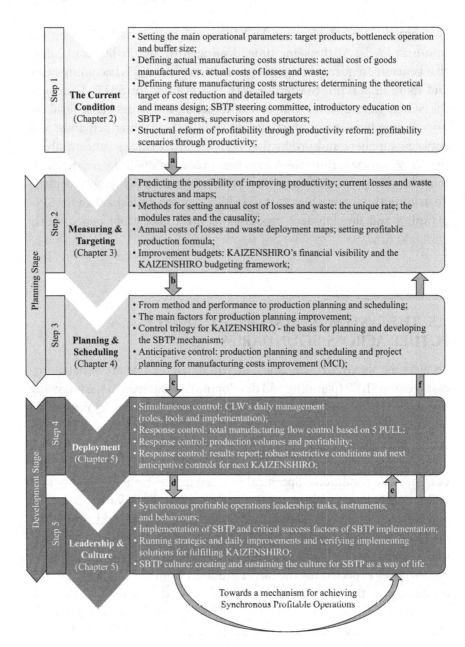

FIGURE 1.14
Planning and developing SBTP steps.

production mix, production constraints, minimum and maximum compliance, etc.); the characteristics of bottleneck operations in connection with the current and future takt time level (cycle time variations, ergonomics, behavior of new products and new processes in connection with takt time, etc.); the possibilities of achieving the OPF state [if any, understanding the parallel operations, analyzing the distances between operations, analyzing the operations without value, analyzing the elements of basic function (BF) and auxiliary function (AF), etc.]; the possibilities of material stocks reduction (the way of knowing the real material stock at any time, standardizing the withdrawal of material from the stock, respecting the minimum and maximum stock, etc.); clarification of the causes of WIP occurrence above the established standards (WIP analysis throughout the processing and of the phenomena that trigger the WIP occurrence above the minimum and maximum standards established and over the standard stay time).

- *Productivity:* the level of losses and waste for each operation; causal relationships between losses and waste, between operations; the current level of manufacturing tempo (products/shift) for the target products – analyzing and understanding in detail the bottleneck operation.
- *Costs:* the level of CLW; establishing the CCLW (losses and waste that cause the appearance of other losses and waste upstream and downstream of manufacturing flow; sometimes they are different from those of the bottleneck operation).
- *Setting objectives and determining the potential for improvement for SBTP fulfillment* (as a basis for potential productivity reform for profitability): for WIP; manufacturing lead time; for losses and waste; manufacturing time; CLW and return-on-sales ratio which is used to indicate the profit ratio for establishing target profit for each target product (or for each product).

Based on the corporate plan developed by the corporate planning department, the production planning establishes the annual production plan taking into account both takt profit and takt time, on the processing capabilities of each operation (especially bottleneck operations), as well as the current level and probably at the CLW (defining actual and future manufacturing costs structures).

In step 2, only profitable production planning is accepted. In order to shape the annual production plan, the production planning department presents the engineering planning department, the continuous improvement department, and the cost accounting department with its needs regarding the type of profitable products to be planned in production, the structure of the CLW, and future production tempo based on the design of the future state of the takt profit which is convergent to the annual- and medium-term profit plan. This is discussed at the annual production planning meeting with top management and the production planning proposal is detailed.

All the data and information necessary to develop a feedforward control based on the production instructions are provided:

1. Instructions for bottleneck operations:
   - volume instructions;
   - target cycle time (TCT);
   - occupancy rate (%);
   - yield (%);
   - automation/digitization rate (%);
   - lead time of the bottleneck operation (CT × WIP);
   - production order/types of priorities;
   - types of fine adjustments for production;
   - instructions for set-up;
   - instructions for start-up, etc.; and
2. Instructions for nonrestrictive operations (similar to those above for bottleneck operations).

Subsequently, the managers responsible for profitable target products detail this plan and establish the basic plan for improving the CLW and production tempo in the bottleneck operation – based on predictions of opportunities to improve productivity by developing current losses, waste structures, and maps. At this stage, all KPIs related to losses and waste are developed and/or reviewed, their current and likely level (based on feedforward controls to anticipate potential restrictions) is analyzed for the types and volumes of products that are planned by the production. At the same time, the cost accounting department estimates the unit costs and the CLW ratio of the total unit costs and the total planned production, investigates whether the production plan can reach the target profit taking into account the bottleneck operation capacity and helps to develop the CLW maps for each production flow – the CLW is determined using one of the three possible methods of transforming losses and waste into costs: the unique rate method, the modules rates method, and the causality method. When production planning does not appear to be profitable, the production planning department requests adjustments. Only profitable production planning is adopted based on the concomitant planning of product volumes and bottleneck improvements (effectiveness) and CLW (efficiency). Once the profitable planning is completed, the annual master budget is developed that comprises annual manufacturing improvement budgets (AMIB) and annual manufacturing cash improvement budget (AMCIB) – to visibly capture the level of KAIZENSHIRO (the target of reducing annual and multiannual manufacturing costs by reducing CCLW) and the development of KAIZENSHIRO budgeting framework at the financial level.

In step 3, the basic plan for production planning and scheduling is determined, especially for the target products chosen, which must make a significant contribution to the annual profit plan.

The production planning manager will analyze and deeply understand the potential restrictive conditions related to fluctuations of customer requests, profit request (stakeholder requirements), bottleneck, and CLW.

The three major factors of CLW (see Figure 1.15) are determined and targets for CLW are set. The production planning manager asks each department involved to review the material requirements and the manufacturing process, and to estimate the CLW and the potential level of the capacity of the bottleneck operation. Depending on the answers received from each department and the levels of the future average prices of the target finished products received from the sales departments, SBTP is calculated in total and for each target product. Following this analysis, the target planning method will be implemented. Target planning method determines the level of the target external profit based on sales (on increasing the capacity of the bottleneck operation) and the level of the target internal profit based on reducing the CLW (KAIZENSHIRO).

This step defines *control trilogy for KAIZENSHIRO* (feedforward controls, concurrent controls, and feedback controls) – the basis for planning and developing the SBTP mechanism – as follows:

1. Control over the actual effects of the production instructions for the bottleneck and non-bottleneck operation and for the CLW to achieve the takt profit and implicitly takt time targets – (*feedforward controls*).

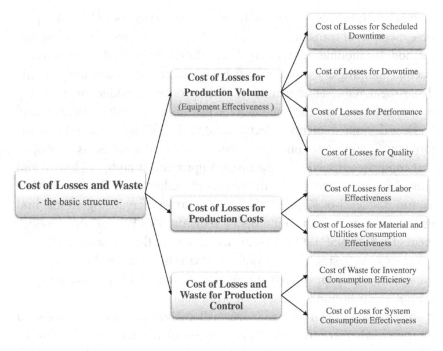

FIGURE 1.15
The basic structure of cost of losses and waste.

2. Daily manufacturing control and CLW control to check the progress of profitable production at short intervals (24/8/4/2 hours, *concurrent controls* or correct problems as they happen – confirmation of production volumes and the results of the improvements; CLW's daily management).
3. Control based on production management (verification of actual results obtained; *feedback control* or correct problems after they occur).
4. The three types of controls (see Figure 1.16) and their actions of continuous reconciliation constitute the SBTP mechanism.

At the same time as the SBTP calculation, the targets for improving the CLW for each operation and the targets for improving the bottleneck operations capabilities are set. These goals become the basic tasks of the top managers and of each employee for the area in which he/she is involved. A special role is played by the plans to increase people's motivation regarding their daily behavior toward these targets.

The basis for establishing these targets are the studies and analyses of systematic (kaizen) and systemic (kaikaku) improvements. The planning

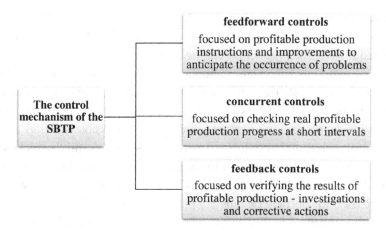

FIGURE 1.16
The control mechanism of the SBTP.

of all strategic kaizen and kaikaku projects and their effective and efficient improvement targets are planned in this step (feedforward controls – improvement project planning for MCI. In this step also, the expectations related to the visible reductions of cycle time are planned with the help of methods design concept (MDC) for the radical improvement of the productivity of bottleneck operations, without investments and with a creative/innovative approach (development of SOP).

Once the production plan based on SBTP has been approved, the entire annual management is developed to achieve the annual target profit. The SBTP review is done at short control intervals to provide a quick and correct feedback to deviations and to achieve stabilization of profitable production planning and provide a basis for an appropriate problem-solving process. Also, the department of continuous improvement plans in detail the development in time of all the improvement projects in order to meet the targets set. During the year, if there is a gap between the initial and the current SBTP, the continuous improvement department plans new actions and the SBTP level is adjusted accordingly. After repeating this process several times, the default SBTP level is reached – it should not be violated in any form in the next period.

Further, after verifying the status of the production equipment, bottleneck capacity planning, material input planning, standard delivery times, current and required lead time, etc., the production, production engineering, maintenance, quality assurance, development and design, sourcing and resource management, and cost management departments provide the production planning and control department with all the information necessary for it to make the final estimates of the SBTP according to the required model. The production engineering department sets the standard values for materials, direct labor hours, planned equipment time according to the routing, etc. At the same time, the production engineering department sets the standard values of losses and waste for scheduled downtime, admissible set-up and adjustment losses time, admissible start-up losses time, admissible tool change losses time, admissible scrap and rework losses, etc. These values are presented in the factory to be assumed by all involved.

These standard values, along with other probable losses and waste values, are used for bottleneck capacity planning (for material requirements planning – MRP) and CLW (to size the ratio of CLW to total costs). They are fixed for one year and with multiannual projections.

Further, for feedforward controls, each department now has a clear annual and multiannual plan for visible cost reductions, a detailed plan at the level of improvement budgets (AMIB and AMCIB) to support SBTP as follows:

- The purpose of decreasing the material costs (through the targets of the kaizen, MDC, and kaikaku projects):
  - the department of development and design of new products has targets to reduce the current costs of the products through effective but also efficient designs of new product and new equipment;
  - the department of sourcing and resource management has multiannual and annual targets for reducing the costs of current and future products through successive negotiations with suppliers and by identifying alternative material and supplier; and
  - the departments of production, production engineering, maintenance, and quality assurance have annual targets for reducing costs with process materials; some companies that have WIP between 40% and 60% of total stocks have cost increases between 5% and 10%.
- The purpose of decreasing the transformation costs: All departments are involved for this purpose (often the CLW ratio of total transformation costs is 35–45%; often 3–6% targets are set per year for the reduction of CLW-related transformation costs).

At this stage, production can begin and profitable order planning can be made in SBTP's logic of thinking only after setting targets to improve bottleneck processes' capabilities and CLW. At the same time, as a consequence, the targets for kaizen, MDC, and kaikaku improvement projects are set, which are effective and efficient targets at process level and are visible at the level of improvements for productivity, inventory, and delivery to meet takt profit and takt time. An example of final targets from the SBTP perspective is: a CLW improvement goal of $98 per product and OEE of the bottleneck operation increase from 69–80% (see Figure 1.12).

In step 4, we move from planning stage to developing stage, from feedforward controls to concurrent controls and feedback controls, through the deployment of effective production planning based on SBTP and running improvement projects to support target profit (both externally – by reaching the planned sales level and internally – by reaching planned cost reductions).

Effective production planning must ensure tracking designed targets by information management of the two basic PULLs (PULL for profit and PULL for clients; see Figure 1.10) through:

- ensuring full freedom of accepting and planning orders that contribute to the takt profit and takt time. For this, analyses are made and measures are taken to mitigate internal and external fluctuations in order to mitigate their impact on the results;
- ensuring the balanced loading of the production on the basis of profitable orders. For this, the transition from the state of production on the basis of the order of the type "it would be good to bring the order, but ..." to planning decisions in the previous week and added in the following week is sought; all calculations of profitability, capacity, and delivery made at least one week in advance; any order planning requires a clear connection with the probable results, which requires a daily reflection on SBTP and on takt profit (concurrent control – CLW's daily management). In this way, we move from monthly reporting, often late to daily reporting of profitability results. Moreover, all stock structures tend to fall dramatically, as does lead time and number of operations.

Therefore, the production planning and control department must:

- connect bottleneck PULLs to PULLs from stakeholders (takt profit) and customers (takt time);
- establish the volumes on the time axis and the production indications based on profitable orders;

- ensure the control of orders in the order of profitability and customer requirements;
- ensure the continuous evaluation of the results of the orders and of the improvements.

Therefore, SBTP deployment is done through concurrent control (or CLW's daily management) and feedback control (total manufacturing flow control based on 5 PULL – production volumes and profitability control, results report, robust restrictive conditions control, and next feedforward controls for next KAIZENSHIRO).

Step 5 is an important step because it coordinates the mechanism to produce as much as it is profitable (based on takt profit) and necessary (based on takt time). In order to continuously achieve and sustain the previous four steps, and implicitly the SBTP mechanism, it is necessary to develop an effective leadership (tasks, instruments, and behaviors) and a consistent culture – creating and sustaining the culture for SBTP as a way of life.

This mechanism of SBTP can be seen in Figure 1.14a–f. Therefore, to ensure continuous SPO you need:

- to fully understand the current state (step 1: the current condition) to have the necessary inputs for robust scientific planning (Figure 1.14a);
- the *planning and scheduling stage* in order to realize the SBTP specific measurements and to establish the real and scientific potential of the profitability of the operations and feedforward controls, in particular of the bottleneck operations (Figure 1.14b) and to carry out the planning and scheduling of future profitable production and the operational targets necessary to achieve the takt profit and implicitly takt time, taking into account the main current and future restrictions (Figure 1.14c); and
- the *developing stage* to achieve SBTP deployment by offering full freedom of product planning to meet target profit and by carrying out annual strategic improvement projects to support the need for market demand and the need for cost reduction by visibly reducing the CLW and to run concurrent and feedback controls (Figure 1.14d) based on consistent leadership and a pro-profitability culture through productivity and feedback controls checking from step 2 (Figure 1.14f).

If the continuous evaluation of SBTP performance (achievement of the takt profit), after the planned profitable products have been produced, deviations are identified with respect to the takt profit, investigations are made to clarify where the responsibility lies, in what processes and where the deviations come from or root causes. In fact, the production planning and control department requests details from the continuous improvement, production, production engineering, maintenance, quality assurance, development and design, sourcing and resource management, and cost management departments to have 5G-based investigations (Gemba – real site, Gembutsu – real thing, Genjitsu – real condition, Genri – theory, and Gensoku – standards). Therefore, the effectiveness and efficiency of the activities of improving bottleneck capacity and the CLW are investigated first and any new activities (Figure 1.14e) are planned and exceptionally and rarely (e.g., during an economic crisis) data and information are offered for restoring profitable production instructions during the year – feedforward controls (Figure 1.14f).

1.6 EXPECTED RESULTS

In line with the above, a pertinent question arises: What kind of tangible and intangible results can be expected by introducing the SBTP system? In order to answer this question simply, one must start from the premise that the continuous fulfillment of the *takt profit* is the main necessary output of the production systems of the companies that apply SBTP.

As shown in Figure 1.17, the main expected results of SBTP implementation are found at the level of three areas that are discussed in the subsequent text.

1.6.1 Tangible Financial Effects

The main merits resulting from the SPO through SBTP are at the financial level. Based on the careful planning and control of the bottleneck for *takt profit*, it is possible to achieve only the necessary products that fit into takt time and are profitable. The effects of SPO are found in passing from an inconsistent way of achieving the operational profit targets (with volumes of production that could not be realized, with volumes of finished

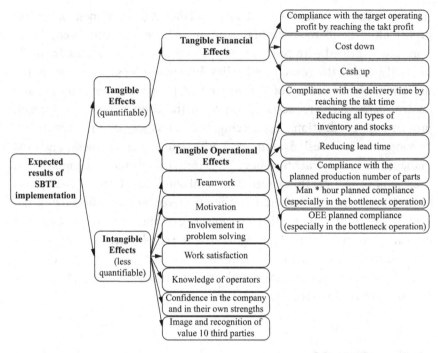

FIGURE 1.17
The main expected results of SBTP implementation.

products in stock that do not have clear orders, with losses of orders due to the inability of production or which were considered unprofitable due to the non-approaching CLW, with a cash flow with syncope and with additional costs with financing activities, with increasing costs based on a high level of storage of finished products and materials, with an oversize of the number of people, etc.), toward a consistent, continuous, and scientific way of obtaining the target of operational profit (with the reduction/elimination of the production volumes that could not be made, with only producing the profitable products required/requested by customers, with a volume of products sold almost equal to the volume of products made, with maximizing cash inflows on time, minimizing unnecessary or too early cash out, with a low ratio of CLW of total costs, with a correct and scientific dimensioning of the number of people required, etc.). In short, performing the operation target profit based on providing only the necessary costs/cost down and cash-up to realize the takt profit. These are visible at the level of AMIB and AMCIB (see steps 1 and 2 from Figure 1.14).

1.6.2 Tangible Operational Effects

The main effect of performing SPO through SBTP at operational level is the continuous assurance of the use of the bottleneck capacity to produce only what is profitable and requested by the customers – *takt time*. The effects of SPO are found in the transition from a constrained production planning based on the respect of the delivery times and on the ability of the bottleneck operation to a production planning that is free to choose only the profitable orders requested by the customers having continuously available data and the necessary information. Therefore, the freedom to choose only profitable orders and order them for shipment is the great benefit of SBTP at operational level (see step 3 from Figure 1.14). Moreover, the continuous planning and development of systematic and systemic, efficient and effective improvement projects, continuously convergent to the takt profit, is another unique benefit of SBTP (see steps 4 and 5 from Figure 1.14). Therefore, the development of operational profitable production formula to meet takt profit and implicitly takt time, even under the conditions of order fluctuations and the need to control the dynamic profitability of bottleneck operation for maximum takt profit and maximum or minimum takt time are unique tangible benefits go to SBTP.

1.6.3 Intangible Effects

Establishing the basic capabilities required to achieve manufacturing cost improvement concurrently with bottleneck capacity growth requires the development and strengthening of a company culture based on improving the knowledge, skills, and attitude of all people in the company and beyond and improving the capabilities of its equipment [assessing the management level through return on assets (ROA)]. Implementing the five steps of SBTP to perform SPO requires a systematic and systemic approach to assessing the progress and rate of improvement of activities. All of this requires the development and consolidation of excellence by employees who acquire high qualifications, in which the company has real concerns for continuous learning in order to support a high level of creativity and innovation at the level of all the people in the company. Strengthening the flexibility of the workforce (as many employees qualified to operate on at least three or four different production processes), the diversity of learning methods, the implementation, and continuous support of a real system of convergent suggestions to KPIs and implicitly to takt profit are just a few essential directions for:

- strengthening teamwork skills based on changing attitudes and skills of employees in increasingly pleasant working environments;
- increasing the motivation to make continuous and beneficial changes;
- ensuring the total and real involvement of all the people in the company, especially the managers; and
- increasing work satisfaction and trust in the company and its own forces at all levels of the company.

The tangible results of the SBTP are recorded even after the first six months after implementation, after the plan for systemic and systematic restructuring has already been developed. The intangible results begin to be better seen after the first two to three years of using SBTP.

More specifically, some of the most important results of SBTP implementations are:

- reduction of the unit cost of manufacturing by 30–45%;
- reduction of WIP by 50% through increased productivity;
- increase in labor productivity by lowering man × hour/product by 50–60%;
- increase in the flexibility level by reducing the average set-up time for the equipment and assembly lines by 60–75%;
- increase in the cycle time especially in bottleneck operations with a minimum of 200% through the innovative redesign of the working methods;
- the OEE average improvement of 150–200% – in particular for bottleneck operations to synchronize them at takt time; and
- process defect ratio cut 1/10; customer complaints have been eliminated on most products.

By adopting the SBTP system to maximize the efficiency and effectiveness of resource utilization, as a way of life and a unit speed of target profit improvement ethos at all hierarchical levels, companies will be able to consistently achieve unit speed of target profit in the bottleneck process for fulfilling multiannual and annual target profit as a unique and effective way through a new profitable production planning paradigm that operates according to its own production system.

1.7 CONCLUSION: SYNCHRONOUS PROFITABLE OPERATIONS FROM PRODUCTION PLANNING STAGE

The SBTP concept focuses on performing SPO by preventing, in particular, the occurrence of CLW and by preventing the restriction of capacity utilization in the operation bottleneck by planning the right things at the beginning. This type of effective planning (the right things at the beginning) is based on a scientific approach because bottleneck levels are measured continuously, as well as the CLW; they are classified and then their root causes are identified and clarified.

The effects of effective planning can be found in addressing and solving/improving three types of major challenges:

1. *Usual challenge 1 in the planning stage:* coupling bottleneck capacities and the level of CLW to the annual and multiannual profit plan.
   SBTP approach: Their scientific establishment and deep understanding of their associated constraints creates the premises for a more stable and robust monthly, weekly, and daily production framework and better stock control; the daily plan of the machining and assembly operations is more predictable and more stable.
2. *Usual challenge 2 in the planning stage:* fluctuations in customer orders, profit requirements, bottleneck, and CLW.
   SBTP approach: Mitigating these fluctuations through SBTP contributes to tighter sales control, a more secure annual budget and a more stable (annually and 3 months) production plan.
3. *Usual challenge 3 in the planning stage:* an approximate knowledge of losses and waste and almost none of their associated costs.
   SBTP approach: Through feedforward cost restriction control for CLW, the design targets for bottleneck and CLW are planned which supports continuous profitable planning.

The effects of an effective development at the level of jobs are found in addressing and solving/improving four types of major challenges:

1. *Usual challenge 1 in the developing stage:* OPF and continuous flow do not cover the entire flow.
   SBTP approach: continuous improvement of CLW and bottleneck capacity reduces/eliminates delays; performing set-ups often with

reduced times to ensure takt profit and flexibility for customer orders and reduces/eliminates unprofitable and/or large lots.

2. *Usual challenge 2 in the developing stage:* deliveries that track quantities and delivery times that still offer multiple "opportunities" for the occurrence of losses and waste, their associated costs and bottlenecks.

   SBTP approach: Beyond just providing deliveries that aim to meet volumes, load capacity, and ensure timely deliveries, the production is more focused on real profitability; the freedom in planning profitable orders requires a consistent set-up plan for smaller and profitable orders; in SBTP thinking, the purpose of the set-up is not only limited to ensuring the production flexibility to meet the demands, but also aims at the planning and production of the lots that have an adequate takt profit that will contribute to the daily, weekly, and monthly profit plan.

3. *Usual challenge 3 in the developing stage:* production evaluation on quantitative criteria, on-time deliveries and stock levels.

   SBTP approach: The production evaluation is based on the respect of takt profit; standardization, and improvement of bottleneck operations, and CLW contributes to effective and efficient control and feedback control to ensure an assessment of the productivity of the production (efficient – takt profit met and effective – takt time met).

4. *Usual challenge 4 in the developing stage:* organizational culture based mainly on client satisfaction.

   SBTP approach: Fully respecting the need for customer satisfaction, the production culture is focused on the need for continuous fulfillment of the profitability target by establishing cost down and cash-up priorities and then meeting the delivery deadline, stocks, lead time, etc.

In conclusion, the future status of SPO is largely decided in the production planning phase (the right things at the beginning). In order to reach the future state of the SPO, it is essential to focus on the unseen side of things, i.e., the essence of the SBTP system. There is a need for a consistent approach to CLW (especially CCLW) and not just losses and waste (the visible part of the shop floor and beyond). The SBTP approach is first of all an "inside out" type approach and then an "outside in" type approach (the need to fulfill the takt profit target). Through the "inside out" approach, the SBTP system is first interested in designing a production plan to prevent the occurrence of CLW/CCLW in the next period from the beginning and not to fight the CLW that is already manifesting. This is why the planning of strategic improvement projects is done concurrently with the planning of production. Moreover, the SBTP system continuously measures and monitors all CLWs but is mainly interested in the types of CLWs that have a high chance of manifesting in the next period and that can decisively influence the expected results (especially CCLW, which has high chances of occurrence in the future and can be improved effectively and efficiently). In this context, the key success factors of the SBTP implementation are as follows: (1) qualified project team, (2) choosing a good promotion program, (3) clarification of purpose in detail, (4) preventive approach, (5) strive to raise awareness, and (6) access to information and people. All these key factors can be fulfilled continuously only through strong leaderships and by involving skilled management consultants.

2

Develop Your Speed-Based Target Profit Mechanism and Start to Live It

Often the top managers make statements, such as: "We tried everything we could, but we feel that we have reached the limit for further improving both value-adding operating time in bottleneck operation, in order to increase production volume and the necessary reductions of unit costs"; or "We are not sure that we will be able to maintain or increase enough the current favorable profit in the future". In these cases and in many others, it is obvious that companies need a robust mechanism to support the target profitability both annually and especially multiannually by implementing and continuously improving a real system of productivity.

In this chapter, starting from the presentation of the approach to managerial commitment in SBTP, we present speed-based target profit (SBTP) mechanism, determination of profit demand and customer demand, how to establish the main operational parameters, simple determination of current costs of losses and waste (CLW) and their effects, establishing future manufacturing costs structures to meet SBTP expectations, and at last but not the least, how to approach structural profitability reform through productivity reform.

Therefore, this chapter presents the basic ingredients of the SBTP mechanism.

2.1 REAL MANAGERIAL COMMITMENT

If the concurrent fulfillment of both the annual and multiannual profit needs as well as the clients' needs are desired based on the fulfillment of consistent synchronous profitable operations, through a scientific, systematic, and systemic approach based on the cooperation between the production planning and control department and the cost management department with the other key departments (production, production engineering, maintenance, quality assurance, development and design, sourcing and resource management), then there must be full and continuous managerial support within the organization so that all resources are made available when needed. In addition to the financial resources (which are not required often) and resources that do not involve investments, the management team needs to provide the resources needed for training (especially ensuring the time needed for people to participate in improvement projects), the resources needed for periodical comparative analysis and evaluation, the sources of information, etc., to enhance people's creativity and innovation. So, it all starts with an active and visible commitment of the management team and not just a formal and declarative support. Continued support for SBTP is not a caprice but a perennial necessity of companies for increasing productivity.

From the SBTP perspective, each manager must be fully aware of who he is and what his position is in the company, and use this understanding to identify the main issues and to know how to approach them to reduce or eliminate them. Managers must be able to mobilize their staffs, colleagues, superiors, and those outside the company to bring about the desired results of SBTP. The main purpose of the managers is to use the power of their workers by directing them to the measurable objectives of the SBTP and by continuously assisting its workers to achieve the objectives set. Moreover, from the SBTP perspective, a manager must have the skills to convince and mobilize his superiors, to discuss with the managers of the other departments in order to achieve his objectives through full cooperation with them and to be able to organize those at his level, as well as those above him. Figure 2.1 shows in antithesis the managerial style that does not use SBTP and the one that uses SBTP.

Therefore, SBTP provides management with the necessary communication tools and reports, integrates the practices necessary to obtain consistent synchronous profitable operations in the current practices of profitable production planning and daily management, tests sales and profitability scenarios, and standardizes so that all people in the company continuously understand what their role is in achieving SBTP goals. Figure 2.2 shows the area of action of the management commitment in support of the SBTP mechanism.

The transition of managerial style from:	To:
Management is based on experiences and intuition;	The management is based on real facts, real data, real condition, theory, standards of cost of losses and waste and of the real use of the capacity of the bottleneck operations;
Management uses too abstract and less practical concepts;	The management uses clear concepts of non-productivity (net processing production per unit in bottleneck operation, cost of losses and waste, etc.);
Management sets targets and means that tend to be capricious based on simple ideas of higher management;	The management always sets goals and means scientifically based and which are convergent with the vision and the mission of productivity of the company;
Management does not use or use precarious analytical methods and statistical management methods;	The management understands continuously and deeply the evolution and the trend of cost of losses and waste and of the real use of the capacity of the bottleneck operations;
Managers are not educated enough to make things move as the company demands, especially from the perspective of profitability and customers;	The managers are constantly aware of the level of costs of losses and waste and the capacity used of the bottleneck operation and as a result they are sufficiently convincing to make things move in the expected direction;
Planning and realizing the profitability and improvements is the task of some people;	Planning and realizing the profitability and improvements is the task of all the people in the company and those beyond;
Functional/departmental organization generates struggles for authority and limiting the full use of all resources continuously, resources directed toward reaching KPIs targets, objectives, productivity mission and productivity vision of the company.	The main managerial purpose is the flow. The specialists in each discipline, all material and non-material resources are channeled toward the fulfillment of the expectations of annual and especially multi-annual profit and of full and continuous customer satisfaction.

FIGURE 2.1

The transition to SBTP management style.

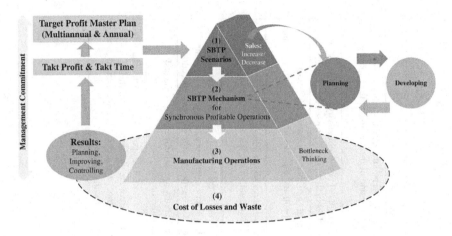

FIGURE 2.2
The role of management commitment in supporting the SBTP mechanism.

As can be seen, the role of the commitment of all managers in the thinking logic of SBTP is essential to continuously support the target profit master plan. The entire SBTP mechanism is based on the real, total, and visible involvement of managers in defining and supporting takt profit and takt time, and planning, improving, and controlling the bottleneck operations and CLW.

Furthermore, as shown in Figure 2.3, in order to plan and develop the SBTP mechanism, it is necessary to define inputs (current state:

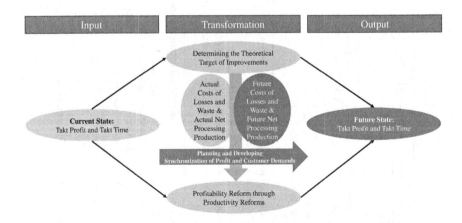

FIGURE 2.3
The SBTP mechanism: Planning and developing the synchronous profitable operations mechanism.

takt profit and takt time) and outputs (future state: takt profit and takt time) based on sales scenarios, increasing or decreasing. SBTP is not too interested in the current mode of transformation itself. It is desired for continuous measurement and deep understanding to prevent potential non-productivity. Transformation is the transfer from state/condition A or input to state/condition B or output. A solution is a means of achieving the desired transformation from A to B. It is hard to believe that a problem/transformation has only one possible solution (or it happens less often). The current level of CLW and net processing production are not problems as it refers to a situation already concluded. A problem involves more than finding a solution because it requires finding a feasible means of achieving the required transformation to the expected output in the future. The required solution is the required output that is based on the theoretical level of possible improvements of current CLW and of net processing production, but the transformation is based on modeling future operations so as to design future CLW and future net processing production in order to meet takt profit and takt time. Further, it is difficult to imagine a transformation problem where there are no restrictions on solutions. A restriction in the SBTP mechanism is something that must significantly or decisively influence a solution (transformation). The identification of the basic characteristics of the problems and their associated restrictions (e.g., time, money, knowledge, space, technical constraints, etc.) are necessary to take into account when designing the SBTP mechanism for the next period and implicitly the necessary transformation.

When designing the SBTP mechanism based on the analysis of the operations there are some points of interest, such as:

- defining the objectives of developing the SBTP mechanism:
  - connecting outputs with the expected results of the company both in the short term, and especially in the medium and long term by understanding both profit demand and customer demand;
  - defining the operations that will be the object of the SBTP mechanism by product categories and especially the bottleneck operations;
  - defining the types of cost and losses feasible to improve; and
  - defining the losses and waste needed to be improved – especially those in bottleneck operation;

- defining theoretical target of improvements:
  - defining losses and waste at the level of each operation;
  - defining the current ratio of CLW from the manufacturing costs; and
  - establishing future critical CLW;
- designing detailed targets for:
  - profit demand;
  - customer demand; and
  - synchronization of profit demand with customer demand;
- designing detailed targets for improvements:
  - analysis and ranking of improvements; and
  - setting up improvements;
- designing a new manufacturing cost structure:
  - structural reform of profitability through productivity reform; and
  - establishing the plans of the effectiveness and efficiency of improvements; and
- developing the mechanism implementation plan to achieve synchronization of profit demand with customer demand.

Therefore, the SPTB mechanism is a simple, unique, and abstract representation of the company. It is essential to obtain the initial confirmation of the mechanism from the top management and to understand in detail the current operating methods and to design them for a definite moment in the future (in order to evaluate company transformation design by implementing the SBTP mechanism).

2.2 UNDERSTANDING OF PROFIT AND CUSTOMER DEMANDS

The variation of the capacity of the production flow to satisfy the profit demand and the customer demand is not a reason to avoid applying SBTP in order to achieve the profit plan by achieving consistent synchronous profitable operations. Understanding and analyzing target profitability and customer expectations must be a particularly important concern when determining both the *takt profit (or the pace of profit demand)* and the *takt time (or the pace of customer demand)*.

To establish the level of takt profit it is necessary to determine the value of internal profit (i.e., the profit obtained by improving the CLW; computed as a bottom-up estimate) as a difference between manufacturing target profit (planned by a top-down approach) and external manufacturing target profit (i.e., the profit obtained by sales requested by customers – planned by a top-down approach; sales supported by a net processing production per unit in bottleneck operation optim – computed as a bottom-up estimate; Posteucă, 2019, pp. 13–15).

The takt profit level is established according to the two possible scenarios of the sales evolution:

- Expected increase in sales: Aims at focusing on fulfilling the multiannual and annual manufacturing target profit, especially through external manufacturing profit through maximizing outputs of bottleneck operation (productivity growth through improving effectiveness – reducing losses or not effectively used input).
- Expected decrease in sales: Aims at focusing on multiannual and annual manufacturing target profit fulfillment, particularly through internal manufacturing profit through minimizing inputs (productivity increase through improving efficiency – waste reduction or excess amount of input; Posteucă, 2019).

To support takt profit, at the level of profit-per-unit, sales growth by increasing sales price is less likely than sales growth based on sales volume growth. The decision to increase or decrease prices differs from one context to another and is only a strategic decision. That is why the control of variable costs is much more important regardless of the probable evolution of prices, up or down (even if to generate cost avoidance and cost savings, the continuous improvement of the CLW takes into account both the improvement of variable costs and fixed costs). So, the improvement projects [methods design concept (MDC), kaizen and kaikaku] of bottleneck operation and of CLW will aim to improve both variable costs, in particular direct costs with raw materials and labor, but also fixed costs, especially those with depreciation of equipment by increasing their degree of use. Beyond the takt profit, in the sales and administrative departments, the value of the CLW improvement is set for fixed costs [approaching selling, general, and administrative (SG&A) expenses is not the subject of this book – it is the sphere of productivity growth in the office].

Therefore, continuing the example of "AA Plant" (in the field of automotive components; manufacturing regime is the manufacturing and assembly industry), during the SBTP mechanism development meetings, in order to fulfill the annual profit plan in accordance with the multiannual profit plan, two phases are discussed mainly (current state – A and future state – B):

A. The current state of the previous period, such as:
   a. Profit per product in last period:

$$\text{Amount of actual profit per product in last period (\$)}$$
$$= \frac{\text{Amount of actual profit in last period (\$)}}{\text{Actual production in last period (units)}} \qquad (2.1)$$

$$\$138 = \frac{\$8,159,949}{59,130}(\text{units})$$

   b. Takt profit established in the last period (the pace of profit demand):

$$\text{Takt profit} = \frac{\text{The contribution profit per unit (\$)}}{\substack{\text{Net processing production per unit in} \\ \text{bottleneck operation (seconds)}}} \qquad (2.2)$$

$$\text{Takt Profit} = \$138/394 \text{ seconds/unit or takt profit}$$
$$= \$138/6.57 \text{ minutes/unit}$$

   Note: Every 6.57 minutes of net processing production per unit in bottleneck operation must generate a contribution profit per unit of $138.

   c. Takt time established in the last period (per month on a shift; in bottleneck; the pace of customer demand):

$$\text{Takt time} = \frac{\substack{\text{Net available processing production time} \\ \text{in bottleneck (minutes)}}}{\text{Total monthly quantity required (units)}} \qquad (2.3)$$

   Takt time (per month on a shift) = 10,798 minutes/1,643.5 units
   = 6.57 minutes (394 seconds)

Takt time (daily on a shift) = 360 minutes/54.78 units = 6.57 minutes (394 seconds)

Takt time (per hour) = 45 minutes/6.84 units = 6.57 minutes (394 seconds)

d. The SBTP in last period:

$$SBTP = \frac{V \times [P - (E + C + A + RT)] \, (\$/\text{period})}{B \, (\text{minutes}/\text{period})} \tag{2.4}$$

where:

V is the target volume of quality products (units/period),

P is the target sales price ($/period),

E is the target SG&A expenses (per period),

C is the target basic manufacturing cost (per period),

A is allowable CLW (per period),

RT is reduction target for CLW (per period),

B is target for net standard operating time (minutes) in bottleneck operation (per period).

Monthly average SBTP in the last period (average over the last 12 months; target fulfillment):

$$SBTP = \frac{1{,}642.5 \, \text{units} \times [\$1{,}150 - (\$126 + \$532 + \$300 + \$54)]}{10{,}798 \, (\text{minutes}/\text{shift}/\text{month})}$$

$$= \frac{\$226{,}665/\text{shift}/\text{month}}{10{,}798 \, (\text{minutes}/\text{shift}/\text{month})} = \$20.99/\text{minute}$$

Note:

- Speed-based target profit = $20.99/minute;
- Standard cycle time = 394 seconds/unit (or 6.57 minutes);
- Net standard operating time (minutes) in bottleneck operation (average over the last 12 months; the average overall equipment effectiveness (OEE) per shift was 74%; target fulfillment) = 10,798 minutes;

- Total units/year = 59,130 units/year;
- Net operating profit per year = $226,665/shift/month × 3 shifts/day × 12 month = $8,159,949/year (see point "A" part "a").
- Therefore, production planning in the bottleneck operation must have been completed (at the same time):
  - Takt profit (per unit) = $138/6.57 minutes/unit (every 6.57 minutes of net processing production per unit in bottleneck operation must generate a contribution margin per unit of $138);
  - SBTP reconciliation with takt profit is accomplished ($20.99/minute × 6.57 minutes/unit = $138/unit);
  - Takt time (per hour) = 45 minutes/6.84 units = 6.57 minutes (394 second) (a unit of product must be made in 394 seconds; or the net hourly capacity in the bottleneck must be 6.84 units).

- In order to achieve the SBTP (takt profit and takt time), 12 strategic improvement projects were planned and implemented (with a 10 week-average deadline for defining, analyzing, finding solutions, and implementing solutions); as the sales kept increasing trend according to the planning, the 12 selected projects focused mainly on achieving the target for net processing production in bottleneck operation, including reduction of cycle time in bottleneck operation, but also on the CLW. The logical thinking of establishing the improvements through the successive running of the profitable improvement scenarios is as follows:
  - If the volume of products will increase by "X"% by increasing the net standard operating time (minutes) in bottleneck operation by "Y"%, and if the CLW will decrease by "Z"%, then an SBTP of $"P"/minute is achieved and a takt profit of $"T"/ "M" minutes/unit is met.
  - To increase the net standard operating time (minutes) in bottleneck operation by "Y"%, it is necessary to reduce the breakdown time by "y1"%, to reduce the setup time by "y2"%, to reduce the start-up time by "y3"%, etc.
  - To reduce the CLW by "Z", it is necessary to reduce the critical CLW by "z1"%, "z2"%, etc.

- B. Future state of the this period, such as:
  - a. Profit per product in this period (see Figures 1.7, 1.8, 1.10, 1.12);

Estimated amount of actual profit in this period (\$) =
amount of actual unit profit in this period (\$) × (2.5)
estimated production in this period (units)

$$(\$)11,826,000 = (\$)150 \times 78,840 \,(\text{units})$$

b. Setting the takt profit for this period (in bottleneck):

$$\text{Takt profit} = \frac{\text{The contribution profit per unit (\$)}}{\substack{\text{Net processing production per unit in} \\ \text{bottleneck operation (seconds and minutes)}}} \quad (2.6)$$

Takt profit = \$150/320 seconds/unit or takt profit
= \$150/5.33 minutes/unit

Note: Every 5.33 minutes of net processing production per unit in bottleneck operation must generate a contribution margin per unit of \$150.

c. Takt time established for this period (per month on a shift; in bottleneck):

$$\text{Takt time} = \frac{\substack{\text{Net available processing production} \\ \text{time in bottleneck (minutes)}}}{\text{Total monthly quantity required}} \quad (2.7)$$

Takt time (per month on a shift) = 11,673 minutes/2,190 units
= 5.33 minutes (320 seconds)
Takt time (daily on a shift) = 389 minutes/73 units = 5.33 minutes (320 seconds)
Takt time (per hour) = 48.6 minutes/9 units = 5.33 minutes (320 seconds) (see Figures 1.7 and 1.10);

d. The SBTP for this period:

$$\text{SBTP} = \frac{2,190 \text{ units} \times [\$1,000 - (\$110 + \$484 + \$211 + \$45)]}{11,673 \text{ (minutes/shift/month)}} \quad (\$/\text{shift/month})$$

$$= \frac{\$328,500/\text{shift/month}}{11,673 \text{ (minutes/shift/month)}} = \$28.14/\text{minute} \quad (2.8)$$

Note:

- Speed-based target profit/per shift/month = $28.14/minute;
- Standard cycle time = 320 seconds/unit (or 5.33 minutes);
- Target for net processing production (minutes) in bottleneck operation (per period) = 11,673 minutes;
- Total units/year = 78,840 units/year;
- Net operating profit per year = $328,500/shift/month × 3 shifts/day × 12 month = $11,826,000/year (see point "B" part "a").
- Therefore, the bottleneck operation must ensure at the same time:
  - Takt profit (per unit) = $150/5.33 minutes/unit (every 5.33 minutes of net processing production per unit in bottleneck operation must generate a contribution margin per unit of $150);
  - SBTP reconciliation with takt profit is accomplished ($28.14/ minute × 5.33 minutes/unit = $150/unit);
  - Takt time (per hour) = 48.6 minutes/9 units = 5.33 minutes (320 seconds) (a unit of product must be made in 320 seconds; or the net hourly capacity in the bottleneck must be 9 units).

- In order to achieve SBTP (takt profit and takt time), as sales trend is expected to increase as planned, 10 improvement projects have been set up that will focus in particular on achieving the target for net processing production in bottleneck operation (to increase the average OEE for the next 12 months from 74% to 80%, including reducing cycle time from 394 seconds/unit to 320 seconds/ unit by running a MDC project for bottleneck operation), but also on the CLW.

Furthermore, as shown in Figure 2.4, in order to accurately collect SBTP data, it is necessary to understand and then continuously improve:

- the bottleneck operations: (1) because there is no point in production planning and shipment planning that are beyond the decided capacity of the bottleneck operation (at least in the case of an assembly line) and (2) it is essential to consider as a priority the level of scrap and rework from bottleneck operation; and

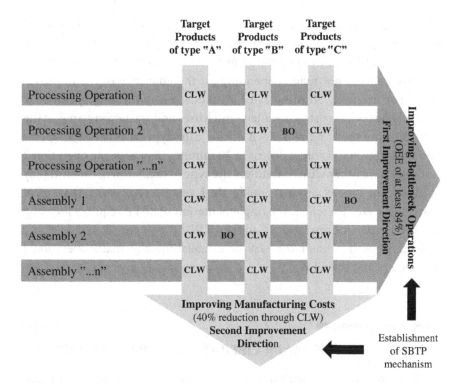

FIGURE 2.4
Two directions of action for planning and developing the synchronous profitable operations mechanism.

- CLW: (1) because it is good to consider that any cost structure has a share of costs of losses or/and waste and (2) the behavior of CLW is dynamic and quite changeable.

Therefore, as shown in Figure 2.4, it is necessary to standardize the types of target products and to continuously measure and improve the bottleneck operation and the CLW for the concurrent realization of the two types of interdependent improvements (CLW and bottleneck operation). Why interdependent? Because, for example, if the OEE level is 65% in process operation 2 (being bottleneck operation), this level generates losses and waste in the respective operation, both upstream and downstream. This type of improvements is in the area of first improvements (bottleneck operation). Furthermore, quantifying and reducing/eliminating CLW is the second direction of improvement. Why isn't the first direction of improvement enough? Is improvement to the ideal state of zero losses and waste enough? The answer is no. In the end, it gets there, through successive systematic and effective systemic improvements, but the choice of these improvements is not made depending on the efficiency of the improvement. For example, 30 minutes of breakdown in *processing operation 2* certainly has other costs associated with losses and waste compared to the same 30 minutes of a breakdown of the same type in processing operation 1. Moreover, two breakdowns of 30 minutes in processing operation 2 certainly have other CLW if it differs the type of breakdown, the shift (day or night), the type of products made, the level of scrap results, the cost of spare parts, etc. Therefore, the implementation of SBTP requires focusing on both bottleneck operations and the CLW.

Next, we will present the way of establishing the main operational parameters and the CLW.

2.3 SETTING THE MAIN OPERATIONAL PARAMETERS

To develop the SBTP mechanism it is necessary to define target products and operations to identify the characteristics of bottleneck operations. Deep understanding of product routes through manufacturing flow is essential (unit routing) for defining and implementing the SBTP mechanism.

2.3.1 Target Products

Companies survive only when they provide the expected output (fulfillment of *takt profit and takt time*). Since, at this moment of the SBTP presentation, both takt profit and takt time aim at the performance of the bottleneck operation, it can be said that they are two faccts of the same coin. Therefore, disputes over what is more important, profit or customer, are unnecessary. A company cannot survive without the concurrent fulfillment of the two dimensions.

The SBTP mechanism is based on planning and developing an effective and efficient production. This means maximizing output while minimizing required inputs (manpower, equipment, materials, utilities, etc.). To achieve this, it is necessary to fulfill the *takt profit* for the target products by:

- increasing the net standard operating time in bottleneck operation (or increase the value-adding operating time in bottleneck operation) by reducing the non-operative time of bottleneck equipment and means to increase output per unit of time of bottleneck equipment; and
- reducing the manufacturing costs by continuously improving the CLW.

Production planning and control is subordinated to the concomitant fulfillment of takt profit and takt time and needs a deep understanding of the entire manufacturing flow and bottleneck utilization capacity. Customers usually define manufacturing flow to make effective products. Consequently, companies must simulate, in detail the total lead time (supply lead time, production lead time, and delivery lead time) to define the possible profitable delivery time for each order. Any error is found in the appearance of more or less visible losses and waste and implicitly in the increase of the costs related to the respective order. Once the products have been accepted to be made, the efficiency of manufacturing flow is the main concern of the company.

Therefore, the moment of accepting orders is a key moment of the efficiency and effectiveness of that order. Accepting the order often creates disputes between the sales department and the production planning department. In order to limit the negative effects of this dispute, which from the SBTP perspective is represented especially by arranging the planning of products in obtaining takt profit (from high to low), and also by the balanced loading of manufacturing flow, loading which is regulated by setup, both for fulfilling the takt profit (setup to ensure the flexibility necessary to satisfy profit demand; inserting a small and profitable order in a large order and less profitable than small order), and for fulfilling the takt time, especially for small orders (setup to ensure the flexibility needed to meet customer demand). Therefore, according to SBTP, the setup activities acquire a double role (see Figure 2.5). The analysis of the opportunity to perform the setup activity will take into account the economic order quantity (EOQ) and the cost of the setup activity.

The selection of target products is a very important activity in the SBTP process. Organizing all the company's products into categories and clarifying the analysis criteria are essential to achieve profitable planning.

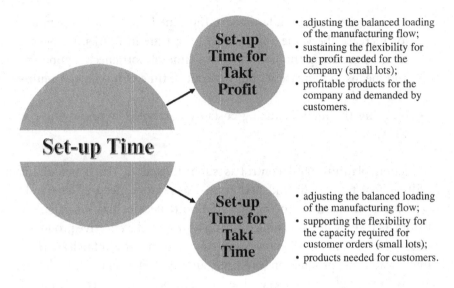

Set-up Time

Set-up Time for Takt Profit

- adjusting the balanced loading of the manufacturing flow;
- sustaining the flexibility for the profit needed for the company (small lots);
- profitable products for the company and demanded by customers.

Set-up Time for Takt Time

- adjusting the balanced loading of the manufacturing flow;
- supporting the flexibility for the capacity required for customer orders (small lots);
- products needed for customers.

FIGURE 2.5
Setup time for takt profit and takt time.

Figure 2.6 shows an example of a standard for target products from the SBTP perspective.

Therefore, it is necessary to continuously update these data on the standardization of target products (profit/loss, manufacturing costs, value of their stocks, number of storage days, delivery time, total lead time, productivity, quality, route confirmation, presence/absence of production outsourcing, etc.) because depending on them, the products responsible for contributing to the fulfillment of takt profit and takt time – implicitly to the fulfillment of target ROI are designated. Moreover, with the help of standardization of target products, planning is done to improve profitability and deliveries by reducing the costs of each product or product family and increasing the used capacity of the bottleneck operation.

2.3.2 Bottleneck Operation

A bottleneck operation is an operation that receives more work requests than it can process to its maximum capacity. This interrupts the manufacturing flow and delays occur. In most cases, the inventory increases before a bottleneck and parts after the bottleneck operation become insufficient. That is why a strict planning and control of the bottleneck operation is

Product:		Date:	Score			Product family:
Category	No.	Items				Evaluation criteria
Effects in Production Volume	1	Product Quantity (PQ) (Frequency)	5	3	1	5 for more than 30 % from volume; 3 for more than 6 % from volume; 1 for less than 5 % from volume;
	2	Product Routing (PR)	5	3	1	5 for more than 80 % from process routes; 3 for more than 60 % from process routes; 1 for less than 60% from process routes;
	3	Overall equipment bottleneck operation capacity utilization	5	3	1	5 for more than 80 %; 3 for more than 70 %; 1 for more than 50 %;
	4	Alternatives for using operational capacity	5	3	1	5 for no alternatives; 3 for the existence of at least 2 alternatives; 1 for the existence of the alternative;
	5	Effects on production failure on other products	5	3	1	5 for causes the production to stop other products; 1 for no effects.
	6	Set-up time for a lot (for the flexibility of profit demand and customer demand)	5	3	1	5 for less than 10 minutes; 3 for less than 20 minutes; 1 for less than 30 minutes.
	7	Mean Time Between Failures (MTBF) for bottleneck	5	3	1	5 for less than one time on month; 3 for more than 3 times on month; 1 for more than 5 times on month;
	8	Mean Time To Repair (MTTR) for bottleneck	5	3	1	5 for less than 2 hours; 3 for longer than 12 hours; 1 for longer than 24 hours;
Effects on Manufacturing Profit/Costs	9	Contribution margin per unit	5	3	1	5 for above average; 3 for medium; 1 for below average;
	10	Overall human work efficiency	5	3	1	5 for more than 80 %; 3 for more than 70 %; 1 for more than 60 %
	11	Material and utilities consumption loss during failures (month)	5	3	1	5 for less than $1000/month; 3 for more than $1000/month; 1 for more than $2000/month.
	12	Cost of quality loss at every product incident	5	3	1	5 for less than $1000/month; 3 for more than $1000/month; 1 for more than $2000/month.
	13	Cost of performance loss (month)	5	3	1	5 for less than $1000/month; 3 for more than $1000/month; 1 for more than $2000/month.
Effects in Production Control	14	Value of raw materials (the monthly value of stocks day)	5	3	1	5 for more than $2 million/month; 3 for more than $1 million/month; 1 for less than $1 million /month.
	15	Value of finished products (the monthly value of stocks day)	5	3	1	5 for more than $2 million/month; 3 for more than $1 million/month; 1 for less than $1 million /month;
	16	Value of packaging materials (the monthly value of stocks day)	5	3	1	5 for more than $1 million/month; 3 for more than $0.5 million/month; 1 for less than $0.5 million /month;
	17	Accident risk	5	3	1	5 for no risk; 3 for medium risk; 1 for great risk;
	18	Pollution risk	5	3	1	5 for no risk; 3 for medium risk; 1 for great risk;
Evaluation						**Target products of Class A, B or C**

The legend:

➤ To use only 5,3 or 1;
➤ Target products of Class A: above 67 points (75 % of maximum points);
➤ Target products of Class B: 45 points – 66 points (50-75 % points of maximum points;
➤ Target products of Class C: Less than 44 points (less than 50 % of maximum points);
➤ Target Class A products will have priority in profitable production planning.
➤ The improvements will focus on the target products of class A, B and C.

FIGURE 2.6

Standard for profitable target products classification (A-B-C analysis).

Operation / Physical area	Cost Center	Profitable Target Products Classification			Number of Products
		A	B	C	
Processing Operation 1	001	15	45	35	95
Processing Operation 2	002	32	34	30	96
Processing Operation 3	003	29	38	23	90
Processing Operation 4	004	11	35	28	74
Processing Operation 5	005	7	17	11	35
Processing Operation 6	006	3	5	8	16
Processing Operation 7	007	2	27	15	44
Total		99	201	150	450
Ratio		22.00%	44.67%	33.33%	100.00%

FIGURE 2.7
Profitable target products route.

needed. The working instructions must consider the actual capacity of the bottleneck operation, both for upstream and downstream operations to support production planning – ordering and processing time.

Figures 2.7 and 2.8 show an example of a profitable target products route and percentages associated with each type of product.

As can be seen, since processing operations 1, 2, 3, and 4 are those that support about 80% of the number of products (in terms of profitability and volume) their improvement is essential (both at the level of CLW and bottleneck, e.g., operation 2 is bottleneck).

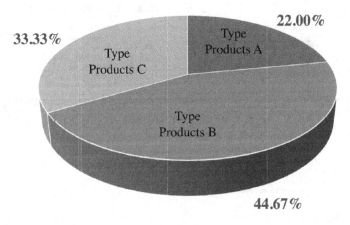

FIGURE 2.8
Percentages associated with each type of product.

The first important element of the SBTP calculation formula is the target volume of quality products – "V" (units/period). As mentioned before, there is no point in a production and shipment planning that is beyond the decided capacity of the bottleneck operation, and it is essential to consider as a priority the level of scrap and rework in the bottleneck operation. The actual capacity of bottleneck operation or the net standard operating time in bottleneck operation – "B" will determine the volume of the entire manufacturing flow and is established by the continuous determination of OEE for the equipment chosen as strategic. Therefore, the takt time fulfillment is in direct connection with the bottleneck operation capability. That is why companies make sustained efforts to achieve a takt time synchronization between equipment and assembly lines and beyond with deliveries. This synchronization is often sought for target products that have the same takt time and an increase in overall line effectiveness (OLE) is sought. The end of the synchronization journey is the ideal one-piece flow (OPF) state in which all losses and waste are eliminated and the equipment and assembly lines are fully synchronized to the takt time.

2.3.2.1 Deep Understanding

Therefore, once the target products have been established, it is necessary to understand the processing paths of each target product (see Figure 2.7) and the capacity of each operation.

In order to understand the capacity of each operation in depth, it is necessary to: understand the inputs and outputs; understand the current working method; continuously measure the operations capacity; understand the evolution of processing and assembly capacities; understand the evolution and trends of the outputs of finished parts and products and the detailing of the causes; the loading and unloading methods of the operations and their associated times; identify and classify potential improvement ideas, etc. All this information is obtained by walking through the factory and by collecting real data. It is necessary to determine the actual load capacity or net standard operating time (*the denominator formulas of SBTP*). Particular attention must be paid to:

- the control indicators of deposits, the operations and transfer times between operations;

- the layout of the areas – placements and way of displaying information and articles;
- the planning methods for processing, the assembly and shipping;
- the way of transmitting the production instructions;
- the methods for capturing production results (volumes): parts, finished products, scrap, rework, etc.;
- the way of planning the necessary direct labor (man × hours);
- the way of planning the activities for the setup required by the takt profit (or the pace of profit demand);
- the way of planning the activities for the setup required by takt time and the need for flexibility (or the pace of customer demand);
- the clarification of bottleneck capacity operation;
- defining the state of overcapacity or subcapacity of the production flow; and
- the clarification of the root causes that determine the appearance of temporary stocks (waste or excess amount of inputs); or in other words: "waste (stocks) elasticity on losses" (Posteucă and Sakamoto, 2017, pp. 236–238, Posteucă, 2018, p. 13).

Beyond collecting and processing the data obtained by walking through the factory, a rigorous office work is also needed:

- to define very clearly the operations/processes that form production lead time (list of equipment and parameters and operating principles of each equipment);
- to establish the types of standard setup activities for each type of product and process, to know the main types of errors of the setup activities compared to the standard operating procedure (SOP) (including errors regarding the order of the setup activities);
- to know the status of ongoing improvement projects for setup (including their improvement targets);
- to know the bill of materials (BOM) for each product;
- to establish the compliance with delivery deadlines;
- to know the average scrap and rework rate;
- to establish the synchronization rate between delivery lead time and production lead time; and
- to know the inventory rate from the raw material warehouse created by the bottleneck capacity operation in the last 3, 6, and 12 months.

Total Contracted Hours																			
Total Working Hours																			Absenteeism and holidays
Non Productive Hours (Shutdown Losses; Hours paid, but no production has been realized)										Productive Hours (Time required to produce)									
Non Productive Hours (NOT engaged on production)					Non Productive Hours (engaged on production, but non producing)					Downtime				Loading Time					
														Production Time					
diseases of employees (sick leave)	injuries at work	short breaks	training	meetings for MDC/Kaizen/Kaikaku	cleaning, checking and lubricating	lack of tasks	waiting time for quality check	waiting for materials	planned maintenance	breakdown	setup, settings, adjustments	fill/refill, replacement, starting	startup	scrap (bad parts)	time to rework	speed loss	minor stops and idling	GOOD PARTS (net standard operating time or net capacity)	
measured	measured	measured	measured	measured	measured	measured	measured	measured	measured	measured	measured	measured	measured	calculation	time with rework	calculation	calculation	measured	measured

FIGURE 2.9
From total contracted hours to net standard operating time for a module.

To clarify bottleneck capacity operations, Figure 2.9 shows how to determine the total or net standard operating time (minutes) for an equipment or module.

Choosing areas for measurements and improvements is very important. From the SBTP perspective, each such area is called the *module* (distinct physical units that contribute to the production of products). In order to establish the modules, the following are considered:

- technological phases (a distinct phase of production; a phase includes all the activities necessary to produce the products);
- types of activities (several series of processes for producing the product according to its characteristics required to be carried out in those activities);
- processes (several series of operations at a workstation to produce the product; these are the detailed elements of an activity); and

- operations (the operation is the clearly defined work unit and is a work unit that cannot be assigned to more than two workers) and work methods associated with activities, processes, and operations.

It is desirable to establish as similar modules as possible in order to easily replicate the improvement solutions. As can be seen in Figure 2.9, of the *total contracted hours*, which represent all paid hours including small breaks, holidays, and absenteeism (for operators, direct support – team leaders off/on production; feeders, finished product movers, etc.), only one part is represented by *good parts*. This production time for good parts is net standard operating time (minutes). The full understanding of the capacity or net standard operating time of the bottleneck operation ("B" in formula SBTP) is actually the capacity that a company can rely on in production planning. Moreover, the quality level of the bottleneck operation is the quality level that should be considered. Furthermore, the net standard operating time is based on standard cycle time (piece/time). The lower the cycle time becomes without affecting the quality level, the more visibly the productivity increases (the denominator of the takt profit formula). In addition to this decrease/improvement of cycle time, all other elements that contribute to the decrease of total contracted hours must be standardized and continuously improved until the feasible elimination of all ineffective activities (losses or not effectively used input). Particular attention should be paid to the differences between the number of units achieved (output/time) and the standard consumption of raw materials/components (inputs; in kg, meters, square meters, etc.) and utilities (inputs; kilowatts, liters, etc.). At the same time, labor productivity must be measured continuously for areas where labor actually ensures production speed (e.g., semiautomatic assembly lines). Determining the capacity or net standard operating time of the bottleneck operation ("B" in the SBTP formula) is similar to that shown in Figure 2.9. *Therefore, the higher the net standard operating time and the longer the cycle time has the chance to manifest, the easier the takt time is fulfilled. Moreover, the higher the net standard operating time, the lower the variable costs tend to decrease (e.g., the reduction of purchase prices from the supply of raw materials, materials and/or components due to a higher volume), and takt profit tends to meet its targets more easily.*

2.3.2.2 The Goals

Currently, the purpose of fully understanding bottleneck capacity operation is to know net processing production capacity in order to deliver on
delivery promises, based on effective and efficient production planning
and rigorous inventory planning. At the same time, in order to support
the planning of production and stocks and to achieve the ROI targets, the
planning and realization of the improvements of losses and waste related to
bottleneck capacity operation are essential. The standardizations of all the
elements in Figure 2.9 aim at the continuous improvement of the net standard operating time (net processing production capacity). The continuous
improvement of net processing production capacity targets both the peace
of profit demand (takt profit) and the peace of customer demand (takt time).

From SBTP's point of view, following are the two main objectives of a
bottleneck operation that must be met concurrently:

1. Ensuring the synchronization between the net standard operating
   time of the equipment and the assembly lines with takt time in order
   to tend toward the ideal state of OPF by eliminating all losses and
   waste (customer demand); for this, objectives are set for the money
   immobilized in the stocks in the warehouses, for the reduction of
   production lead time, for the fulfillment of the delivery terms, and
   for the observance of man × hour according to the planning; and
2. Ensuring the synchronization between the net standard operating
   time with takt profit (profit demand) in order to tend toward the
   ideal state of zero CLW; for this, the SBTP mechanism is established
   to ensure the maximum use of all company resources; the required
   quantity of buffer stock before the bottleneck operation and the
   dynamic buffer sizing to mitigate any fluctuations due to problems
   in operations are established; the way of adjusting the inputs of raw
   materials, materials, and components to the bottleneck operation is
   established in order to carry on with the bottleneck operation when
   there is lack of raw materials/components. Moreover, improvement
   targets are set for each cost structure of losses and waste.

Following the full understanding of the bottleneck operation and the
establishment of its objectives, the frame of reference for the production is
determined, the production being approached holistically. Specifically, it
is decided that the capacity of production system in bottleneck operation

is necessary to be ensured in accordance with production quantity for the next period, the level of strategic capacity reserve necessary to mitigate variations in customer demand and variations in manufacturing system capacity (usually between 20% and 30%), and last but not least, the determination of the state of over- or under-capacity for the next period (depending on which the systematic – kaizen and systemic – MDC and kaikaku improvements are established).

2.3.3 Buffer Size

Once the target products and bottleneck capacity operation have been determined and understood, in order to truly support profit demand and customer demand (the OPF status is not fully realized) it is necessary to establish a temporary measure on the required inventory quantities for bottleneck operation, for target products in particular, and the establishment of the buffer inventory size to ensure timely supply of bottleneck operation. All this to support the target volume element of quality products (per period) (see "V" from SBTP formula). The buffer helps to ensure the satisfaction of the demand for profit and the demands of customers in all conditions. Buffer inventory is a means of responding to customer requests when there are manifestations of internal constraints. The additional stock needed to meet takt time when customer demands vary is a distinct element of production planning. Both the buffer inventory and the additional stock caused by order fluctuations are forms of waste (excess inventories). In the case of buffer inventory, it is sought to determine the causality of its occurrence based on the company's internal events. In other words, the clarification of the types of losses that cause the appearance of buffer inventory or waste (stocks and inventory) elasticity in losses (Posteucă and Sakamoto, 2017, pp. 236–238; Posteucă, 2019, p. 38). In this context, each module will generate both losses and waste.

Therefore, in order to establish the buffer size and limit the negative effects of the manifestation of the internal constraints of the bottleneck capacity operation, including the occurrence of at least sporadic schedule overtime, a detailed analysis of the fluidity level of the bottleneck capacity operation is needed based on records from equipment computers. For this, the following are analyzed:

- the downtime history (breakdowns; setup, settings, adjustments; startup, etc.) of the process before the bottleneck capacity operation (see Figure 1.3);

- the longest time of a repair of the process before bottleneck capacity operation and not only before bottleneck capacity operation;
- the average time of process blockages before bottleneck capacity operation;
- the variation of the lower limit of the inventory or the fixed safety inventory (FSI; size × capacity of the bottleneck operation); the setting of the FSI also considers: the requirements of the assembly phase (number of days * daily consumption), problems with equipment during production, the degree of load capacity of the bottleneck operation (estimated level of buffer supply delays and lack of orders), labor power issues, quality problems – especially for target products, power outages, and the like;
- the variation of the upper limit of the inventory or the variable safety inventory (VSI; FSI + quantity required for the following week + quantity required over 2 weeks);
- the variation of the maximum limit: VSI + FSI + the good residues left from the processing;
- the moment of replenishing the buffer inventory depending on the rhythm of the PULLs from the bottleneck capacity operation;
- the frequency and types of buffer controls to minimize stock investments (controls should tend to zero); and
- the way of classifying the types of firm orders received, etc.

The purpose of the detailed buffer size analysis is for:

- establishing/standardizing the minimum and maximum acceptable level for the proper functioning of the bottleneck capacity operation (through continuously improved setup, both afferent profit demand and customer demand, through kaizen for scrap and rework, by reducing cycle time from bottleneck operation, etc.);
- limiting to the maximum the money blocked in unnecessary stocks; and
- limiting to the maximum the increase of unit costs caused by the variations of the capacity of the bottleneck operation.

Usually buffer size generates FSI supplementation via VSI by 10–20% to limit the negative effects of internal constraints. It also seeks to load the system with up to 90% (bottleneck operation capacity). Production planning is strict for the first five days of the week; on Saturday it is recovered and one or more safety days are left until shipment (in conditions of market instability the number of these days may increase; this respite is used to fulfill takt profit for the target products of class "A" and "B"; profitable products have priority by shortening to the maximum setup time to meet profit demand). The continued support to prevent bottleneck capacity operation is also essential to simplify control in the area.

2.4 DEFINING ACTUAL MANUFACTURING COSTS STRUCTURES

After the presentation in the previous sections of the main elements of the SBTP formula that contribute to the support of the target volumes, respectively target volume of quality products ("V") and net standard operating time (minutes) in bottleneck operation ("B"), without addressing the level of target sales price in the period ("P"), as they are in the sphere of marketing activities and cannot be influenced too much to increase (under the conditions of free pricing in a global market; we do not get into the logic of dumping policies and other such policies) and without addressing the target SG&A expenses in the period ("E"; which is addressed by increasing productivity in offices areas, subject outside this book). In order to support the fulfillment of SBTP, we will further present manufacturing cost (calculation of "C" or the target basic manufacturing cost per period form the SBTP formula), and then how to determine the CLW to identify the ratio of CLW from total manufacturing costs in order to understand the theoretical and practical target of improvements for future CLW (see Figure 2.3; determining "A" or the allowable CLW per period form the SBTP formula), and finally the feasible annual target of CLW (or setting "RT" or reduction target for CLW per period) in order to meet the target SBTP and takt profit.

So, two costing systems are commonly used in manufacturing:

- *Process costing* (preferred by manufacturing companies that produce many units of a single product and when one output unit is not clearly distinguished from another output unit; an average cost system is used to determine the cost of the product); and

- *Job-order costing* (is preferred by manufacturing companies that produce many different products in each period; when the products are in accordance with the specific requirements of each customer; each order is tracked and cost allocations are made for each process/operation/department; average cost computed by process/operation/department).

As is well known, the schedule of cost of goods manufactured covers three cost elements, namely direct materials, direct labor, and manufacturing overhead which currently includes indirect materials and indirect labor as well as other manufacturing costs, such as the power used to run the equipment in the factory. These manufacturing overheads cannot be traced directly to certain processes/operations/departments, but are distributed using predetermined rates [including by using an activity-based costing (ABC) method].

2.4.1 Actual Cost of Goods Manufactured

The basic purpose of a cost and managerial accounting system is to continuously support operations by planning and controlling their profitability and by providing the data and information needed for decision-making.

Even if this book does not aim to detail the management and cost accounting fundamentals (job-costing systems, process-costing systems, cost allocation, determining how costs behave, etc.), we will briefly address how to determine the actual cost of goods manufactured, in order to later describe in detail how to determine the actual CLW.

Therefore, the purpose of manufacturing costing is to calculate the cost of raw materials, direct labor, and manufacturing overhead used in production. In addition, manufacturing costs associated with goods that were finished during the period are determined. The cost of raw materials is not simply the cost of raw materials purchased during that period (considering the yield ratio). Raw materials cost or direct materials cost is the cost of the materials used in the respective period by each cost center separately (for each object cost: operation, equipment, activity, product, etc.). The purchases of raw materials made during the period are added to the beginning raw materials inventory balance to determine the cost of materials available for use during the period. The ending materials inventory is deducted from this amount to arrive at the cost of raw materials used in production. After determining the raw materials cost, the transformation costs (also called conversion costs; direct labor and manufacturing over-head) are determined to get the total manufacturing costs for the period. After calculating the total manufacturing costs, we move to work-in-process inventory add to that, total manufacturing costs, and we get the total work in process for the period. Finally, the work in process for the period is lowered by ending work-in-process inventory to get the cost of goods manufactured. Further, the cost of goods manufactured is added to the beginning finished goods inventory to get the cost of goods available for sale. The ending finished goods inventory is subtracted to obtain the cost of goods sold. The cost should be close to the actual (a robust standard costing system can be very helpful).

Therefore, in manufacturing cost systems two terms are used when approaching process costs: *prime costs* and *transformation costs*. Prime costs are all direct manufacturing costs (most often only direct material costs are included). Transformation costs are all manufacturing costs other than direct materials costs. Transformation costs are all indirect manufacturing costs (other terms: manufacturing overhead costs and factory overhead costs) and fixed manufacturing costs for transforming direct materials into finished goods (sometimes labor costs).

From the perspective of allocating direct materials costs to cost objects (departments/cost centers/products) there are no particular difficulties. The BOM developed based on product design and associated material lists is used (yield ratio is considered).

Instead, allocating indirect manufacturing costs and fixed manufacturing costs to cost items is often a challenge. Indirect cost depends on cost allocating standard. Some fixed manufacturing costs can be allocated relatively easily to cost centers (e.g., depreciation of equipment). The indirect manufacturing costs allocating standard is one of the important components that decides a price offer for a product. Often companies set this standard considering volumes (direct labor hours, equipment hours), activities (activity drivers as in the case of activity-based costing), price level, product pricing strategy, etc.

Therefore, the purpose of actual cost of goods manufactured from the perspective of determining the actual CLW is:

- to compute unit product costs:
  - in the absorption costing variant (in which all manufacturing costs are considered product costs, regardless of whether they are

variable or fixed costs; the cost of a unit of product consists of direct materials, direct labor, and both variable and fixed overhead; variable and fixed selling and administrative expenses are treated as period costs and are deducted from revenue as incurred); and

- in variable costing variant (in which only those production costs that vary in tandem with production as product costs are addressed; the cost of a unit of product consists of direct materials, direct labor, and variable overhead; fixed manufacturing overhead, and both variable and fixed selling and administrative expenses are treated as period costs and deducted from revenue as incurred;

- to determine the cost of one minute for each cost center, both with non-productive hours, and with productive hours (see Figure 2.9); and

- to determine material costs for each cost center with scrap, spare parts, utilities consumed, etc.

From the manufacturing costs perspective, the main challenges are:

- deep understanding of the fluctuations in manufacturing cost (direct materials costs, direct labor costs, and manufacturing overhead costs) caused by the change in the volume of activity, the change in the cost structure and the change in purchase prices; and

- practicing an effective feedforward control regarding manufacturing cost fluctuations (even if companies practice an elaborate standard cost system), feedforward control to prevent the occurrence of such significant fluctuations (i.e., overhead absorption and labor hour variances) so that contribution margin and net operating income targets are continuously met.

For example, in order to address manufacturing cost fluctuations by developing a standard costing method, the following is done:

1. *The correlation between fluctuation in quantity and fluctuation in cost*: For example, *direct labor cost* for more than 100 kpcs/month is 120% productivity coefficient and for less than 10 kpcs is 90% productivity coefficient; between the coefficient of 90% and 120% productivity

are other categories (4–6 categories); for example, for *indirect manufacturing cost* more than 100 kpcs/month, the cost decreases 10% and for less than 5 kpcs, the cost increase 10%; volume efficiency is reflected).

2. *The calculation of depreciation cost that makes it possible to reinvest*: Depreciation cost is calculated by straight-line of acquisition cost of assets since it has a possibility to reinvest; but, usually, the products are produced by depreciating assets – so it becomes more profitable than the quotation on accounting book).

3. *The allocation of indirect manufacturing cost:* Allocation by volume or direct/indirect ratio is not appropriate; volume allocation often targets large volume ranges and does not match reality; moreover, high-volume products should bear more of the costs; direct/indirect allocation does not provide the opportunity to identify opportunities for cost reductions and "selling" indirect costs to the customer becomes difficult).

Therefore, from the SBTP perspective, the direct materials costs are allocated to each module (or operation) and then to each product, and the transformation costs (indirect manufacturing costs and fixed manufacturing costs) are allocated in the lump sum according to the net standard operating time per unit in bottleneck operation (minutes) – to the standard passing speed of bottlenecks operation for each product. For example, transformation cost ÷ total shots of tooling/month ÷ quantity/shot of tooling.

Resuming Figure 1.7, in Figure 2.10 the way of determining the unit profit by directly distributing materials costs per operations and by distributing the transformation cost based on bottleneck speed per operations is presented.

However, it would be desirable for each cost to be drawn directly on the products, for example, tool cost, die and jig cost, energy cost etc. These costs should be estimated individually from process cost because there are two cases of quotation that includes in the unit price or excludes from the unit price. Moreover, SG&A ratio is based on past result of SG&A. SG&A includes part of development cost. For example, 20–25% would be for fundamental research and development ratio. Therefore, development cost allocated to manufacturing cost (transformation costs) can be 75–80% (industrial development ratio).

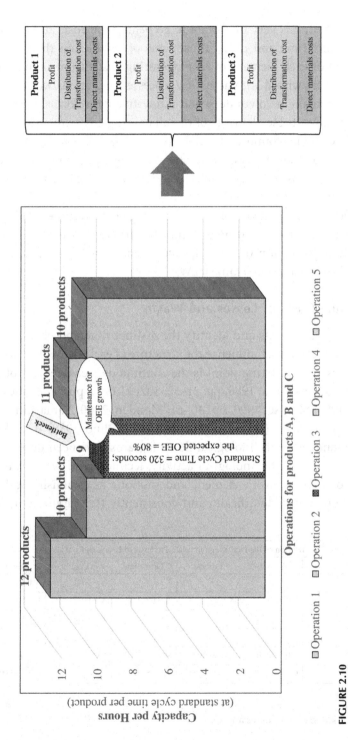

FIGURE 2.10
Capacity of operations and allocation of costs per product – distribution of transformation cost based on bottleneck speed.

In this context, it is very important to go behind the costs and to identify the distinct time and physical elements of production that include the structure of each element of manufacturing costs. Controlling these cost elements associated with activities/processes/operations/work items/ movements actually involves deep and innovative job reforms. From the SBTP perspective, these elements of manufacturing costs are represented by CLW, and the profound and innovative reform concerns the innovative approach to productivity of each job by implementing transformations based on continuous systematic (kaizen) and systemic (MDC and kaikaku) improvements.

In conclusion, the purpose of manufacturing cost from the SBTP perspective is to determine and understand the structure of unit costs and their mode of formation on modules (cost centers; activities/processes/ operations) in order to determine CLW.

2.4.2 Actual Costs of Losses and Waste

In order to go after costs and identify the distinct time and physical elements of production that influence the structure of each element of manufacturing costs, the starting point is the continuous measurement of the level of losses (Nakajima, 1988, pp. 21–52; Suzuki 1994, pp. 21–44, Sekine and Arai, 1998; Shirose, 1999, pp. 40–61; Monden, 2000; Yamashina and Kubo, 2002) and waste (Ohno, 1978; Ohno, 1982; Ohno, 1988) at the level of each module (after technological flow diagrams have been developed: technological phases; technological activity, technological process; technological operations; work element and motion) to establish the level of non-productivity scientifically and consistently (see Figure 2.11; MC

Classification of the measurement related to costs of losses and waste					
Technological Phases	Activity	Process	Operation	Work element	Motion
X	X 1	X 1-1	X 1-1-1	X 1-1-1-1	X 1-1-1-1-1
	X 2	X 1-2	X 1-1-2	X 1-1-1-2	X 1-1-1-1-2
	X 3	X 1-3	X 1-1-3	X 1-1-1-3	X 1-1-1-1-3
....	....	....	....	....	....
MC: $10,000	MC: $9,000	MC: $8,000	MC: $7,000	MC: $6,000	MC: $5,000
	CLW: $1,000	CLW: $2,000	CLW: $3,000	CLW: $4,000	CLW: $5,000

FIGURE 2.11
Uncovering hidden cost of losses and waste.

is manufacturing cost; CLW is CLW – included in the MC structure; Posteucă and Sakamoto, 2017; Sakamoto, 2010).

After 6, 12, and 18 months of measuring losses and waste, it is possible to understand the manifestation of losses and waste for each cost object (phase, activity, process, product, etc.) in part and especially for the bottleneck operation. CLW at the activity level are represented by the CLW created at the system level (e.g., production changes/adjustments plan loss, new equipment delays installing loss, new products development delay release loss, obsolete equipment loss, surface/square meters loss, etc.). CLW at the process and operation level are measured with the help of OEE and improved through MDC, kaizen or kaikaku projects. CLW at the work element and motion level are in the industrial engineering area and are measured and improved with the help of MDC.

But some pertinent questions arise such as: What are losses and waste? What are CLW? What is non-productivity?

As it is known, one of the ways to measure productivity is:

$$\text{Productivity} = \frac{\text{Output}}{\text{Input}} \tag{2.9}$$

An analytical approach to the content of productivity through three factors is (Posteucă and Sakamoto, 2017, pp. 295–312):

$$\text{Productivity} = M, \text{methods} \times P, \text{performance} \times U, \text{utilization} \tag{2.10}$$

Another way to measure productivity is:

$$\text{Productivity} = \text{Effectiveness} \times \text{Efficiency} \tag{2.11}$$

In other words:

$$\text{Effectiveness} = \frac{\text{Output (maximized)}}{\text{Input resources (constant)}} \tag{2.12}$$

The lack of output maximization (management results) is determined by not effectively used input or *losses*.

Concurrently:

$$\text{Efficiency} = \frac{\text{Output (constant)}}{\text{Input resources (minimized)}} \qquad (2.13)$$

The lack of minimization of resource input is determined by excess amount of inputs or *waste*.

Therefore, it can be said that the higher the level of losses and waste, the higher the level of non-productivity and the higher the manufacturing costs. The non-productivity is found both at the level of methods (especially losses or non-effectiveness), at the level of performance (waste or non-efficiency), and at the level of utilization (losses or non-effectiveness). Continuous measurement of losses and waste (especially at the level of activity, process, and operation) is essential to understand the current and potential level of non-productivity. Moreover, the continuous transformation of all losses and waste into costs helps to financially dimension non-productivity.

In this way, managers become more aware and engaged in reducing this level of non-productivity in a feasible way to:

- maximize the external profit, especially against the background of increasing sales volume (in other words by reducing non-productivity related losses in particular); and
- maximize the internal profit, especially against the background of decreasing sales volume (in other words by reducing non-productivity related to waste in particular).

In this context of non-productivity, a number of pertinent questions arise, such as: What are the main categories of losses and waste that SBTP addresses? How are these losses and waste transformed into costs? How are the most effective and efficient improvement projects chosen in order to reach the future CLW starting from the actual CLW?

To answer these questions succinctly, we will take the example from "AA Plant" (detailed answers to the above questions will be presented in the following sections).

Therefore, AA Plant (in the field of automotive components; manufacturing regime is the manufacturing and assembly industry) has three target product groups ("A", "B", and "C"). In order to fulfill its annual profit plan in accordance with the multiannual profit plan, it continues the analysis of the two faces (current state – A and future state – B; see Section 2.2, "Understanding of Profit and Customer Demands"). All these types of products go through four modules (three processing and one assembly and inspection – bottleneck capacity module; see Figure 1.3).

The management of AA Plant knows the following information related to costs and volumes:

- Average production volume/shift/month: 1,642.5 units;
- Total unit cost: $1,012 ($126 + $532 + $300 + $54; respectively, SG&A expenses – their reduction is not the purpose of this book; target basic manufacturing cost; allowable CLW and reduction target for CLW);
- Total unit manufacturing cost: $886 ($532 + $300 + $54; respectively, target basic manufacturing cost; allowable CLW and reduction target for CLW);
- Total manufacturing cost/month: $1,455,255 ($886 × 1,642.5 units);
- Total manufacturing cost/year: $17,463,060 ($14,552,558 × 12 months);
- Total manufacturing cost per month is composed of raw material costs of $873.153 (60%) and conversion cost of $582.102 (40%);
- The following activities are often carried out to address reductions in raw material costs:
  1. Making profitable designs for future products (by the research and development department; approximately 80% of future costs are set in the design phase);
  2. The search for alternative materials and supplier and through successive negotiations with current suppliers (by the supply chain department, where annual targets for reducing raw material costs between 3% and 5% are set); and
  3. Reductions in the processes of the products made (by all the departments involved in the production process, where annual targets for reductions of raw material costs between 3% and 5% are set).
- The structure of transformation costs per month is presented in Figure 2.12 ($582.102 structure).
  The structure of transformation costs is:
  - *Variable transformation cost ratio (vtcr)*: $28/minute ($407.471/ 14.580 minutes; 14.580 minutes is loading time in bottleneck module; $407.471 is the difference between $582.102 and $174.631; $174.631 is depreciation cost); and

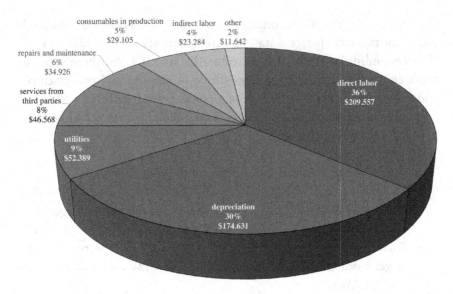

FIGURE 2.12
Example of the structure of transformation cost (percentages and dollars).

- *Fixed transformation cost ratio (ftcr)*: $12/minute ($174.631/14.580 minutes).

Reducing transformation cost [time-related losses and waste (TRLW)] and reducing raw material costs at process level [physical losses and waste (PLW)] is the area of interest and action of SBTP by reducing CLW and increasing net standard operating time (minutes) in bottleneck capacity module (per period).

Therefore, the management of "AA Plant" knows the following initial information related to bottleneck equipment losses measurement [measurements and calculations for six months; working hours (WH) – 14.950/month (with overtime of 550 minutes/month); the total number of parts produced (N): 1,680.5 pieces; total pieces of scrap (S) (pieces): 38 pieces; standard cycle time (Sct) (seconds/piece): 394 seconds per piece (or 6.57 minutes); real time cycle (Rct) (seconds/piece): 404 seconds per piece (or 6.73 minutes)]. Figure 2.13 shows the OEE calculation for bottleneck equipment losses (module 4 for assembly and inspection – see Figure 1.3).
Notes:

(*) Ls = N × Rct – Sct = 1,680.5 pieces × (404 seconds – 394 seconds) = 1,680.5 × 10 seconds = 16,805 seconds = 280 minutes.

	Are given as the conditions	Calculation of loss of effectiveness of equipment	monthly average (min.)	no. of events/ month	average time/ event (min.)	scrap
1	Yes	Monthly working hours (30 days * 8 hours * 60 minutes = 14.400 minutes; 550 minutes is overtime)	14.950			
2		Scheduled downtime (a+b+c+d+e+f)	250			
3		Admissible Losses during the period (g+h+i)	120			
g	Yes	Admissible set-up and adjustment time	120	10	12	0
h	Yes	Admissible tool change time	0			
i	Yes	Admissible start-up time	0			
4		Loading time [LT] (1)-(2)-(3)	14.580			
5	Not	Breakdown overtime (j+k+l)	1300			
j	Not	Mechanical failure overtime	450	10	45	10
k	Not	Electrical failure overtime	600	15	40	20
l	Not	Waiting for repairs overtime	250	25	10	0
6	Not	Set-up & adjustment overtime	180	10	18	8
7	Not	Cutting tool replacement overtime	60	12	5	0
8	Not	Start-up & yield overtime	84	12	7	0
9		Actual Operating time [AOT] (4) - (5) - (6) - (7) - (8)	12.956			
10	Not	Loss of speed [Ls] (*)	280			
11	Not	Minor stops and idling [MSI] (**)	1920			
12	Not	Net Operating Time [NOT] (Sct * N)	11.035			
13	Yes	Rework time	0			
14	Not	Total loss with scrap [TLS] (***)	250			
15	Not	Value-adding operating time [VAOT] (****)	10.786			

FIGURE 2.13
Overall equipment effectiveness calculation for bottleneck module.

(**) MSI = WH − (2 + 3 + 5 + 6 + 7 + 8 + 13 + 14) − VAOT = 14.950 − 2.244 − 10.786 = 1920 minutes.

(***) TLS = Sct × S = 394 seconds/piece × 38 pieces = 14,972 seconds = 250 minutes.

(****) VAOT = [Sct × (N − S)] = 394 seconds/piece × (1,680.5 pieces − 38 pieces) = 10.786 minutes.

OEE = Availability × Performance × Quality = AOT/LT × NOT/AOT × VAOT/NOT = 12.956/14.580 × 11.035/12.956 × 10.786/11.035 = 0.89 × 0.85 × 0.98 = 0.74 or OEE = VAOT/LT = 10.786/14.580 = 0.74 or 74%.

Transformation of losses in costs for bottleneck capacity module is done as follows:

a. Breakdown losses = *ftcr* × breakdown time = $12/minute × 1,300 minutes = $15,600/month.

b. Setup and adjustment losses = $ftcr$ × setup and adjustment time = $12/minute × 180 minutes = $2,160/month.

c. Cutting tool replacement losses = $ftcr$ × cutting tool replacement time = $12/minute × 60 minutes = $720/month.

d. Start-up and yield losses = $ftcr$ × start-up and yield time = $12/minute × 84 minutes = $1,008/month.

e. Speed losses = ($vtcr + ftcr$) × loss of speed = ($28/minute + $12/minute) × 280 minutes = $11,200/month.

f. Idling and minor stoppage losses = ($vtcr + ftcr$) × minor stops and idling losses = ($28/minute + $12/minute) × 1,920 minutes = $76,800/month.

g. Rework losses = ($vtcr + ftcr$) × rework time = ($28/minute + $12/minute) × 0 minute = $0/month.

h. Scrap losses = ($vtcr + ftcr$) × total loss with scrap = ($28/minute + $12/minute) × 250 minutes = $10,000/month.

i. Waste of scrap (material) = 38 pieces × $886/product = $33,668/month.

j. Total costs of volume/operation losses: (a) + (b) + (c) + (d) = $15,600 + $2,160 + $720 + $1,008 = $19,488/month.

k. Total cost of efficiency losses and waste: (e) + (f) + (h) + (j) = $11,200 + $76,800 + $10,000 + $33,668 = $131,668/month.

l. Total CLW = $19,488/month + $131,668/month = $151,156/month.

m. Total CLW as a percentage of the transformation cost = 25.97% (transformation cost is $582.102).

n. Value-adding cost = ($vtcr + ftcr$) × value-adding operating time = ($28/minute + $12/minute) × 10,786 minute = $431,440/month.

o. Total CLW + value-adding cost = $582,596 (or $581,102 or without the impact of rounding calculations).

Note 1:

This way of determining the CLW afferent to the bottleneck capacity module can be extended to the other modules to fully determine the CLW structure of the total manufacturing costs; it often reaches a percentage between 30 and 40% of CLW in the structure of manufacturing costs (it will be presented in Sections 3.2 and 3.3 of Chapter 3 and in Section 4.5 of Chapter 4).

Note 2:

The current OEE rate of 74% has been the result of several kaizen projects for loss reduction in recent years (see Figure 2.14). The initial OEE

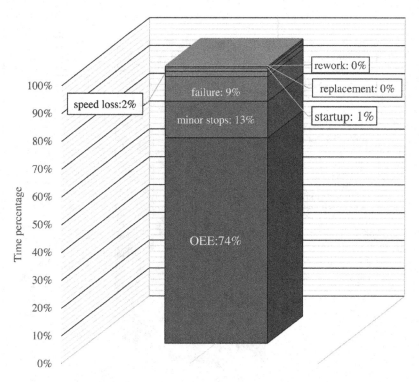

FIGURE 2.14
Overall equipment effectiveness as a percentage for bottleneck capacity module.

level was 54%, and the average initial CLW level for the three products was 43% of the processing cost.
Note 3:

All improvement projects (MDC, kaizen, or kaikaku) now start from the CLW level in module 4 considered bottleneck capacity to achieve both the reduction of CLW and the increase of net standard operating time in bottleneck capacity module to support SBTP (see Figure 2.15).
Note 4:

In addition to the 25.9% percentage of CLW in the bottleneck capacity module (assimilated with cost of losses for production volume – equipment effectiveness; see Figure 1.15), "AA Plant" also has the following CLW in terms of transformation costs (assimilated with cost of losses for production costs; see Figure 1.15): 2% cost of utility losses (over standard value of utilities), 1.5% costs of auxiliary material losses (over standard value of auxiliary material); 1% costs of maintenance material losses (over standard

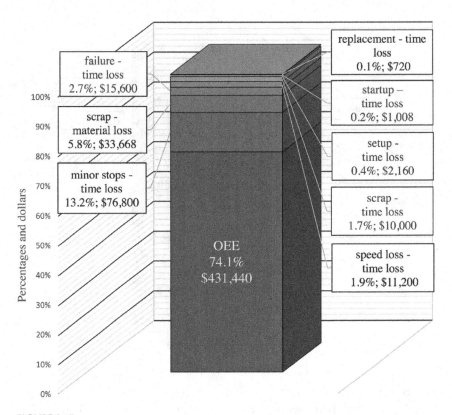

FIGURE 2.15
From overall equipment effectiveness to cost of losses and waste as a percentage value and
dollars for bottleneck capacity module.

value of maintenance material). Therefore, CLW become 30.4% of transformation costs.

The structure of transformation cost per unit (average per month)
for products A, B, and C [the total number of parts produced (N):
1,680.5 pieces] is shown in Figure 2.16.

Moreover, the level of loss of speed (Ls) and of minor stops and idling
(MSI) determined an increase of the work in progress level compared to
the standard by 10% that generated an increase of raw material costs by
3%, generated an increase of near-to-the-lines stock by 20% which generated an increase of raw material costs by 1%, and also generated an increase
of raw material and components in the warehouse by 20% which in turn
generated an increase of raw material costs by 5% (these are assimilated to
the CLW for production control losses – see Figure 1.16).

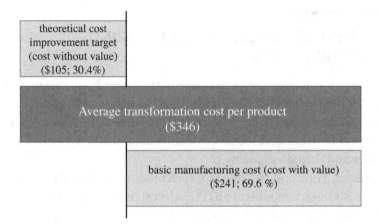

FIGURE 2.16
Unit transformation costs without value (cost of losses and waste) vs. unit manufacturing costs without value (from unit transformation costs).

Note 5:

The level of CLW is of 30.4% from transformation costs (or $105 at unit level; see Figure 2.16) and of 9% from raw material costs (or $46.76 at unit level). Total CLW at unit level is of $152 (or 17.16% from $886 unit manufacturing cost).

Even if the percentage of 17.16% of the total unit manufacturing cost of $886 is relatively small compared to what can be obtained (we will present in Chapter 3 the methods for setting annual CLW), the advantages of this way of determining CLW, called the *unique rate method* are: the information is relatively easy to obtain; often the annual level of CLW identified is acceptable (from year to year other creative phenomena of CLW appear); the calculations are quite simple; it is an easy way to implement CLW; it is often a sufficient approach to the reporting needs of the company's CLW level, etc.

However, there are some notable disadvantages. The biggest disadvantage is that bottleneck capacity modules (purpose: fulfillment of takt time) may be different from bottleneck profit modules (purpose: fulfillment of takt profit).

Therefore, a more detailed approach to the current CLW is needed to facilitate the targeting of CLW improvements and the net standard operating time in bottleneck module to strengthen the planning and continuous development of synchronous profitable operations. These details will be presented in Chapter 3.

2.5 DEFINING FUTURE MANUFACTURING COSTS STRUCTURES

To support SBTP from the perspective of the target basic manufacturing cost ("C"; per period), the allowable CLW ("A"; per period), and the reduction target for CLW ("RT"; per period), it is necessary to determine the theoretical target of cost reduction and its detailing by types of CLW on modules and then on products.

Therefore, a unit cost is defined for each product unit based on the definition of costs in each module of SBTP. Each cost in each module can contribute to obtaining a product unit or not. A cost that contributes to a unit of product is called a basic manufacturing cost ("C"; per period), and if a cost does not contribute to a unit of product, it is called a cost of losses and waste (CLW). This cost sharing must be done continuously and scientifically.

By continuously measuring and analyzing the CLW at the level of each module, it is necessary to classify the costs continuously. For this, it is necessary to perform the following:

- Defining and clarifying the current functions of each module for each activity. Then, the role of each activity must be described (What does it do and what is the role of the activity?).
- After clarifying the current functions of each module, check whether the current functions are functions that contribute to obtaining a product or not. The main types of CLW are now defined and classified (presented in Chapter 3 in detail; Section 3.2).

The purpose of determining the CLW level as accurately as possible is to predict the possibility of improving unit costs by improving productivity (reducing or eliminating losses and waste). Therefore, the basic manufacturing cost ("C"; per period) represents the cost structures that are directly responsible for the conversion from input to output. The lack of a cost or an incomplete cost in this structure determines the loss of the value of the activities in a module and implicitly of the characteristics and functions of a product. At the same time, CLW represents the parts of the basic manufacturing cost that are affected by losses and waste. Some of the losses and waste are necessary to support the basic manufacturing cost, they are not useless, but some are useless and must be eliminated in time as much as possible. This part of losses and waste transformed into costs that is useless is subject to a reduction target for the CLW ("RT"; per period). Therefore, RT is determined on the basis of the current level of basic manufacturing cost based on the level of losses and waste converted into costs. In order to establish the RT improvement targets, it is considered that the ideal state of CLW that can be approached effectively and efficiently is the state of zero CLW (ideal costs or theoretical cost improvement). Therefore, having this reference point of ideal costs, it is possible to make a continuous comparison between the current state, the future state (which will be improved in the next period), and the ideal state for each manufacturing flow, for each module, and especially for each product family or product.

2.5.1 Determining the Theoretical Target of Cost Reduction

In this above approach, only the bottleneck capacity module, the main area of interest to achieve target-oriented manufacturing cost improvement is the cost area of losses and waste (theoretical cost improvement target is of $105; ideal costs). Figure 2.17 shows how to set an annual and multiannual

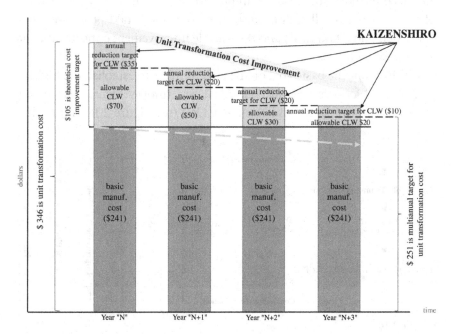

FIGURE 2.17
KAIZENSHIRO for unit transformation cost improvement.

reduction target for CLW through successive improvement projects in order to meet the expected level of SBTP. Over time, the level of basic manufacturing cost (cost with value) often tends to decrease, as a result of: (1) the implementation of kaizen project solutions to reduce the theoretical cost improvement target; (2) the manifestation of the experience effect; (3) the increase in product volumes and the emergence of economies of scale (cost per unit of output tends to decrease based on increasing scale of operation – measured by the amount of output produced).

Figure 2.17 considers that the determined CLW level is fully available for improvement. But most of the time, the scientifically determined CLW level cannot be fully attacked because some of the CLWs are needed to support the basic manufacturing cost, and another part is not feasible to make improvements. In this case, taking into account the objective restrictions (the difficulty of approaching an improvement, the level of amounts involved in making improvements, the need for systemic change to make certain improvements, the long time to implement the improvement, etc.), a lower level of theoretical cost improvement target can be established (ideal costs).

The determination of the theoretical target of cost reduction must take into account both the need for improvement established by the market (the concurrent fulfillment of both profit demand – takt profit and customer demand – takt time) and the feasible improvement opportunities at the level of modules.

At this point, the basic goal of SBTP thinking is to establish the highest possible and feasible level of theoretical cost improvement target based on critical cost of losses and waste (CCLW) (see Figure 2.18). From this

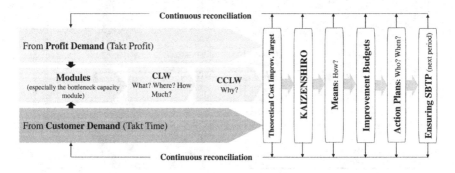

FIGURE 2.18
From profit demand and customer demand to KAIZENSHIRO and annual action plan to ensuring SBTP.

theoretical cost improvement target is established the annual reduction target for CLW or KAIZENSHIRO (it means improvable value as a target in Japanese; CCLWs that can be prevented for the next period).

The KAIZENSHIRO concept was created and developed by Dr. Shigeyasu Sakamoto, in the area of industrial engineering, a concept inspired by machine tool work (more precisely from yield metal processing), as a fundamental point of the technology developed by him, a technology called methods design concept (MDC) (Sakamoto, 2010; Posteucă and Sakamoto, 2017). The KAIZENSHIRO concept developed and used by Dr. Shigeyasu Sakamoto is at the micro-level (at the level of cycle time; approaching the basic and auxiliary functions of the work elements of a new and innovative method of work; KAIZENSHIRO focuses on reducing time associated with the auxiliary functions of the work elements). The KAIZENSHIRO concept developed and used in this book aims especially at macro-level (CCLW size that can be prevented from the total manufacturing costs of the next period), and also at micro-level (CCLW dimension related to auxiliary functions of the work elements within a cycle time).

Therefore, the more intensified the identification of as many CLW (true cost improvement opportunities) and further CCLW as accurately as possible the links between the cause-effect of CLW, the annual KAIZENSHIRO increases and the opportunity to reach a reduction target for the CLW ("RT" per period) increases. It is always sought to have the highest possible level of KAIZENSHIRO. By summing up the annual KAIZENSHIRO, the multiannual KAIZENSHIRO or the multiannual strategic cost reduction target based on improving the CLW level is obtained. Therefore, KAIZENSHIRO is not a simple goal setting by management. The fulfillment of KAIZENSHIRO is based on the entire SBTP mechanism to establish feasible means to achieve KAIZENSHIRO by continuously reconciling managerial expectations with effective and efficient opportunities at the level of SBTP modules (see Figures 2.2–2.4). Therefore, in SBTP logic, KAIZENSHIRO can be assimilated with the "scrap" level of annual transformation costs and material costs or annual CLW feasibly approached.

2.5.2 Detailed Targets and Means Design

Often, setting goals and targets to make improvements (or means) is a challenge for many companies and management teams. According to

SBTP, when setting objectives, the first decision is to establish SBTP's contribution to the company's basic policy and how to achieve medium and long-term business objectives. In other words, the objectives of SBTP must be convergent with the company's basic policy (annual and multianuual targets and means or policy) (Akao, 1991, p. 5).

Therefore, in order to meet the annual KAIZENSHIRO (annual reduction target of CLW) (see Figure 2.17; e.g., the year "N" of $35 per unit) it is necessary to detail each CLW targets. KAIZENSHIRO needs to be divided into several targets achieved through smaller improvement projects. It is very important to take into account the CLW targets related to meeting the target for net standard operating time (minutes) in bottleneck operation (per period) ("B" from the SBTP formula).

Therefore, starting from the structure of CLW presented in Figure 1.15, the way of fulfilling the annual KAIZENSHIRO is detailed (see Figure 2.19). As you can see, the KAIZENSHIRO of $35 for "N" year is focused on getting mostly out of the cost of losses for production volume, which means that the future level of sales will tend to increase for the "N" year for the products produced in the respective modules and the volume level must increase. Consequently, concerns for systematic and systemic improvements and allocated resources will focus in particular on the visible reduction of cost of losses for production volume (fulfillment of target for net standard operating time in bottleneck operation – "B" in formula SBTP). Examples of convergent objectives toward KAIZENSHIRO can be:

1. equipment losses of 35% per day decrease at 19% per day, from 165 minutes per day to 85 minutes per day on equipment, so that CLW contributes to the KAIZENSHIRO fulfillment; and
2. man × hour losses of 40% per day decrease at 20%, from 150 minutes per day per man to 65 minutes per day per man.

If the level of sales was expected to be declining, then the main concern would have been to improve cost of losses for production costs and CLW for production control and then for cost of losses for production volume. Even in the case of reduced sales volumes, increasing the net standard operating time in bottleneck operation ("B" in the SBTP formula) can be a goal if the aim is to reduce the number of equipment used and the optimal loading of those kept. Therefore, increasing productivity is a perennial goal of any company, regardless of whether sales volume is increasing or decreasing.

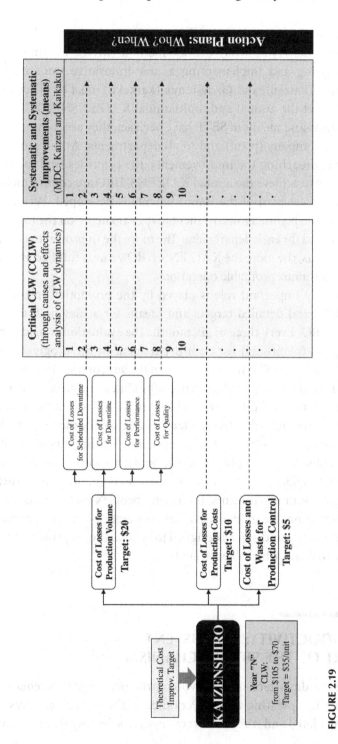

FIGURE 2.19

From KAIZENSHIRO to targets and means detailed.

Irrespective of future sales growth scenarios, increasing or decreasing, all improvements (1) innovative work method (MDC; for time-related losses; designing and implementing a new innovative work method); (2) systematic (kaizen); and (3) systemic (kaikaku) must be effective and efficient to meet the annual and multiannual KAIZENSHIRO. Once the detailed targets and means of SBTP have been set, they are communicated to the entire company (plant) and to all departments. At the same time, the way of approaching the improvements, the priorities, and the strategies necessary to achieve the annual KAIZENSHIRO are communicated – the annual master plan of the improvements is developed. Periodically, the results of the planned improvements are evaluated – on the total company (plant) and for each department. The more the improvement projects reach their goals, the more the KAIZENSHIRO value is fulfilled and tends toward synchronous profitable operations.

An extremely important role is played by the promotion in the company of SBTP and detailed targets and means for achieving the annual KAIZENSHIRO. Every three or six months the evaluation is made on the total company (plant) and for each department of the progress toward reaching the annual SBTP, more precisely of the level of reaching the targets established at the level of departments/modules/products. When this progress is not met as planned, the SBTP team should review the situation, identify objective and subjective obstacles, issue appropriate instructions, and redesign the outlook for SBTP compliance. The benefits of SBTP can be both tangible and intangible. Tangible benefits are expressed in quantities, while intangible benefits cannot be expressed quantitatively (such as, improving work in small teams, increasing people's motivation, increasing job satisfaction due to increased real cooperation between people and against the background of jobs designed to be relaxing, improving people's knowledge to deal with problems, etc.).

2.6 PRODUCTIVITY: CONSISTENT SUPPORT OF THE SBTP MECHANISM

Corporate headquarters often have control over costs, revenues, and investments in operating assets. Periodically the return on investment (ROI) is calculated and it shows how changes in sales, expenses, and assets affect ROI. Any investment center's performance is often evaluated using a measure called ROI. ROI is defined as net operating income divided by average operating assets. Net operating income is income before taxes and is sometimes referred to as earnings before interest and taxes. Operating assets include cash, accounts receivable, inventory, plant and equipment, and all other assets held for operating purposes. The operating asset base used in the formula is typically computed as the average operating assets (beginning assets + ending assets) divided by 2.

Examining the components of ROI is essential, namely margin and turnover. Margin (net operating income divided by sales) is improved by increasing sales or reducing operating expenses (costs). The lower the operating expenses per dollar of sales, the higher the margin earned. Turnover (sales divided by average operating assets) is one of the essential elements because it represents the investment in operating assets. Excessive funds tied up in operating assets depress turnover and lower ROI. Therefore, ROI is margin multiplied by turnover. Any increase in ROI must involve at least one of the following: (1) increased sales; (2) reduced operating assets; or (3) reduced operating expenses (costs).

2.6.1 Structural Reform of Profitability Through Productivity Reform

The starting point for improvement is to measure the opportunity for improvement in line with business expectations. Then, the awareness of need comes almost by itself. Figure 2.20 shows the approach to profitability scenarios in SBTP logic, through productivity, in order to achieve profitability reform through productivity reform by influencing (1) increased sales, (2) reduced operating expenses (costs), or (3) reduced operating assets.

The legend:

- R&D costs (1.3) are the costs of research and development.
- SG&A expense (1.4) is selling, general, and administrative expense.
- RM, Comp., Pack (3.1) are raw materials, components, and packaging materials.
- OEE/OLE (3.4) are overall equipment effectiveness and overall line effectiveness.
- MDC ("f") is method design concept.

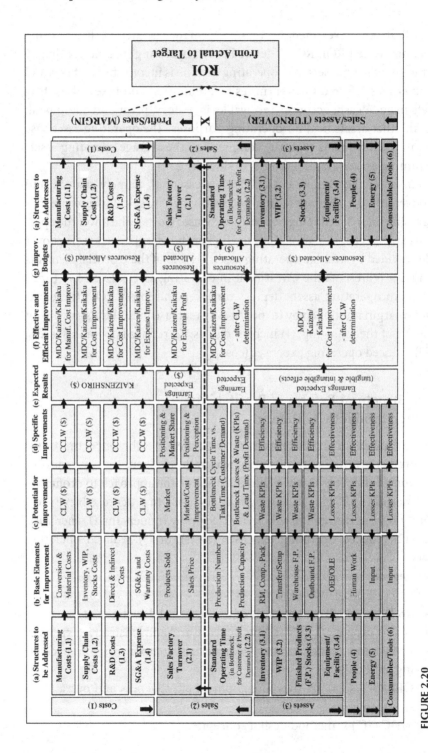

FIGURE 2.20
Profitability scenarios through productivity.

The approach to profitability scenarios through productivity is a systemic one to meet the annual and multiannual ROI target. It is the opposite of random approaches to systematic and systemic improvements.

As can be seen, the calculation formula of SBTP is integrated into profitability scenarios through productivity.

Respectively (from Figure 2.19):

- The target volume of quality products ("V") and the target sales price ("P") are assimilated with sales factory turnover ("2.1").
- The target SG&A expenses ("E") are the SG&A expenses ("1.4")
- The target basic manufacturing costs ("C") are the manufacturing costs ("1.1").
- The allowable CLW ("A") are assimilated with the potential for improvement ("c") and with the specific improvements ("d").
- The reduction target for CLW ("RT") are assimilated with the expected results ("e").
- The target for net standard operating time (minutes; "B") in bottleneck operation are assimilated with standard operating time (in bottleneck; for customer and profit demands; "2.2").

As can be seen, the approach of profitability reform through productivity using profitability scenarios through productivity supports the SBTP mechanism because it helps managers make decisions based on the detailed elements of current ROI to meet the target ROI as follows (see Figure 2.19):

- For the *increased sales* (or sales factory turnover; 2.1) it is necessary to meet the target of standard operating time through effective and efficient improvements ("f"; for external profit and for cost improvement – after CLW determination); after the expected earnings are established scientifically based on the CLW and CCLW (causality analysis for CLW in dynamics) ("e"), the resources needed to be allocated are planned and controlled using the improvement budgets (resources allocated; "g").
- For *reduced operating assets* (or assets; from "3.1" to "3.4") the continuous measurement of productivity is needed (efficiency × effectiveness; specific improvements; "d") with the help of waste key performance indicators (KPIs) and losses KPIs (potential for

improvement; "c"); then based on expected earnings (tangible and intangible effects; "e"; to support the reduced operating assets) the effective and efficient improvements ("f") are established and the resources needed to be allocated are planned and controlled with the help of the improvement budgets (resources allocated; "g"); people, energy, and consumables/tools are assimilated with the assets.

- For reduced operating expenses (costs) the continuous transformation of losses and waste and of critical losses and waste (determined by waste KPIs and losses KPIs) in costs are needed in order to have continuous information about CLW and CCLW (their location, evolving trends, their ratio of total costs, etc.); then based on the expected results (KAIZENSHIRO; "e") the effective and efficient improvements ("f") are established and the resources needed to be allocated are planned and controlled with the help of the improvement budgets (resources allocated; "g").

The development of profitability scenarios through productivity in the short, medium, and long term can contribute to the scientific support of SBTP and target ROI fulfillment. At the same time, the development of profitability scenarios through productivity ensures the verification of the relevance of the designed targets of SBTP. Any investment can be tracked by detailing the efficiency of its capacity utilization.

Knowing the reports on net operating income, average operating assets, and sales and operating expenses (costs), one can calculate the actual ROI. Then, in addition to this information, knowing continuously the total level of the actual CLW, CCLW, and standard operating time (in bottleneck capacity module; for customer demand and profit demand) the potential to improve productivity can be established to meet ROI target (increasing ROI scientifically). In this way, the financial visibility of the improvements is ensured before starting any improvement project (it is known as the money stake of any improvement; any improvement must be both effective and efficient) and after the implementation of the improvement solutions (by developing improvement budgets; details will be presented in Chapter 3).

Therefore, sustaining target profitability through target productivity is essential in SBTP thinking.

2.6.2 The Productivity Implementation and Improvement Design

In order to meet SBTP and implicitly target ROI by meeting KAIZENSHIRO and expected earnings (tangible and intangible effects) it is necessary to develop a multiannual and annual master plan of productivity to achieve the improvement of CLW and standard operating time (in bottleneck; for customer and profit demands) scientifically and consistently.

As shown in Figure 2.20, future productivity design (through the development of the productivity master plan) is based on:

- the continuous measurement and awareness of the *potential for improvement* ("c"; more precisely of CLW);
- developing the causal analysis of CLW throughout the entire manufacturing flow in order to establish *specific improvements* ("d"; more precisely of CCLW that can be feasibly prevented by subsequent improvements);
- establishing the *expected results* ("e"; more precisely improvable value as a target: KAIZENSHIRO and expected earnings);
- establishing the *effective and efficient improvements* ("f"; means for achieving improvable value as a target; more precisely of MDC, Kaizen and Kaikaku projects); and
- development of *improvement budgets* ("g"; more precisely of allocated resources).

If the potential for improvement is the result of accurately measuring the waste and losses KPIs and their transformation into costs (resulting in CLW), whether the *specific improvements* are determined by an analysis of the causality between CLW's behavior along the entire manufacturing flow, then the *expected results* are set to achieve SBTP and the *improvement budgets* are developed to support improvements, and a special place is occupied by the logic of establishing *effective and efficient improvements* to achieve *future productivity improvement design* scientifically, feasibly, and consistently.

Therefore, after developing the productivity basic policy, respectively the productivity vision and mission planning system level (Posteucă, 2018; Posteucă, 2019), and strategic planning system level (Posteucă and Sakamoto, 2017) one proceeds to the development of manufacturing

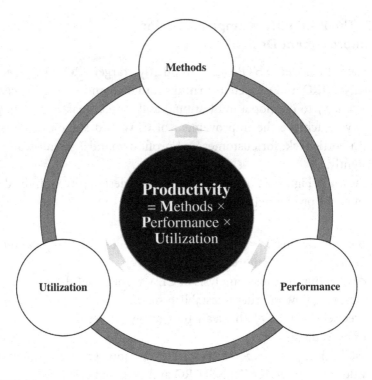

FIGURE 2.21
The three factors of productivity for the implementation and improvement of manufacturing processing.

processing plan system level (see Figures 1.3 and 1.10) and to manufacturing processing implementation (Sakamoto, 2010) and an improvement system level by using three factors of productivity ("Productivity = M, methods × P, performance × U, utilization") (Posteucă and Sakamoto, 2017, p. 295).

As shown in Figure 2.21, to fully embrace total productivity improvement at manufacturing processing implementation and improvement system level, the future productivity improvement design aims at following (Posteucă and Sakamoto, 2017, pp. 295–312):

- *Manufacturing processing method*: The development of methods is the starting point of organizing the implementation and improvement of productivity and is the most dominant dimension of productivity because it ensures the robustness and safety of the modules.

Establishing the method of interaction between people, equipment, and materials is essential to ensure: reducing the cycle time, increasing bottleneck machine/facility capacity, products design contents (redesign for easy assembly work), reducing changeover/setup time, reducing shop floors' manning, etc.

- *Manufacturing processing performance*: Refers to the efficiency of the method previously established by establishing a standard time and by identifying and addressing the difference between standard and actual cycle time per unit and the small stops. From the SBTP perspective, it is about net standard operating time per unit in bottleneck operation (minutes) from the takt profit formula.
- *Manufacturing processing utilization*: Refers to the time planned to perform the activities that create value. From the SBTP perspective, it is about standard operating time (in bottleneck capacity module; for customer demand and profit demand; see 2.2 from Figure 2.20) or "B" from the SBTP formula. Production planning and control, equipment maintenance, and quality control are activities related to the "U" dimension of productivity.

Therefore, *methods* and *performance* aim to establish standard time, while *utilization* refers to the planning of the planned time in order to carry out activities that create value (quality products made according to customer and profit demands).

2.7 CONCLUSION: SPEED-BASED TARGET PROFIT MECHANISM AT PRODUCTION PLANNING STAGE

Therefore, SBTP mechanism first aims at understanding profit demand and customer demand through the continuous and real involvement of the top managers, of all the people in the company and beyond. Continuous measurement of losses and waste parameters at the module level to establish the current level of CLW and the standard operating time in bottleneck capacity modules are essential to design a future winning state of the SBTP mechanism.

The basic approach of the SBTP mechanism is that everything is decided in the production planning stage. Recognizing that productivity is the engine that maintains the robustness of the SBTP mechanism, it must be planned in the production planning stage. Designing the best working methods, setting standard time, and increasing capacity utilization are essential elements of planning and improving productivity to support both takt profit and takt time.

Section II

Planning Synchronous Profitable Operations

3

Support Striving for
Speed-Based Target Profit

Sometimes CEO statements are heard in companies such as: "We are aware that our company has a high cost structure compared to other companies and that profitability can be improved, but we do not know now what the possible level of improvement in costs and profitability is because we do not continuously know the level of non-productivity in detail".

Therefore, an important step in addressing SBTP is to establish the quantitative potential to prevent non-productivity and to establish potential feasible improvements. The aim is to scientifically identify the maximum potential for feasible prevention of non-productivity by continuously measuring the level of losses and waste and by transforming them into costs; then by establishing annual costs of losses and waste (CLW) deployment maps, by establishing a profitable production formula, and by developing improvement budgets to provide guidance on how to address the most feasible productivity improvements to support profitable production planning. All these topics will be addressed in turn in this chapter.

3.1 PREDICTING THE POSSIBILITY OF IMPROVING PRODUCTIVITY

For the measurement and improvement of productivity to be a permanent activity, a systematic approach is needed (continuous and in-depth measurement of losses and waste) and not just a temporary idea – a sudden promotion or a fashion that is in line with world fashion. It is no exaggeration to say that this second step of SBTP development is the most important (see Figure 1.14; Step 2: Measuring & Targeting). It is known that what cannot be measured cannot be fully understood and consequently cannot be improved.

Understanding the real situation of productivity involves determining productivity and non-productivity indicators. Usually, the manufacturing productivity is measured by *overall equipment effectiveness (OEE)* (as a percentage) and the *setup time* (minutes) related to the selected equipment as important in ensuring the expected takt profit and takt time, by *man × hour by product,* by *lead time, overall line effectiveness (OLE),* etc.

Regarding the productivity of the processing method in manufacturing (method), it is sought to explore the efficiency of the processing method in modules. From the perspective of the functions (basic functions and auxiliary functions) that are performed for each task (of people or equipment), the effectiveness of the task processing method is explored. Regarding the efficiency of manufacturing processes (*performance*), the aim is to investigate the possibility of measuring work and improving performance (variability and level) of the manufacturing operations.

Regarding the processing plan in manufacturing (*utilization plan*), it seeks to clarify the real situation of the way in which the activity is carried out systematically and then seeks to clarify the possibility of improving capacity utilization by awareness of the level of losses and waste and of the CLW. So, first of all, we need a clarification of how the products are made in a concrete way.

After a deep understanding of the real productivity situation, a comparison with an official standard is needed [such as, methods-time measurement (MTM) for setting the standard time or the world-class OEE level of 85%]. Beyond these standards, improving productivity being an eternal theme, the current level may be far from the ideal state (the ideal state being the one that can be met). In this context, it is necessary to make a comparison. In order to establish the quantitative potential for preventing non-productivity and establishing potential feasible improvements, it is not enough to capture only the current state of productivity and non-productivity (losses and waste) and to look for potential points to prevent losses and waste possible to appear in the next period. It is necessary to understand the differences between current productivity and world standards in depth. Productivity level awareness not only indicates the potential level of feasible productivity improvement, but also the management technology that needs to be introduced for each type of productivity improvement, and ensuring awareness from all people in the company about the need to improve productivity to meet the goal of each type of losses and waste.

In this context, the only way to understand the current level of losses and waste and to compare this level with world standards is to make a continuous diagnosis. The purpose of diagnosing the current level of losses and waste is to predict the potential for this increase in productivity. Quantitative diagnosis of losses and waste aims at the individual approach of each type of losses and waste by measuring the time consumed [frequency of an event multiplied by the average time of an event; time-related losses and waste (TRLW)], measuring the unnecessary material consumption [e.g., scrap level; measured in quantity multiplied by the value; physical losses and waste (PLW)], and how and how much productivity can be improved. It must be predicted in percentages. It also predicts not only how much productivity will be improved for each target module, but also how it will affect productivity across the company, addressing critical losses and waste (those that are the root causes of other losses and/or waste).

Productivity is not only measured by performance (achievement) nor is it measured only by the degree of use of resources. It must be measured by a combination of both. In other words, it is desirable to achieve the highest performance with the least amount of resources. For example, even if business results (performance) tend to decline, if resource inflows continue to decline, productivity as a ratio must increase. From the perspective of losses and waste, productivity is analyzed as a productivity index, as follows:

$$\text{Productivity index} = \frac{\text{Productivity for the target period}}{\text{Baseline productivity}}$$

$$= \frac{\dfrac{\text{Results for the target period}}{\text{Productivity for the target period}}}{\dfrac{\text{Results for the reference period}}{\text{Resources for the target period}}} \qquad (3.1)$$

$$= \ldots \times 100$$

Measuring the real state of productivity is necessary regardless of the industries or the probable scenarios of sales evolution (increase or decrease of sales) (see Figure 3.1).

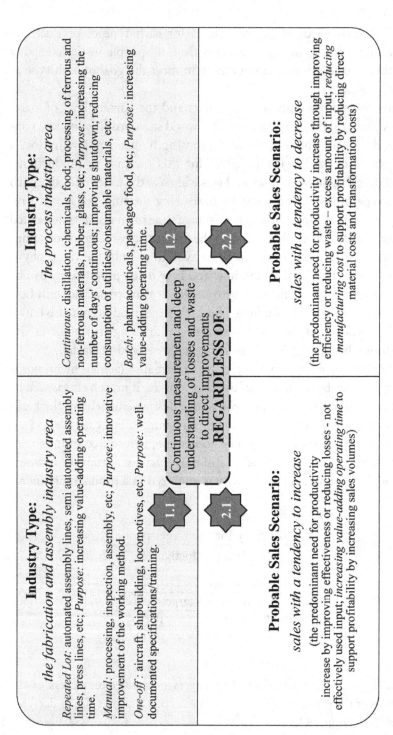

FIGURE 3.1

Measuring and improving productivity regardless of industry and sales trend.

To measure productivity, five categories of measurements are set and a productivity index is calculated for these five results. The five categories are as follows: (1) overall index (e.g., sales/employees); (2) target achievement ratio (e.g., number of new products released in production/number of new products planned to be released in production); (3) cost ratio (e.g., sales/cost); (4) manufacturing processing unit [e.g., machine operation time/setup time; actual input/planned input (per unit)]; (5) standard time ratio (e.g., production/working day; profit from product/input time).

From the perspective of losses and waste, the main purpose of the SBTP approach is to measure and understand the level of the actual costs of losses to estimate theoretical cost improvement target, allowable CLW, and annual reduction target for CLW or KAIZENSHIRO so as to contribute to the concurrent fulfillment of takt profit and takt time.

3.2 CURRENT LOSSES AND WASTE STRUCTURES AND MAPS

Why is it necessary to define the structures of losses and waste? The answer is simple: If they are not defined, then they cannot be measured. If they cannot be measured, then it is not known what needs to be improved. Therefore, based on the continuous measurement of losses and waste, the management can trigger improvement activities (kaizen) and actions (kaikaku) to bring the level of productivity to a desired level. Therefore, measuring losses and waste should not be the goal. These measurements are just a result of the past. Measurement is not an improvement activity but a starting point. The stronger the starting point, the more effective and efficient targeting and improvement can be expected.

Productivity measurement can be done at the micro and macro level. The micro level refers to the productivity of the processing volume (throughput productivity), after the working method has been defined (manufacturing processing method; improve manufacturing processing methods to increase effectiveness) and then the working time has been standardized (manufacturing processing efficiency; through implementation of standards time to increase efficiency). The macro level refers to the productivity of the degree of contribution of manufacturing processing (contribution productivity) or more precisely, the level of use of available capacity to meet managerial objectives to improve productivity.

Therefore, manufacturing productivity is divided into two categories:

- *Throughput (efficiency) productivity*: measures the productivity of each SBTP module in terms of processing time – especially the bottleneck mode (waste; see dimension 2.2 in Figure 3.1); it actually measures the operational productivity; measurement based on an objectively established standard; and
- *Contribution (effectiveness) productivity*: measures the productivity from the perspective of the physical contribution of each SBTP module – especially the bottleneck mode; the degree of contribution regarding the supply of quality finished parts/products (losses; see dimension 2.1 in Figure 3.1); actually measures total productivity (target productivity; a measurement based on a productivity index – an index that measures relative and continuous productivity in relation to a certain reference period).

Thus, without measuring the two factors of productivity, throughput and contribution, measuring productivity in manufacturing and SBTP would be meaningless.

As part of the performance improvement activity, the measurement of losses and waste must be directly related to the day-to-day management activities in order to subsequently make improvements for each type of losses and waste.

Therefore, in order to predict the improvement of productivity, it is necessary to first understand the real situation of productivity. It is necessary to capture the real situation as quantitatively as possible in order to make quantitative predictions.

However, the manufacturing operations are not only complex and diverse, but also vary depending on the type of product made. Therefore, the real state of productivity must be measured continuously in order to: (1) capture the phenomena that create losses and waste; (2) understand the dynamics and causal relationships between each type of losses and waste from the same module and especially between the modules; and (3) understand the manifestation of the operating principles of the equipment and of the entire manufacturing flow with impact in losses and waste.

As shown in Figure 1.15, the basic structure of losses and waste is:

- losses for production volume;
- losses for production costs; and
- losses and waste for production control.

These will be detailed in the following sections. Each structure of losses and waste must be adapted to the real circumstances of each company.

3.2.1 Losses of Production Volume

For manufacturing companies, losses of production volume (equipment effectiveness) are those that obstruct output maximization (management results) – not effectively used input (or losses). These are mainly in the category of contribution (effectiveness) productivity and aim at increasing value-adding operating time of equipment to support profitability by increasing sales volumes (dimension 2.1 of Figure 3.1).

In the SBTP approach, there are four major categories of losses of production volume (scheduled downtime losses, downtime losses, performance losses, and quality losses). Even if they are well known and addressed in manufacturing companies, by OEE calculation, they are still often at high percentage levels and sometimes inaccurate in terms of their continuous collection and without an accuracy and detailing that allows a clear direction of improvements necessary to be made.

The four main categories of losses of production volume are presented in detail in Table 3.1.

In the first category, *scheduled downtime losses* (independent shutdown equipment conditions), loss categories may be included such as: (1) illnesses losses; (2) work injuries losses; (3) waiting for materials losses; (4) stock counting losses; (5) training losses; (6) losses of people's participation in improvement projects; (7) fulfillment order losses; (8) power interruption losses; (9) missing tasks losses; and (10) short breaks losses.

The first category, *scheduled downtime losses* (admissible stops caused by equipment) may also include: (11) allowable time for cleaning losses; (12) allowable time for checking and lubricating equipment losses; (13) allowable time for planned maintenance losses; (14) allowable time for setup and adjustments losses (for the fulfillment of the necessary flexibility both takt profit and takt time; calculations regardless of the type of

TABLE 3.1

The Main Categories of Losses of Production Volume (Equipment Effectiveness and Efficiency)

Category of Loss	Loss Type	Name of Losses	KPI's for Losses	Units	Measurement Mode	Responsible Managers	Data Collection	Collections Frequency	The Main Effects				
									Time	Production	Distances	Labor	Dollars
1 CP Scheduled Downtime Losses	TRLW, PLW	Scheduling shutdown time	(1) Total time of downtime/ month; (2) Number of defects produced by the downtime (unit)	Time (minutes); number, costs	Total downtime/ month	Autonomous maintenance	Area	Continuous	X	X			
2 Downtime Losses	TRLW, PLW	Breakdown	(1) Breakdown rate of equipment (1/h); (2) Repair rate of equipment (1/h); (3) Number of defects produced by the breakdown (unit)	Time (minutes); number, costs	Total downtime/ month	Planned maintenance	Team	Continuous	X	X	X		

(Continued)

TABLE 3.1 (Continued)

The Main Categories of Losses of Production Volume (Equipment Effectiveness and Efficiency)

Category of Loss Type	Loss Type	Name of Losses	KPI's for Losses	Units	Measurement Mode	Responsible Managers	Data Collection	Collections Frequency	The Main Effects				
									Time	Production	Distances	Labor	Dollars
	TRLW, PLW	Setup, settings, adjustments	(1) Number of setups in a period; (2) Setup time of equipment (min); (3) Number of defectives produced during the adjustment (unit)	Time (minutes); number, costs	Total downtime/month	Autonomous maintenance	Area	Monthly	X	X			
	TRLW, PLW	Tool changes	(1) Number of units produced between the two tool changes of equipment (unit); (2) Tool changing time of equipment (min); (3) Number of defectives produced during the adjustment (unit)	Time (minutes); number, costs	Total downtime/month	Autonomous maintenance	Team	Weekly	X	X			

(Continued)

TABLE 3.1 (Continued)

The Main Categories of Losses of Production Volume (Equipment Effectiveness and Efficiency)

Category of Loss Type	Loss Type	Name of Losses	KPI's for Losses	Units	Measurement Mode	Responsible Managers	Data Collection	Collections Frequency	The Main Effects				
									Time	Production	Distances	Labor	Dollars
	TRLW, PLW	Equipment start-up time	(1) Number of start-ups in a period (unit); (2) Start-up time of equipment (min); (3) Number of defectives produced during the adjustment (unit)	Time (minutes); number, costs	Total downtime/ month	Autonomous maintenance	Team	Monthly	X	X			
3 TP Performance Losses	TRLW	Equipment cycle time (speed down)	(1) Theoretical cycle time of equipment; (2) Actual cycle time of equipment;	Time (minutes); number	Total downtime/ month	Autonomous maintenance	Team	Quarterly	X	X			
	TRLW	Equipment minor stoppages	(1) Minor stoppages rate of equipment (1/unit); (2) Total repair time of equipment (min);	Time (minutes); number	Total downtime/ month	Autonomous maintenance	Team	Weekly	X	X	X		

(Continued)

TABLE 3.1 (Continued)

The Main Categories of Losses of Production Volume (Equipment Effectiveness and Efficiency)

Category of Loss	Loss Type	Name of Losses	KPI's for Losses	Units	Measurement Mode	Responsible Managers	Data Collection	Collections Frequency	Time	Production	Distances	Labor	Dollars
4 CP Quality Losses	PLW, TRLW	Scrap and rework	(1) Scrap rate of equipment / module (1/unit); (2) Rework rate of equipment/ module (1/ unit)	Quantity; time, costs	Total downtime/ month	Quality	Team	Monthly	X	X	X		
	TRLW	Replanning	(1) Total time of replanning/ month	Time (minutes); number, costs	Total downtime/ month	Quality	Area	Monthly	X	X			

CP, contribution (effectiveness) productivity; PLW, physical losses and waste (e.g., defects, useless production resource consumption, useless inventory, useless stocks, useless space, unnecessary equipment, etc.); TP, throughput (efficiency) productivity; TRLW, time-related losses and waste (missed opportunity of realized production; labor paid without production, etc.).

setup, for profit or for clients); (15) allowable time for start-up losses; and (16) allowable time for tool change losses, etc.

As scheduled downtime losses are not included in the OEE calculation, respectively they will affect from the start the available capacity to be used in production planning; they must be continuously measured, standardized, and improved.

To approach the third category, performance losses, it is first necessary to innovate the design of the manufacturing processing method, to support increased manufacturing effectiveness, and then to increase the manufacturing processing efficiency through implementation of standard time [standard operating procedure (SOP)] to increase efficiency (it is the area of measurement and improvement of productivity at the micro level).

By measuring, standardizing, and subsequently improving the four major categories of losses of production volume, one can answer following questions: How can equipment effectiveness be increased? How can output be increased per unit of time? How can the continuous decrease of not effectively used input or losses be made? Also, how can production time be extended and quality be improved by reducing defects and rework, minimizing quality variation, and improving product quality?

Both for contribution (efficiency) productivity and for throughput (efficiency) productivity, it is necessary to develop the planning and control of manufacturing processing (effective use of equipment-hours and man-hours by managing various capacity utilization plans) to meet targets of takt profit and takt time (production planning is done on the basis of productivity planning).

3.2.2 Losses of Production Costs

As already mentioned, measuring and improving productivity means maximizing area output [management results: parts, products, services; contribution productivity (CP)/effectiveness] while minimizing the necessary inputs, benefiting from the use of a more innovative working method to combine materials, manpower, equipment, utilities, etc.; throughput productivity (TP)/efficiency. The stake of CP and of TP is increasing added value (effectiveness) and reducing manufacturing costs (efficiency). In the previous section were presented the four major categories of production volume losses (see Table 3.1 and value-adding operating time from Figure 2.13), which have as main purpose increasing added value (effectiveness). We now continue to present losses and address the main losses of production costs aimed at minimizing inputs or reducing manufacturing costs (efficiency) (section 2.2 of Figure 3.1).

In the SBTP approach, there are two major categories of losses for production costs (manual or semi-automatic assembly lines – human work losses and material and utilities efficiency).

The two main categories of losses for production costs are presented in detail in Table 3.2.

By measuring, standardizing, and subsequently improving the two major categories of losses for production costs, one can answer following questions: How to increase the number of operations allocated to an operator by increasing the SOP robustness? Also, how can the workforce be reduced by improving work, reducing manual labor, or promoting digitalization? How can control over material and utilities efficiency be increased? How can production planning be done to facilitate the growth of production resource efficiency? How can losses of production volume be reduced by decreasing losses of production costs?

3.2.3 Losses and Waste of Production Control

In the SBTP approach, there are two major categories of losses and waste of production control (inventory consumption efficiency and system consumption efficiency and effectiveness). The basic purpose of reducing or eliminating losses and waste of production control is to promote and achieve unsupervised production and to identify solutions to increase production volume and reduce manufacturing costs.

The two main categories of losses and waste of production control are presented in detail in Table 3.3.

By measuring, standardizing, and subsequently improving the two major categories of losses and waste of production control, one can answer questions such as: How can raw materials, components, packaging materials, and spare parts be purchased so that no interruptions in production and/or overstorage occur? How can the number of days of storage of finished products be reduced/eliminated? How can it be reduced in flow inventory – work-in-progress (WIP) and near-to-line inventory? How can the distribution losses be minimized? At the same time, how can system resource losses be reduced/eliminated? How can losses of production volume be reduced by decreasing losses and waste of production control?

TABLE 3.2

The Main Categories of Losses for Production Costs

Category of Loss	Loss Type	Name of Losses	KPI's for Losses	Units	Measurement Mode	Responsible Managers	Data Collection	Collection Frequency	Time	Production	Distances	Labor	Dollars
5 CP Downtime Losses (can impede human work effectiveness)	TRLW	Management	Man × hours/month	Time (minutes)	Total Man × hours/month	Continuous improvement	Team	Monthly	X			X	X
	TRLW	Operating/ motion/ walking	Hours/ month	Time (minutes)	Total hours/ month	Continuous improvement	Team	Monthly	X		X	X	X
	TRLW	Internal logistics (handling)	Hours/ month	Time (minutes)	Total hours/ month	Logistics	Team	Monthly	X		X	X	X
	TRLW	Measurement & adjustment	Man × hours/ month	Time (minutes)	Total/month	Continuous improvement	Team	Monthly	X			X	X
	TRLW	Line organization/ balancing	Man × hours/ month	Time (minutes)	Total/month	Continuous improvement	Area	Monthly				X	X
	TRLW	Non-digitalization (distribution & transfer)	Hours/ month	Time (minutes)	Total hours/ month	Engineering	Team	Monthly				X	X
	TRLW	Manual work	Man × hours/ month	Time (minutes)	Total Man × hours/month	Engineering	Area	Monthly				X	X

(Continued)

Losses for Production Costs
Assembly line (human work)

TABLE 3.2 (Continued)

The Main Categories of Losses for Production Costs

Category of Loss	Loss Type	Name of Losses	KPI's for Losses	Units	Measurement Mode	Responsible Managers	Data Collection	Collection Frequency	The Main Effects				
									Time	Production	Distances	Labor	Dollars
6 TP Production Resource Losses (can impede production resource efficiency)	PLW	Material yield	Yield ratio (%)	Dollars	Dollars/month	Continuous improvement	Area	Monthly					X
	PLW	Auxiliary consumables	Theoretical and actual cost for each process	Dollars	Dollars/month	Production	Area	Monthly					X
	PLW	Die, jig, and tool	The number of units produced between the two die, jig, and tool changes for each process (theoretical and actual)	Dollars	Dollars/month	Planned maintenance	Area	Monthly					X
	PLW	Obsolete spare parts	Obsolete ratio (%)	Dollars	Dollars/month	Planned maintenance	Area	Quarterly					X
	PLW	Energy & other utilities	Theoretical and actual cost for each process	Dollars	Dollars/month	Planned maintenance	Area	Monthly					X

Material & Utilities Efficiency

CP, contribution (effectiveness) productivity; PLW, physical losses and waste (e.g., defects, useless production resource consumption, useless inventory, useless stocks, useless space, unnecessary equipment, etc.); TP, throughput (efficiency) productivity; TRLW, time-related losses and waste (missed opportunity of realized production; labor paid without production, etc.).

TABLE 3.3

The Main Categories of Losses and Waste for Production Control

Category of Loss	Loss Type	Name of Losses and Waste	KPI's for Losses and Waste	Units	Measurement Mode	Responsible Managers	Data Collection	Collections Frequency	The Main Effects				
									Time	Production	Distances	Labor	Dollars
7 CP In-flow Inventory	TRLW/PLW	WIP from setup waste	Number of units for each module	Number/time	Average; Index; Dollars/month	Continuous improvement	Area	Monthly					X
	TRLW/PLW	WIP from transfer waste	Number of units for each module	Number/time	Average; Index; Dollars/month	Continuous improvement	Area	Monthly					X
	TRLW/PLW	Near to line inventory waste	Number of units for each module	Number/time	Average; Index; Dollars/month	Logistics	Area	Monthly					X
TP Warehouses Inventory & Stocks	PLW	Raw material inventory waste	Number of units for each zone	Number; Days	Average; Dollars/month	Production planning	Team	Monthly					X
	PLW	Components inventory waste	Number of units for each zone	Number; Days	Average; Dollars/month	Production planning	Team	Monthly					X
	PLW	Packaging inventory waste	Number of units for each zone	Number; Days	Average; Dollars/month	Production planning	Team	Monthly					X
	PLW	Finished products inventory waste	Number of units for each zone	Number; Days	Average; Dollars/month	Production planning	Team	Monthly					X
8 TP System CL Resource Losses	TRLW	Production changes/Adjustments plan loss	Number of changes/month	Number; Minutes	Total time/month	Production planning	Team	Monthly		X			
	TRLW	New equipment delays installing loss	Theoretical vs. actual time for each equipment (time-to-production)	Time (minutes)	Total downtime /month	Planned maintenance	Team	Quarterly					

Losses and Waste for Production Control
Inventory Consumption Efficiency
System Consumption Efficiency and Effectiveness

(Continued)

TABLE 3.3 (Continued)

The Main Categories of Losses and Waste for Production Control

Category of Loss	Loss Type	Name of Losses and Waste	KPI's for Losses and Waste	Units	Measurement Mode	Responsible Managers	Data Collection	Collections Frequency	The Main Effects				
									Time	Production	Distances	Labor	Dollars
	TRLW/ PLW	New equipment inefficiency losses	(1) Theoretical vs. actual cycle time of equipment; (2) Theoretical vs. actual setup time of product equipment; (3) Theoretical vs. actual scrap and rework rate of equipment; (4) Theoretical vs. actual man × hours/product of equipment; (5) Theoretical vs. actual OEE of equipment.	seconds/ minutes/ percentage/ number/ man × hour per product	Total downtime /month	Planned maintenance	Team	Monthly	X	X		X	X
	TRLW	New products development delay release loss	Theoretical vs. actual time for each new product (time-to-market)	Time (minutes)	Total downtime /month	Planned maintenance	Team	Monthly		X			X
	TRLW	New products development inefficiency loss	(1) Theoretical cycle time of new product; (2) Actual cycle time of new product	Time (minutes)	Total downtime /month	Planned maintenance/ Production	Team	Monthly	X	X			X

(Continued)

TABLE 3.3 ***(Continued)***

The Main Categories of Losses and Waste for Production Control

Category of Loss	Loss Type	Name of Losses and Waste	KPI's for Losses and Waste	Units	Measurement Mode	Responsible Managers	Data Collection	Collections Frequency	The Main Effects				
									Time	Production	Distances	Labor	Dollars
	PLW	Obsolete equipment loss	Obsolete ratio (%)	Dollars	Dollars/month	Planned maintenance	Area	Quarterly	X	X			X
	PLW	Surface/Square meters loss	Square meters (%)	Dollars	Dollars /month	Facility	Area	Quarterly			X		X
	TRLW	Internal distribution loss	(1) Theoretical vs. current cycle time of supply to the line/ equipment; (2) Minutes of lack of raw materials/ components supplied to the line/equipment	Time (minutes)	Total downtime /month	Logistics	Area	Monthly	X	X	X	X	X
	TRLW	External distribution loss	(1) Theoretical vs. current cycle time of supply to the line/ equipment; (2) Minutes of lack of raw materials/ components supplied to the line/ equipment	Time (minutes)	Total downtime /month	Logistics	Area	Monthly	X	X	X	X	X

CP, contribution (effectiveness) productivity; PLW, physical losses and waste (e.g., defects, useless production resource consumption, useless inventory, useless stocks, useless space, unnecessary equipment, etc.); TP, throughput (efficiency) productivity; TRLW, time-related losses and waste (missed opportunity of realized production; labor paid without production, etc.).

Therefore, the final objective of operational productivity from the SBTP perspective is the measurement, standardization, and continuous improvement of all losses and waste with clear visibility on the fulfillment of the annual and multi-year target profit. It is obvious that all these structures of losses and waste do not manifest all at once and with the same intensity. It is obvious that a company that has just joined SBTP will use a lower number of losses and waste. However, these losses and waste must be defined and used within companies in order to capture the phenomena that continuously generate losses and waste.

By measuring, standardizing, and improving losses and waste, SBTP seeks to meet:

- *the objective of improving the production effectiveness* (contribution productivity by total productivity measurement) to generate and maintain the use of the necessary capacity of equipment and/or assembly lines by harmonizing human-machine capacity, or in other words increasing productivity with value; especially during the sales growth period;
- *the objective of reducing the overall manufacturing costs or the efficiency increase* (throughput productivity by increasing operational productivity measurement based on total productivity index); especially during the period of reduced sales (especially through payroll cuts and lowering of subordinate material costs); and
- *by transforming losses and waste into CLW and further CLW into CCLW, the two objectives merge to meet SBTP.*

Thus, if productivity is constantly reached in a certain area that has been the subject of improved losses and/or waste, the next move is to clearly define the following areas. Productivity measurement must be done with a standard of comparison. This is not a comparison with the outside world. The standards are determined taking into account the maximum defined level of feasible use of current capacities (an index is established as a standard) and based on the assumption that the latest equipment (automation or digitization) is installed for the respective SBTP modules (an index is established as standard).

Therefore, even if losses and waste are measured, it must be known at all times at what level our company is compared to the desired level to meet takt profit and takt time. In other words, there is a need for an audit of the productivity system that aims at "dream digitalization factories".

Therefore, the system for measuring losses and waste consists of these two mechanisms: understanding losses and waste to improve productivity in order to achieve SBTP according to established standards and verifying the levels of achievement of standards over time. Measurement is the basis of standardization, and standardization is the basis of continuous improvement.

3.2.4 Losses and Waste Maps: Location, Magnitude, and Causality

After defining the production system model (see Figure 1.3), as well as the types of losses and waste that need to be measured, the measurement of losses and waste is performed at the same time as investigating the types of losses and waste related to each module of each manufacturing flow. Figure 3.2 shows the location and magnitude of each type of losses and waste related to each SBTP module.

The magnitude refers to:

- *TRLW*: the average time of a certain type of event creating losses and waste and the frequency of that type of event for each module; and

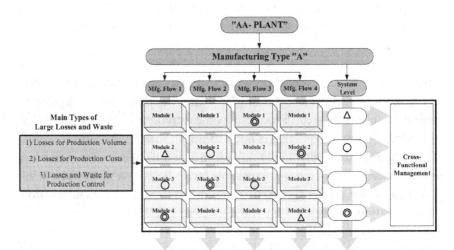

Input 1: for the causal analysis of losses and waste that can be prevented in the near future
Input 2: for planning and developing costs of losses and waste map

FIGURE 3.2
The map of locations and magnitude of losses and waste.

- *PLW*: defects, useless production resource consumption, useless inventory, useless stocks, useless space, unnecessary equipment, etc.

Each of the three types of losses and waste in Figure 3.2 is evaluated by three types of markings that represent the initial priorities of improving losses and waste. Unmarked modules mean that no significant improvements are needed for that module in the next period.

Each of the three types of losses and waste can occur at the module level or at the system level. An example of system-level losses can be waiting for repairs losses – the average waiting time between announcing a breakdown event to a module and the time of arrival of the maintenance professionals in the module, multiplied by the frequency of breakdowns in the module. This type of loss is often included in breakdown losses on modules, but is actually a systemic loss as sometimes the maintenance department does not have the capacity to intervene promptly or does not have a clearly established intervention prioritization system (e.g., bottleneck modules are priority). In order to address this type of losses, a systemic approach is needed, more precisely to reorganize and standardize the activity of the maintenance department and not to make an improvement to a specific module (Posteucă and Zapciu, 2015b; Posteucă and Sakamoto, 2017 pp. 116–132; Posteucă, 2018, pp. 173–180; Posteucă, 2019, p. 106–111;). The outputs in Figure 3.2 represent: (1) the input for the causal analysis of losses and waste that can be prevented in the near future (see Figure 3.3); and (2) planning and developing CLW map (see Figure 3.20). Cross-functional management refers to the departments: quality, cost, engineering, production, sales, office personnel, etc.

Furthermore, based on the information in Figure 3.2, it is necessary to identify and analyze the root source that generates losses and waste both along the modules of a manufacturing flow, upstream and downstream of the module in which the event creating losses and waste occurs, as well as at the systemic level. The causal relationships between losses and waste are often obvious. For example, for manufacturing flow 1 in Figure 3.3 (which is a follow-up to the example from "AA Plant" described in the previous chapters; module 4 being bottleneck – assembly and inspection) a delay in supplying module 2 with raw materials or components (*waiting for material losses*) causes losses and waste for module 1 (such as equipment minor stoppages loss; speed down loss, energy and other utilities losses, WIP from transfer waste, near to line inventory waste, etc.), as well as for modules 3

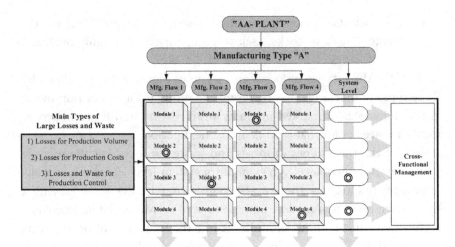

Input for conversion of losses and waste into manufacturing costs

FIGURE 3.3
The map of causal relationships between losses and waste.

and 4 (such as minor stoppages loss; speed down loss, operating/motion/ walking losses, energy and other utilities losses, WIP from transfer waste, near to line inventory waste, etc.). At system level, the following losses and waste may occur: (1) internal logistics (handling) – for unnecessary material handling around the module; (2) internal distribution loss – for delays in the distribution of raw materials and/or components to modules, regardless of whether the raw materials and/or components were available in the warehouse or not; (3) energy and other utilities losses; (4) management losses, etc., and last but not least the production opportunity (profit) losses (see Figure 3.3). Therefore, the search for effective and efficient solutions in module 2 *for waiting for material losses* is unlikely. Focusing on causal losses and waste is essential (holistically).

Capturing causal relationships is done continuously and is recorded from shift to shift in *shift report*. The two team leaders from the last and the starting shift are responsible for meeting, about 5–15 minutes, to exchange information and to briefly analyze the previous shift and business information needed to start the next shift. The goal is to ensure that the team leader who starts the production knows the past performance and all relevant current issues that may affect the future performance, such as downtime, quality, or changeovers. At the same time, the team leader from the last shift records and validates in the *shift report* the structure of losses and waste for each module and product and especially their causality. The manufacturing flow/line boards and team board contain performance information and are also to be used as an information source for losses and waste.

Therefore, the improvement priority in Figure 3.2 moves from module 4 to module 2. Module 2 is considered the main module that causes losses and waste along manufacturing flow 1 and at system level. Continuous and early identification of losses and wastes that cause other losses and wastes along the manufacturing flow is the key to effectively and efficiently address subsequent improvements to prevent probable losses and wastes and to avoid a fight against the effects and not with root causes (Posteucă, 2019, pp. 111–116). The output in Figure 3.3 represents the input for conversion of losses and waste into manufacturing costs (see Figure 3.20).

3.3 METHODS FOR SETTING ANNUAL COST OF LOSSES AND WASTE

Converting losses and waste into costs is an inevitable challenge for any company that uses SBTP. The approach of the CLW addresses following two major activities:

1. Continuous measurement of CLW in order to know their current status (presented in this section based on the presentation in Figure 3.2); and
2. Establishing the annual CLW that need to be improved (will be presented in Section 3.4).

After the presentation of the approach of losses and waste in Figures 3.2 and 3.3, now it is the turn of the presentation of the conversion of these losses and waste into costs to be able to direct the necessary improvements in order to concurrently fulfill the takt profit and the takt time by fulfilling each component element of the SBTP mechanism.

The approach of converting losses and waste into costs can be done gradually, from simple to complex. Figure 3.4 shows the three stages of the development of a system for transposing losses and waste into costs (usually in 3–5 years):

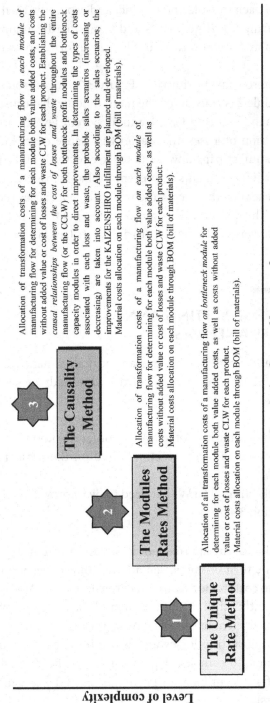

The Unique Rate Method

The Modules Rates Method

Allocation of all transformation costs of a manufacturing flow both module both value added costs, as well as costs without added value or cost of losses and waste CLW for each product.
Material costs allocation on each module through BOM (bill of materials).

The Causality Method

Allocation of transformation costs of a manufacturing flow *on each module* of manufacturing flow for determining for each module both value added costs, as well as costs without added value or cost of losses and waste CLW for each product.
Material costs allocation on each module through BOM (bill of materials).

Allocation of transformation costs of a manufacturing flow *on each module* of manufacturing flow for determining for each module both value added costs, and costs without added value or cost of losses and waste CLW for each product. Establishing the *causal relationships between the cost of losses and waste* throughout the entire manufacturing flow (or the CCLW) for both bottleneck profit modules and bottleneck capacity modules in order to direct improvements. In determining the types of costs associated with each loss and waste, the probable sales scenarios (increasing or decreasing) are taken into account. Also according to the sales scenarios, the improvements for the KAIZENSHIRO fulfillment are planned and developed. Material costs allocation on each module through BOM (bill of materials).

Level of complexity

Setting and analysis of cost of losses and waste

FIGURE 3.4
The three stages of evolution of a system of conversion of losses and waste into costs.

- *The unique rate method*: All losses and waste of a bottleneck module are converted into the transformation costs of a clearly identifiable manufacturing flow.
- *Modules rates method*: All losses and waste of each module are converted into the transformation costs related to each module of a clearly identifiable manufacturing flow.
- *Causality method*: All losses and waste of each module are converted into the total costs related to each module of a clearly identifiable manufacturing flow, taking into account the causal relations between the way of manifestation of losses and waste in dynamics and taking into account the probable evolution of sales.

3.3.1 The Unique Rate Method

The sales department coordinates with the production planning and control department to achieve concurrently the takt profit and the takt time (to perform synchronous profitable operations) by determining CLW.

In order to be able to significantly influence the concomitant fulfillment of takt profit and takt time it is necessary to:

- fulfill the target of contribution profit per unit for the period (e.g., one year); there is no point in planning this contribution that is above the level of effectiveness and efficiency of the theoretical cost improvement target; the goal is to meet the KAIZENSHIRO level (annual reduction target for CLW); and
- fulfill the net standard operating time per unit in bottleneck module (minutes); there is no point in planning production and shipments that is above the capacity decided in bottleneck module and no level of quality that is above the quality possibilities in bottleneck module.

By continuously determining and then continuously improving the CLW, the SBTP mechanism targets are met, both meeting the target of the contribution profit per unit for the period and, concurrently, meeting the net standard operating time per unit in bottleneck module (more exactly, the pace of profit demand and the pace of customer demand).

As presented in Chapter 2, when the example from "AA-Plant" of converting losses and waste into costs was presented, transformation costs (conversion costs) is the main manufacturing cost structure that are subject to the connection with losses and waste (of course material costs are also addressed).

As shown in Figure 3.5, the CLW by this method aim to determine the level of CLW from the transformation costs, first at the level of the bottleneck module (module 4 – assembly and inspection; stage 1), then determining the level of CLW at the product level (stage 2) and then planning and developing improvements to meet the annual level of KAIZENSHIRO. The material costs are determined at the level of each module based on the bill of materials (BOM). The level of losses related to material and components is found in the material yield loss (measured as yield ratio in %; see Table 3.2; production resource losses).

This method can initially meet the CLW approach to meet SBTP requirements. This method is often sufficient when:

- the sales volumes are growing steadily;
- the diversity of products made on a manufacturing flow is relatively low; and
- the product competition in certain markets is acceptable.

However, when using this method, to meet the annual theoretical cost improvement target (KAIZENSHIRO) by reducing a certain structure of CLW, for example, cost of breakdown losses, erroneous conclusions can sometimes be reached, as the fulfillment KAIZENSHIRO can never be guaranteed. Specifically, the attempt to reduce the cost of breakdown losses, calculated by multiplying the breakdown reduced time (hours) with the degree of loading of the equipment in the module ($/hours), for the scenario of decreasing sales for the next period (the actual production quantity for the period is less than the capacity of manufacturing flow or the capacity of the production system) can lead to the increase of transformation cost on the background of bearing the cost to achieve the improvement of breakdown losses, because an increase of capacity is obtained that was already in surplus. Even if the level of saved costs of breakdown losses may be higher than the costs of achieving the improvement, we can still talk about a lost opportunity to make another much more visible improvement of reducing the CLW (e.g., in the category of losses for production costs and losses and waste for production control, see Tables 3.2 and 3.3) and the lost opportunity to make a profit by directing resources into operational activities.

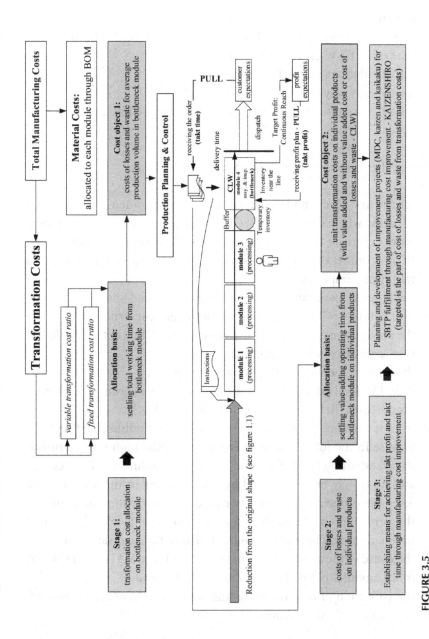

FIGURE 3.5

The unique rate method for setting costs of losses and waste.

Therefore, the advantages of this global way of determining CLW are:

1. the information is relatively easy to obtain;
2. often the annual level of CLW identified is acceptable (from year to year other CLW creative phenomena occur);
3. the calculations are quite simple;
4. it is an easy way to implement CLW; and
5. it is often a sufficient approach to the company's CLW level reporting needs.

However, there are some notable disadvantages such as:

1. for the first three modules CLW was not determined. It can reach a situation where one minute of CLW from any of the three modules is more expensive than one minute of module 4 considered bottleneck; in this context the takt profit perspective is less approached than the takt time perspective;
2. the types of losses and waste are relatively limited and may not provide details of CLW for each manufacturing cost structure;
3. the products may not attract the same level of CLW; detailed calculation is required for each product;
4. the improvements directing may be erroneous;
5. the CLW level does not take into account the lost profit opportunity proportional to the losses (opportunity cost) level;
6. some losses and waste are visible in bottleneck modules, but they have a cause in modules 1, 2, or 3. For example, the high level of minor stops and idling (MSI) from the bottleneck module (see Figures 2.13 and 2.14) may be determined by the problems in modules 1, 2, or 3, by the problems of internal or external distribution loss, and by the problems of production changes/adjustments plan loss; these problems are independent of module 4 and it is necessary to identify the cause of these MSI effects in order to achieve KAIZENSHIRO in other modules of SBTP and not in module 4; and
7. the collection of data on losses and waste may have errors, is brief, and not standardized enough.

In conclusion, in order to fulfill takt profit and takt time and implicitly SBTP, after establishing the CLW it is necessary to take into account: (1)

the arrangement of the products in the order of the profit speed of each product (from high to low); (2) the continuous check of the load balancing capacity of the bottleneck module; and (3) adjusting the load balance and the profit balance by combining the setup time for both takt profit and takt time fulfillment.

3.3.2 The Modules Rates Method

Therefore, against the background of the disadvantages related to the unique rate method, more refined approaches are required to determine the CLW (modules rates method and causality method).

Modules rates method is more appropriate when:

- sales volumes have significant fluctuations;
- the diversity of products made on a manufacturing flow is increasing (it is necessary to ensure the level of flexibility through the setup activity for fulfilling the takt time);
- the products have significant differences between the processing time cycles for each module;
- some products do not cover the entire manufacturing flow;
- the competition of products on the markets is increasing (the need for profitable price reduction is pressing); and
- there are tendencies to increase the level of transformation cost, both of its variable part (especially of overhead costs), and especially of its fixed part (especially the depreciation of equipment in each module), etc.

In this context, it is obvious that total working time from bottleneck module is no longer sufficient as the basis for allocating the transformation costs and it is necessary to allocate the transformation costs on each module of a manufacturing flow and then convert each loss and waste of each module into the equivalent transformation costs.

As shown in Figure 3.6, the CLW by this method aim to determine the level of CLW from transformation costs, first at the level of each of the four modules (stage 1), then to determine the level of CLW at product level (stage 2), and then improvements are planned and developed to meet the annual level of KAIZENSHIRO by meeting the annual level of KAIZENSHIRO at the level of each module. The material costs are determined at the level of each module based on the BOM. The level of losses

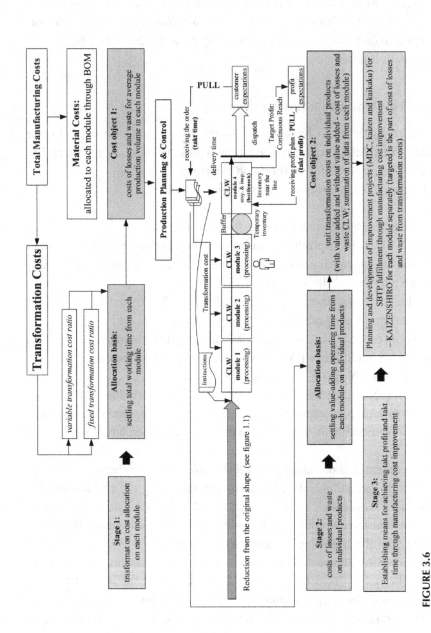

FIGURE 3.6

The modules rate method for setting costs of losses and waste.

related to material and components is found in material yield loss (measured as yield ratio – %; see Table 3.2; production resource losses).

The modules rates method uses all loss and waste measurements (see Tables 3.1–3.3) for each module. The calculations are quite similar to those presented in Chapter 2 (see Sections 2.4 and 2.5).

Figure 3.7 shows how to transform losses and waste into costs from the perspective of reaching the planned levels of profits – a process called profit planning. Profit planning is done by preparing numerous budgets, which, when put together, form an integrated business plan known as a master budget. An innovative part of the budgeting process is represented by the annual budgets for manufacturing cost improvement to ensure planning (involves the development of objectives for the annual reduction target for CLW or KAIZENSHIRO for each module, per total modules of a manufacturing flow, per products and per total company) and controlling (involves the steps taken by the management to ensure the achievement of KAIZENSHIRO at each level – module, manufacturing flow, product, and total company) of the annual fulfillment of KAIZENSHIRO.

From this perspective of profit planning, in Figure 3.7, the total cost structures are approached at the level of variable costs and fixed costs (columns from "h" to "w"). As can be seen, in order to obtain a higher percentage of the CLW that can be improved as efficiently and effectively as possible, the module rates method addresses costs beyond manufacturing costs, namely selling, general, and administrative expense (SG&A). Also, in Figure 3.7 are presented losses and waste structure (columns "a" and "b"; see Tables 3.1–3.3 for KPIs for losses and waste which are now presented in column "d"). Column "c" presents the detail of the module for which the transformation of losses and waste into costs is made (see Figure 2.11). Furthermore, in columns "e", "f", and "g" is presented the new structure of total costs from the perspective of identifying CLW, respectively: basic manufacturing cost or value-added costs (column "e"), annual allowable cost of losses and waste (CLW; column "f"; or part of CLW that will not be targeted for improvement in that year) and finally, the establishment of annual reduction target for CLW (or KAIZENSHIRO) at activity, process, or operation level (actually the basic purpose of this figure; column "g").

To support the determination of KAIZENSHIRO for each module it is necessary to establish KAIZENSHIRO for each manufacturing flow, product family, or for a specific product. This is the time of top-down reconciliation (Figure 3.8) with bottom up (Figure 3.7) and vice versa

For each module (M) of a manufacturing flow: activity (A), process (P), operation (O)

Losses and Waste Structure	For module (M): Activity (A); Process (P); Operation (O) (A1; P1.1; ...“n”) (c)	KPIs for losses: TRLW & PLW (d)	basic manuf. cost ($) (e)	annual allowable CLW ($) (f)	annual reduction target for CLW ($) (g)	DMC (h)	IMC (i)	DLC (j)	ILC (k)	TC (l)	DJC (m)	EC (n)	FC (o)	MC (p)	DC (q)	MMC (r)	BFC (s)	AC (t)	IC (u)	RDC (v)	DLC (w)
Production Volume — Equipment Losses — Scheduled Downtime Losses	......	TRLW & PLW	......	......	......									X	X	x					
Downtime Losses	......	TRLW & PLW	......	......	......									X	x	x			x	x	
Performance Losses	......	TRLW	......	......	......			X		x	x	x	x		x			x	x	x	
Quality Losses	......	TRLW & PLW	......	......	......	x	x	X		x	x	x	x						x		x
Production Costs — Labor Losses	......	TRLW	......	......	......			X	X								x				
Material and Utilities Consumption Losses	......	PLW	......	......	......		X	X				X	X				x				
Production Control — Inventory Consumption Waste	......	TRLW & PLW	......	......	......											x	X		x		x
System Consumption Losses	......	TRLW & PLW	......	......	......	X		x	x			x	x		x		x				
Total (a)/(b)	(c) $	(d)	(e) $	(f) $	(g) $	$	$	$	$	$	$	$	$	$	$	$	$	$	$	$	$

Total Cost Structure — Product Cost: Manufacturing Cost (MC): Variable Costs (including Manufacturing Overhead Costs - MO) = DMC, IMC, DLC, ILC, TC, DJC, EC, FC; Fixed Costs (MO) = MC, DC, MMC. Period Cost: SG&A Expenses (variable & fixed) = BFC, AC, IC, RDC; Distribution and Logistic Costs (DLC).

Direct Material Cost (DMC); Indirect Material Cost (IMC); Direct Labor Cost (DLC); Indirect Labor Cost (ILC); Tool Cost (TC); Die and Jig Cost (DJC); Energy Cost (EC); Fuel Cost (FC); Maintenance Cost (MC); Depreciation Cost (DC); Maintenance Materials Cost (MMC); Bank and Financial Cost (BFC); Administrative Costs (AC); Inventory Costs (IC); R&D Costs (RDC); Distribution and Logistic Costs (DLC)

KAIZENSHIRO

FIGURE 3.7

From losses and waste and their associated costs to KAIZENSHIRO for each module.

For each manufacturing flow, product family or product

From KAIZENSHIRO to KAIZENSHIRO for each manufacturing flow, product family, or product.

Losses and Waste Structure			For 4 modules of target manufacturing flow: Module 1 + Module 2 + Module 3 + Module 4	KPIs for losses: TRLW & PLW	Total Cost Structure			Total Cost Structure														
									Product Cost											Period Cost			
									Manufacturing Cost (MC)												SG&A Expenses (variable & fixed)		
									Variable Costs (including Manufacturing Overhead Costs - MO)								Fixed Costs (MO)						
				basic manuf. cost ($)	annual allowable CLW ($)	annual reduction target for CLW ($)	Direct Material Cost (DMC)	Indirect Material Cost (IMC)	Direct Labor Cost (DLC)	Indirect Labor Cost (ILC)	Tool Cost (TC)	Die and Jig Cost (DJC)	Energy Cost (EC)	Fuel Cost (FC)	Maintenance Cost (MC)	Depreciation Cost (DC)	Maintenance Materials Cost (MMC)	Bank and Financial Cost (BFC)	Administrative Costs (AC)	Inventory Costs (IC)	R&D Costs (RDC)	Distribution and Logistic Costs (DLC)
Production Volume	Equipment Losses	Scheduled Downtime Losses	……	TRLW & PLW	……	……	……									×	×						
		Downtime Losses	……	TRLW & PLW	……	……	……									×	×	×	×		×		
		Performance Losses	……	TRLW	……	……	……																
	Quality Losses		……	TRLW & PLW	……	……	……	×	×	×	×					×	×						
Production Costs	Labor Losses		……	TRLW	……	……	……		×	×	×												
	Material and Utilities Consumption Losses		……	PLW	……	……	……	×		×			×	×	×								
Production Control	Inventory Consumption Waste		……	TRLW & PLW	……	……	……			×				×	×		×	×	×	×	×	×	×
	System Consumption Losses		……	TRLW & PLW	……	……	……	×	×							×		×		×			×
(a)	(b)	Total	(c)	(d)	(e) $	(f) $	(g) $	(h) $	(i) $	(j) $	(k) $	(l) $	(m) $	(n) $	(o) $	(p) $	(q) $	(r) $	(s) $	(t) $	(u) $	(v) $	(w) $

FIGURE 3.8

From KAIZENSHIRO for each module to KAIZENSHIRO for each manufacturing flow, product family, or product.

(catchball process; until an acceptable KAIZENSHIRO is established at the top management level in order to meet SBTP and at the shop floor level for acceptance of improvement projects – MDC, kaizen, and kaikaku). At this moment, the planning of the most effective and efficient improvement projects to fulfill KAIZENSHIRO is already starting. Therefore, keeping the explanations from Figure 3.7, in Figure 3.8 is presented the sum of the modules (see column "c") to establish the necessary KAIZENSHIRO on a manufacturing flow, product family, or for a product (see column "g").

Now, the data in Figure 3.8 become information of SBTP thinking because through the stratification analysis the following can be visualized graphically:

- loss and waste type vs. module;
- module vs. loss and waste type;
- cost of losses and waste vs. module;
- module vs. cost of losses and waste; and
- KAIZENSHIRO vs. module, etc.

Therefore, one of the major differences from the unique rate method is that modules rates method recognizes that bottleneck capacity module (purpose: takt time fulfillment) may be different from bottleneck profit module (purpose: takt profit fulfillment). As can be seen in Figure 3.9, the bottleneck profit module is the module that accumulates the most CLW – module 3 (bottleneck capacity module remaining module 4). For example, in this module 3 you can find expensive piece of equipment, expensive equipment, with a high level of CLW, but which is not a bottleneck capacity module. However often the bottleneck capacity module is similar to the bottleneck profit module.

Moreover, the root causes of the CLW visible in bottleneck profit module can be in the previous modules (modules 1 and/or 2) and/or in the next module (module 4 – bottleneck capacity module). For this reason, taking into account the trend of sales volumes in the next period, increasing or decreasing, we can move to a more refined method of determining CLW – the causality method (next section).

At the same time, with the help of a module rate method, the structure of each product can be determined from the perspective of opportunities to improve manufacturing costs (Figure 3.10). In a less refined form, this product-level structure is also possible in the case of the unique rate method.

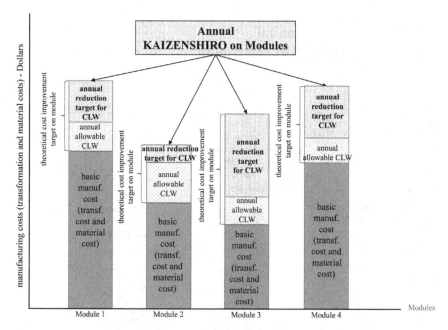

FIGURE 3.9

The annual manufacturing cost improvement targets cost from each module across the entire manufacturing flow.

The SBTP approach accepts that one of the challenges facing any manufacturing company is to allocate overhead costs (as part of transformation costs) to cost objects, such as products and services based on the activities undertaken to produce each product or service. For this, companies that use SBTP can often use activity-based costing (ABC). ABC refines cost systems, focusing on individual activities as fundamental cost objects. An activity is an event, task, or work unit with a specified purpose, for example, product design, setup, and so on. ABC focuses on indirect costs, as direct costs can be tracked relatively easily for products and jobs, but do not determine the level of CLW to drive improvements. ABC is only a costing system that focuses on the distribution of overhead costs based on causal relationships between costs and activities, but not the causal relationships between CLW in activities/processes/operations (see Figure 2.11).

Therefore, in SBTP thinking, the identification and approach of the bottleneck capacity module remains a priority in order to be able to plan and fulfill the targets set for takt profit and SBTP (see the denominator of the takt profit and SBTP formulas; the net standard operating time per unit

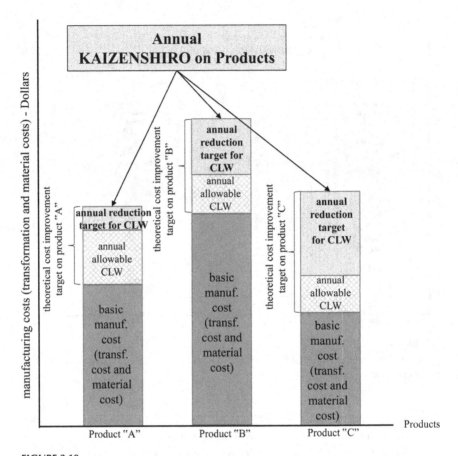

FIGURE 3.10
The annual manufacturing cost improvement targets cost from each product of the same manufacturing flow.

in bottleneck operation – takt profit; the net standard operating time in bottleneck operation – SBTP), but there is also a major concern regarding bottleneck profit module in order to maximize the CLW (numerator of takt profit and SBTP formulas).

Therefore, the main advantages of the modules rates method are: (1) a more refined identification of the CLW and KAIZENSHIRO; (2) a better targeting of improvements; (3) establishing KAIZENSHIRO for each module; (4) establishing KAIZENSHIRO for each product family separately to support competitiveness through price, volume, and profit; and (5) establishing KAIZENSHIRO for each product separately to support competitiveness through price, volume, and profit, etc. Disadvantages include: (1) the spread of CLW is high; (2) there is no causal relationship between losses and waste throughout the entire manufacturing flow; and (3) there is no causal relationship between the types of costs associated with losses and waste depending on the sales scenario – increasing or decreasing, etc.

To address these main disadvantages, the module rates method raises the level of complexity and we move on to the method of causality.

3.3.3 The Causality Method

Since the purpose of SBTP is to plan and develop a production management that concurrently fulfills both takt profit and takt time, an even more detailed approach to the CLW at the level of the entire manufacturing company is needed for:

- maximizing the contribution profit per unit by minimizing the CLW (reduction/elimination of costs without value especially from the bottleneck profit module); and by
- maximizing the net standard operating time in the bottleneck capacity module also by minimizing the CLW (reduction/elimination of costs without value in bottleneck capacity module). As can be seen in Figure 2.8, to increase the net standard operating time or net capacity (good parts; production volume with the expected quality) it is necessary to reduce/eliminate all losses and waste (e.g., downtime, non-productive hours, etc.) which translate into CLW.

Therefore, the fulfillment of the SBTP mechanism depends on the visible and consistent reduction/elimination of CLW.

For this, the causality method goes beyond modules rate method which recognized the existence of the bottleneck capacity module (purpose: takt time fulfillment) and the bottleneck profit module (purpose: takt profit fulfillment) and that these two types of bottleneck can be in different modules sometimes. The causality method aims to identify the root causes of the two different types of bottleneck and then provides support for identifying, planning, and implementing the most effective and efficient cost improvement solutions of losses and waste considered critical (CCLW).

In this context, it is obvious that the total working time from bottleneck module/each module is no longer sufficient to be the basis for allocating transformation costs as was the case with the unique rate method and the modules rates method. The causality method uses as allocation bases (see Figure 3.13):

- settling total working time from each module; and
- the cause-effect relationship between CLW in a particular module and the cause-effect relationship between CLW of different modules and capacity/sales.

The result in Figure 3.3 is represented by the *input for the causal analysis of losses and waste that can be prevented in the near future*. More precisely, based on Figures 3.2 and 3.3, we can now establish the principles of how losses and waste occur and their place of occurrence by establishing the relationship between critical losses and waste (cause) and the effects losses and waste (*multiple; in the mirror and stratified*) to clarify the cost structures that are affected (increase unnecessarily) following the occurrence of each type of losses and waste (see Tables 3.1–3.3).

Why multiple effects losses and waste? As can be seen in Figure 3.11, where an example of the analysis of the relations between the *internal logistic loss or critical loss or waste* [or losses due to the lack of raw materials and components at the time required for the production of module 3 (bottleneck profit modules) and especially the provision of the minimum and maximum level of buffer – temporary inventory before module 4 – bottleneck module capacity; it is considered that module 3 has the task of ensuring the optimal level of the buffer] and the *effects losses and waste*, the impact of the internal logistic loss is felt not only at the level of module 3, but both upstream (warehouse – raw materials; modules 1 and 3) and downstream (module 4 and system level). The purpose of any solution to a problem is to identify the root cause and not fight the multiple effects of the problem. Therefore, the identification of *critical loss and waste and the establishment of their impact on the effects losses and waste,* from shift to shift, requires a transition from a simple collection of losses and waste for each module to identifying the phenomena that create losses and waste and the total impact of these phenomena.

Furthermore, why effects losses and waste in the mirror? Because in establishing the cause-effect relationships, the impact of each loss and waste in costs is immediately determined (see Figure 3.11). Based on the previous establishment in the system of theoretical (or standard) costs for

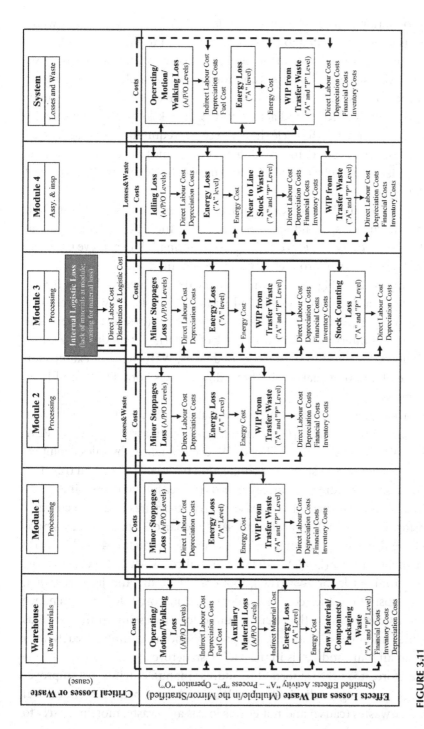

FIGURE 3.11

Causal relationships between critical losses, multiple effects losses and waste and attracting specific cost structures.

the production of a product in a module (1, 2, 3, 4, and warehouse; warehouse is a module related to the supply chain, not to the production area) or system, a distinction is made between theoretical (or standard) costs and actual cost (including losses and waste). For example, for energy costs the difference is made between theoretical (or standard) costs ($/unit; kilowatt-hour(s) – Kwh) and actual cost ($/unit; kilowatt-hour(s) – Kwh). Specifically, knowing the cycle time in seconds required to process, assemble, or inspect a product in a module that consumes electricity (Kwh), the time consumed unnecessarily is determined to determine the costs of energy losses.

Why stratified effects losses and waste? Because as shown in Figure 2.11, the approach to losses and waste and implicitly the CLW is done at least at the level of *Activity "A", Process "P", and Operation "O"* to achieve uncovering hidden reserve of productivity and profitability.

The approach in Figure 3.11 underlies the development of Figure 3.3.

To more easily convert losses and waste into costs, they are classified into two types (KPIs for losses and waste): TRLW (measured in terms of time, such as internal logistic loss or lack of materials at module or waiting for material loss) and PLW (number of defects; WIP, etc.). For example, in the case of an event that creates breakdown losses both TRLW and PLW will appear.

Another question arises: Can the probable evolution of sales influence the level of transformation costs (variable and fixed) associated with TPLW and PLW? The answer is yes. The CLWs are influenced by sales evolution scenarios. Figure 3.12 shows the connection between TRLW and transformation cost depending on sales scenarios (increasing or decreasing).

Regarding PLW, they will increase all cost structures (material cost and transformation costs) regardless of sales scenarios. For example, scraps resulting from setup, settings, adjustments loss in module 4, will increase direct material cost (DMC), indirect material cost (IMC), direct labor cost (DLC), indirect labor cost (ILC), tool cost (TC), die and jig cost (DJC), energy cost (EC), fuel cost (FC), depreciation cost (DC), maintenance materials cost (MMC) that were required for processing in the previous modules (modules 1, 2, and 3). The part of time spent unnecessarily with scrap in all four modules is in the TRLW structure.

Therefore, it is very important to address manufacturing cost improvement by reducing or eliminating CLWs which have behind them critical losses or wastes (cause) and not effects losses and waste, more precisely to

The scenario of future sales	The scenario of production planning		The connection between TRLW and transformation cost	
	Production formula	General explanation	Cost structure	Effect
Increasing Sales (under capacity)	actual production quantity for the period > last capacity of production system	the time of losses and waste will generate the increase in the transformation costs (variable and fixed; beyond the standard cost) based on the need for capacity to satisfy the volumes demanded by the customers	Direct Labor Cost (DLC)	Will Increase (the lack of production capacity)
			Indirect Labor Cost (ILC)	Will Increase (the lack of production capacity)
			Maintenance Cost (MC)	Will Increase (the lack of production capacity)
			Energy Cost (EC)	Will Increase (the lack of production capacity)
			Fuel Cost (FC)	Will Increase (the lack of production capacity)
			Depreciation Cost (DC)	Will Increase (the lack of production capacity)
Decreasing Sales (overcapacity)	actual production quantity for the period < last capacity of production system	the time of losses and waste will generate variable transformation cost increase (beyond the standard cost) and will not increase the fixed transformation cost (depreciation cost; against a reduced need for capacity to meet the volumes requested by customers)	Direct Labor Cost (DLC)	Will increase (as the loading time is extended due to the occurrence of losses and waste)
			Indirect Labor Cost (ILC)	Will increase (as the loading time is extended due to the occurrence of losses and waste)
			Maintenance Cost (MC)	Will increase (as the loading time is extended due to the occurrence of losses and waste)
			Energy Cost (EC)	Will increase (as the loading time is extended due to the occurrence of losses and waste)
			Fuel Cost (FC)	Will increase (as the loading time is extended due to the occurrence of losses and waste)
			Depreciation Cost (DC)	It will not increase (the planned production quantity can be assured)

FIGURE 3.12

The connection between time-related losses and waste and transformation cost depending on sales scenarios (increasing or decreasing).

address critical CLWs by setting effective and efficient targets for the concurrent fulfillment of takt profit and takt time (KAIZENSHIRO). In order to fulfill KAIZENSHIRO it is necessary to identify, clarify, and classify all the effects losses and waste related to a critical loss or waste (cause).

Normally, a number of pertinent questions may arise regarding the relationship between critical losses and waste (cause) and effects losses and waste (*multiple; in the mirror and stratified*), respectively: Who makes the connections between critical losses and waste (cause) and effects losses and waste? When? How? All these questions are answered in the organization of daily management or shop floor management (discussed in detail in Chapter 6).

Therefore, in order to reduce CLW in a scientific, systematic, and systemic way, it is necessary to clarify the principles and parameters related to each loss and waste that contribute to the unnecessary increase of manufacturing costs.

As can be seen in Figure 3.13, this causality method aims to:

1. determine the CLW for average production volume in each module (cost object 1), and then
2. critical costs of losses and waste (CCLW) for bottleneck profit module and for bottleneck capacity module (cost object 2) to obtain

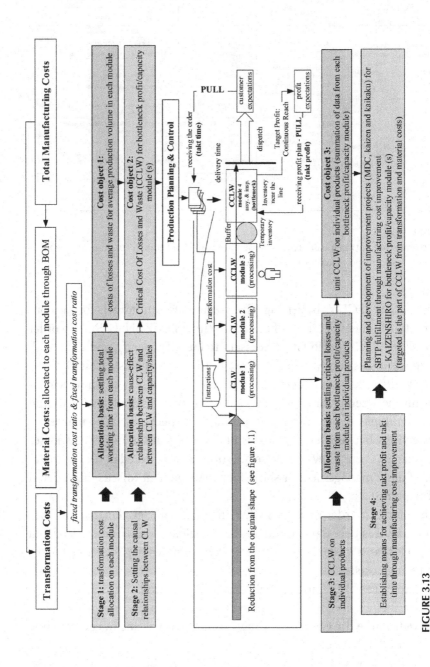

FIGURE 3.13

The causality method for setting costs of losses and waste.

3. unit CCLW on individual products (summation of data from each bottleneck profit module and bottleneck capacity module) (cost object 3; allocation basis is settling critical losses and waste from each bottleneck profit module and bottleneck capacity module on individual products) by
4. planning and development of improvement projects (MDC, kaizen, and kaikaku) for SBTP fulfillment through manufacturing cost improvement or of KAIZENSHIRO for bottleneck profit/capacity module(s) (targeted is the part of CCLW from transformation and material costs).

Again, as in the case of both the unique rate method and the modules rate method, the material costs are determined at the level of each module based on the BOM. The level of losses related to material and components is found in material yield loss (measured as yield ratio – %; see Table 3.2; production resource losses). The difference is now that the level of costs of material yield losses is determined at the level of each loss and waste depending on the triggering event of losses or waste (e.g., if a breakdown event caused a scrap, then the cost of scrap losses time and the material yield losses are associated with the cost of breakdown losses). Reducing or eliminating the cost of breakdown losses will also have a positive effect on reducing the scrap rate of the equipment/module (see Table 3.1).

The causality method uses all loss and waste measurements (see Tables 3.1–3.3) for each module. But now, the calculations are no longer similar to those presented in Chapter 2 (see Sections 2.4 and 2.5).

In order to be able to go further, a little emphasis should be placed on how to approach the causality method on the difference between:

- losses and waste related to a bottleneck capacity module (purpose: takt time fulfillment); unlocking a bottleneck capacity module will aim to increase production volume (increase output; increase net standard operating time or net capacity or increase effectiveness) to meet a higher level of takt time especially against the background of increased sales and will seek in particular to reduce losses from Table 3.1; and
- losses and waste related to a bottleneck profit module (purpose: fulfillment of takt profit); in order to unblock a bottleneck profit module, the aim will be to reduce production inputs (reducing manufacturing

costs or increase efficiency) in order to achieve a high level of takt profit especially against the background of declining sales volumes and will seek in particular to reduce losses for production costs (see Table 3.2) and losses and waste for production control (see Table 3.3).

Going beyond the presentation of the main effects of losses and waste (time, production, distances, labor, and dollars; see Table 3.1–3.3), which directed the determination of costs of losses and waste for the first two methods (the unique rate method and the modules rates method), the causality method determines separately costs of losses and waste for the sales growth scenario and for the sales decrease scenario, as the cumulation of costs related to losses and waste are considered to be different.

3.3.3.1 Increasing Sales Scenario

Figure 3.14 presents the way to transform losses and waste into costs in order to contribute to the achievement of planned levels of profits (a process called profit planning) from the perspective of sales growth (or actual production quantity for the period > last capacity of production system; or the under capacity status). Figure 3.14 presents the quantitative analysis of the connections between losses and waste structure and total cost structure on a module compared to the qualitative analysis of losses and waste presented in Figures 3.2 and 3.3.

Again, total cost structure is addressed at the level of variable costs and fixed costs (columns from "j" to "y"). As can be seen, in order to obtain a higher percentage of the CLW that can be improved as effectively and efficiently as possible, the causality method addresses costs beyond manufacturing costs, namely SG&A expense. Also, in Figure 3.14 the losses and waste structure is presented (columns "a" and "b"; see Tables 3.1–3.3 to see KPIs for losses and waste which are now presented in column "d"). Column "c" contains the details of the module (bottleneck profit or capacity module – BM) for which the transformation of losses and waste into costs is made (see Figure 2.11). Further, in the columns "e", "f", "g", "h", and "i" the new structure of total costs from the perspective of identifying CLW is presented, respectively:

- basic manufacturing cost or value-added costs (column "e");
- cost of losses and waste (CLW; column "f");

scenario 1: increasing sales
(actual production quantity for the period > last used capacity of production system/manufacturing flow)

For each bottleneck profit or capacity module (BM) of a manufacturing flow:
activity (A), process (P) and operation (O)

Total Cost Structure

Losses and Waste Structure

KAIZENSHIRO

Losses & Waste Structure (a)	(b)	For module (BM): Activity (A); Process (P) Operation (O) (A1; P1.1; O1.1.1; ..."n") (c)	KPIs for losses: TRLW & PLW (d)	Total Manuf. Cost — basic manuf. cost ($) (e)	Total Manuf. Cost — cost of losses and waste ($) (f)	critical cost of losses and Waste (CCLW) ($) (g)	annual allowable CCLW ($) (h)	annual reduction target for CCLW ($) (i)
Production Volume — Equipment Losses	Scheduled Downtime Losses		TRLW & PLW					
	Downtime Losses		TRLW & PLW					
	Performance Losses		PLW					
	Quality Losses		TRLW					
Production Costs	Labor Losses		TRLW & PLW					
	Material and Utilities Consumption Losses		TRLW					
Production Control	Inventory Consumption Waste		PLW					
	System Consumption Losses		TRLW & PLW					
Total			TRLW & PLW	$ (e)	$ (f)	$ (g)	$ (h)	$ (i)

Total Cost Structure

	Product Cost — Manufacturing Cost (MC)											Period Cost				SG&A Expenses (variable & fixed)
	Variable Costs (including Manufacturing Overhead Costs - MO)									Fixed Costs (MO)						
	Direct Material Cost (DMC)	Indirect Material Cost (IMC)	Direct Labor Cost (DLC)	Indirect Labor Cost (ILC)	Tool Cost (TC)	Die and Jig Cost (DJC)	Energy Cost (EC)	Fuel Cost (FC)	Maintenance Cost (MC)	Depreciation Cost (DC)	Maintenance Materials Cost (MMC)	Bank and Financial Cost (BFC)	Administrative Costs (AC)	Inventory Costs (IC)	R&D Costs (RDC)	Distribution and Logistic Costs (DLC)
Scheduled Downtime Losses	x	x	x							x	x					
Downtime Losses	x	x	x				x	x	x	x	x	x		x	x	x
Performance Losses			x	x		x	x	x	x							
Quality Losses	x	x	x	x	x	x		x	x							x
Labor Losses			x	x									x			
Material and Utilities Consumption Losses	x	x	x	x							x	x		x		x
Inventory Consumption Waste														x	x	x
System Consumption Losses	x	x	x	x					x	x	x	x		x	x	x
Total	$(i)(k)	$(l)	$(m)(n)	$(o)(p)	$(q)(r)	$(s)	$(t)	$(u)(v)	$(w)	$(x)(y)						

FIGURE 3.14

From losses and waste and their associated costs in sales increasing scenario to KAIZENSHIRO for each bottleneck profit or capacity module (BM).

- critical cost of losses and waste (CCLW; column "g"; through cause-effect analysis it is sought to find at least 80% of CLW embedded in CCLW both at the level of bottleneck profit module and bottleneck capacity module – BM);
- annual allowable CCLW (column "h", or part of the CCLW that will not be targeted for improvement in that year); and finally
- setting the annual reduction target for CCLW (or KAIZENSHIRO) at the level of activity, process or operation of each bottleneck profit module and bottleneck capacity module – BM (actually the basic purpose of this table; column "h").

The formulas in the table are:

$$TMC = BMC + CLW \qquad (3.2)$$

where:
   TMC is total manufacturing cost ($/module/period)
   BMC is basic manufacturing cost (or value-added cost) ($/module/period) (column "e"; Figure 3.14)
   CLW is cost of losses and waste (or without value-added cost) ($/module/period) (column "f"; Figure 3.14)

and

$$ART = CCLW - AA \qquad (3.3)$$

where:
   ART is annual reduction target for CCLW (KAIZENSHIRO; those subject to improvements of microproductivity – MDC and macroproductivity – kaizen and kaikaku; $/module/period) (column "i"; Figure 3.14)
   CCLW is critical cost of losses and waste (seeks to concentrate at least 80% of CLW of all modules in the bottleneck profit module and the bottleneck capacity module; CCLWs are those that can be prevented through improvements; $/module/period) (column "g"; Figure 3.14)
   AA is annual allowable CCLW (part of CCLW that will not be targeted for improvement in that year; $/module/period) (column "h"; Figure 3.14).

Furthermore, by breaking down each structure of losses and waste (see Tables 3.1–3.3) at the product unit level, it is possible to identify and understand in-depth the structure and dynamics of the CLW. For example, for the transformation of scheduled downtime losses into unit manufacturing costs, two cost structures are mainly affected: DC and DLC. The calculation formulas per module and per product in the following period are as follows:

- For depreciation cost:

$$CDL = \frac{SDR \times DC}{APC} \qquad (3.4)$$

where:
CDL is unit cost of depreciation losses ($/module/period)
SDR is scheduled downtime rate (%/module/period)
DC is depreciation costs ($/module/period)
APC is actual production quantity (module/period)

- For direct labor cost:

$$CDLL = \frac{NO \times DLC \times SDR}{APC} \qquad (3.5)$$

where:
CDLL is unit cost of direct labor losses ($/module/period)
NO is number of operators (module/period)
DLC is direct labor cost ($/module/period)
SDR is scheduled downtime rate (%/module/period)
APC is actual production quantity (module/period)

Following this causal analysis for the sales growth scenario and the unit cost of losses calculation, the concentration for achieving SBTP is reduced to the fulfillment in particular of the CCLW related to production volume losses. This direction often results in substantial improvement of employees' attitudes and abilities, and working environments have become more pleasant, through full involvement and collaboration of cost management and production departments. At the same time, this direction of improvements toward the fulfillment of SBTP by reducing/eliminating CCLW often determines the increase of the standardization level of losses and waste.

The approach in Figure 3.14 is continued at the level of the summation of modules (see Figure 3.15) to identify both the contribution of each module to the fulfillment of KAIZENSHIRO for that period (see Figure 3.16) and KAIZENSHIRO at the level of each product.

As can be seen in Figure 3.16, taking into account the generally accepted principle that different evaluation methods lead to different results, the causality method identifies more opportunities to improve the CLW for each bottleneck profit module (module 3) or bottleneck capacity module (module 4) than the first 2 methods (the case of the unique rate method and the modules rates method). All improvement projects for the next period will now focus on modules 3 and 4 to meet KAIZENSHIRO.

At the same time, Figure 3.17 shows the way to establish a manufacturing improvement target on each product (see formulas 3.4 and 3.5). Again, the visibility of opportunities to improve CLW is greater.

In conclusion, the essential differences of the CLW approach for the increasing sales scenario compared to decreasing sales scenario (which will be presented immediately in the next section) are:

- losses of production volume (equipment effectiveness and efficiency) are particularly affected (see Table 3.1) which attract only certain cost structures (see Figure 3.14; columns "j" to "y"; "X" represents a cost with high influence on the structure of losses; "x" represents a cost with significant influence on the structure of losses; the lack of marking means that the respective cost structure is not attracted by that loss); and
- manufacturing cost improvement targets the modules that are CCLW carriers, respectively bottleneck profit module and bottleneck capacity module.

3.3.3.2 Decreasing Sales Scenario

Figure 3.18 shows how to transform losses and waste into costs in order to contribute to the achievement of planned levels of profits (a process called profit planning) from the perspective of declining sales (or actual

Scenario 1: INCREASING SALES

(actual production quantity for the period >
last used capacity of production system/manufacturing flow)

For each manufacturing flow, product family or product

(focus on bottleneck profit and capacity module - BM)

Total Cost Structure

Losses and Waste Structure

Losses & Waste Structure			For 4 modules of target manufacturing flow: Module 1 + Module 2 + Module 3 (BM - profit) + Module 4 (BM - capacity)	KPIs for losses: TRLW & PLW	Total Cost — basic manuf. cost ($)	Total Cost — cost of losses and waste ($)	Manufacturing cost improv. — critical cost of losses and Waste (CCLW) ($)	annual allowable CCLW ($)	annual reduction target for CCLW ($)
Production Volume	Equipment Losses	Scheduled Downtime Losses	......	TRLW & PLW	......	......	......	......	......
		Downtime Losses	......	TRLW & PLW	......	......	......	......	......
		Performance Losses	......	TRLW	......	......	......	......	......
		Quality Losses	......	TRLW & PLW	......	......	......	......	......
	Labor Losses		......	TRLW	......	......	......	......	......
Production Costs	Material and Utilities Consumption Losses		......	PLW	......	......	......	......	......
Production Control	Inventory Consumption Waste		......	TRLW & PLW	......	......	......	......	......
	System Consumption Losses		......	TRLW & PLW	......	......	......	......	......
Total			(c)	(d)	(e) $	(f) $	(g) $	(h) $	(i) $
(a)		(b)							

KAIZENSHIRO (annual reduction target for CCLW ($))

Total Cost Structure

	Product Cost — Manufacturing Cost (MC) (including Manufacturing Overhead Costs - MO)								Fixed Costs (MO)			Period Cost — Bank and Financial Cost (BFC)	SG&A Expenses (variable & fixed)			
	Variable Costs															
	Direct Material Cost (DMC)	Indirect Material Cost (IMC)	Direct Labor Cost (DLC)	Indirect Labor Cost (ILC)	Tool Cost (TC)	Die and Jig Cost (DJC)	Energy Cost (EC)	Fuel Cost (FC)	Maintenance Cost (MC)	Depreciation Cost (DC)	Maintenance Materials Cost (MMC)	Bank and Financial Cost (BFC)	Administrative Costs (AC)	Inventory Costs (IC)	R&D Costs (RDC)	Distribution and Logistic Costs (DLC)
	(j) $	(k) $	(l) $	(m) $	(n) $	(o) $	(p) $	(q) $	(r) $	(s) $	(t) $	(u) $	(v) $	(w) $	(x) $	(y) $

FIGURE 3.15

From KAIZENSHIRO for each module in increasing sales scenario to KAIZENSHIRO for each manufacturing flow, product family, or product.

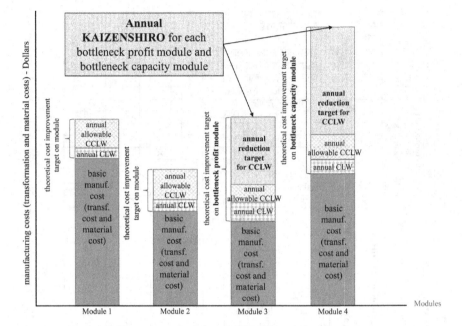

FIGURE 3.16

The annual manufacturing cost improvement targets cost for each module with two types of bottleneck – across the entire manufacturing flow.

production quantity for the period < last capacity of production system; or the overcapacity status).

Again, the total cost structure is approached at the level of variable costs and fixed costs (columns from "j" to "y") as in Figure 3.14. The difference from Figure 3.14 is that now the total level of cost structure related to losses and waste is more comprehensive because companies are in a state of overcapacity, a system that causes losses and waste systemically.

The formulas in Figures 3.18 are similar to those in Figures 3.14 (see formulas 3.2 and 3.3). At the same time, the breakdown of each losses and waste structure at the level of unit product costs is made according to the logic presented in formulas 3.4 and 3.5.

Following this causal analysis for the sales decrease scenario and the unit cost of losses calculation, the focus for achieving SBTP is reduced to fulfilling in particular the CCLW related to losses for production costs (see Table 3.2) and losses and waste for production control (see Table 3.3).

Like the approach in Figure 3.15, the approach in Figure 3.18 continues at the level of summing up the modules (see Figure 3.19) to identify both

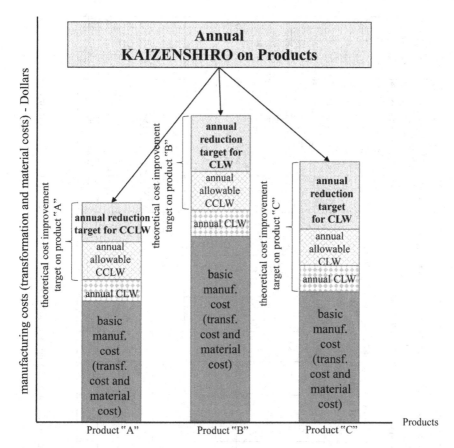

FIGURE 3.17
The annual manufacturing cost improvement targets cost on each product with two types
of bottleneck – across the entire manufacturing flow.

the contribution of each module to KAIZENSHIRO's fulfillment for that
period (similar to Figure 2.12) and KAIZENSHIRO at the level of each
product (similar to Figure 3.17).

Some of the advantages of the causality method are: (1) a greater accuracy in determining the CLW; (2) a better control of the CLW by determining the CCLW; (3) offers the possibility to focus the improvement
efforts and resources on the relevant factors of CCLW; (4) ensures better management of planning and development of improvements related
to synchronous profitable operations by directing the improvement targets for KAIZENSHIRO to be able to be fulfilled continuously, etc. The
main disadvantages are: (1) the cost of implementation and maintenance;

Scenario 2: DECREASING SALES
(actual production quantity for the period < last used capacity of production system/manufacturing flow)

For each bottleneck profit and capacity module (BM) of a manufacturing flow: activity (A), process (P) and operation (O)

KAIZENSHIRO

Total Cost Structure

	Product Cost											Period Cost				
	Manufacturing Cost (MC)											SG&A Expenses (variable & fixed)				
	Variable Costs (including Manufacturing Overhead Costs - MO)								Fixed Costs (MO)							
	DMC	IMC	DLC	ILC	TC	DJC	EC	FC	MC	DC	MMC	BFC	AC	IC	RDC	DLC

Loss and cost association matrix (middle columns):

For module (BM): Activity (A); Process (P); Operation (O) (A1; P1.1; O1.1.1; ... "n")	KPIs for losses: TRLW & PLW	Total Cost – basic manuf. cost ($)	cost of losses and waste ($)	Manuf. cost improv. – critical cost of losses and Waste (CCLW) ($)	annual allowable CCLW ($)	annual reduction target for CCLW ($)
(c)	(d)	(e)	(f)	(g)	(h)	(i)

Losses and Waste Structure

Production Volume	Equipment Losses	Scheduled Downtime Losses	TRLW & PLW
		Downtime Losses	TRLW & PLW
		Performance Losses	TRLW
		Quality Losses	TRLW & PLW
Production Costs	Labor Losses		TRLW
	Material and Utilities Consumption Losses		PLW
Production Control	Inventory Consumption Waste		TRLW & PLW
	System Consumption Losses		TRLW & PLW
	Total		

Column reference letters and units:
(a) | (b) | (c) | (d) | (e) $ | (f) $ | (g) $ | (h) $ | (i) $
(j) $ | (k) $ | (l) $ | (m) $ | (n) $ | (o) $ | (p) $ | (q) $ | (r) $ | (s) $ | (t) $ | (u) $ | (v) $ | (w) $ | (x) $ | (y) $

FIGURE 3.18

From losses and waste and their associated costs in decreasing sales scenario to KAIZENSHIRO for each bottleneck profit or capacity module (BM).

Scenario 2: DECREASING SALES

(actual production quantity for the period <
last used capacity of production system/manufacturing flow)

For each manufacturing flow, product family or product

(focus on bottleneck profit and capacity module - BM)

Losses and Waste Structure			For 4 modules of target manufacturing flow: Module 1 + Module 2 + Module 3 (BM - profit) + Module 4 (BM - capacity)	KPIs for losses: TRLW & PLW	Total Cost		Manufacturing cost improv.		
					basic manuf. cost ($)	cost of losses and waste ($)	critical cost of losses and Waste (CCLW) ($)	annual allowable CCLW ($)	annual reduction target for CCLW ($)
Production Volume	Equipment Losses	Scheduled Downtime Losses	....	TRLW & PLW	$	$	....	....	....
		Downtime Losses	....	TRLW & PLW	$	$	....	....	....
		Performance Losses	....	TRLW	$	$	....	....	....
		Quality Losses	....	TRLW & PLW	$	$	....	....	....
Production Costs	Labor Losses		....	TRLW	$	$	....	....	....
	Material and Utilities Consumption Losses		....	PLW	$	$	....	....	....
Production Control	Inventory Consumption Waste		....	TRLW & PLW	$	$	....	....	....
	System Consumption Losses		....	TRLW & PLW	$	$	....	....	....
(a)	(b)		(c)	(d)	(e) $	(f) $	(g) $	(h) $	(i) $

KAIZENSHIRO

Total Cost Structure

(Total Cost Structure columns — Product Cost / Period Cost)

Product Cost — Manufacturing Cost (MC):
- Variable Costs (including Manufacturing Overhead Costs - MO):
  - Direct Material Cost (DMC)
  - Indirect Material Cost (IMC)
  - Direct Labor Cost (DLC)
  - Indirect Labor Cost (ILC)
  - Tool Cost (TC)
  - Die and Jig Cost (DJC)
  - Energy Cost (EC)
  - Fuel Cost (FC)
- Fixed Costs (MO):
  - Maintenance Cost (MC)
  - Depreciation Cost (DC)
  - Maintenance Materials Cost (MMC)

Period Cost — SG&A Expenses (variable & fixed):
- Bank and Financial Cost (BFC)
- Administrative Costs (AC)
- Inventory Costs (IC)
- R&D Costs (RDC)
- Distribution and Logistic Costs (DLC)

Column labels: (j) (k) (l) (m) (n) (o) (p) (q) (r) (s) (t) (u) (v) (w) (x) (y) — all $

FIGURE 3.19

From KAIZENSHIRO for each module in decreasing sales scenario to KAIZENSHIRO for each manufacturing flow, product family, or product.

(2) the uncertainty of the stability of the future decision-making needs of managers.

3.4 ANNUAL COSTS OF LOSSES AND WASTE DEPLOYMENT MAPS

Once the annual improvement opportunities have been established through one of the three previous methods, in order to achieve the convergence of improvements to meet the SBTP, the *CLW policy deployment* is required at the level of each module, product or product family. CLW policy deployment means setting targets ("expected results") and means ("guidelines for achieving a targets" – how to achieve the targets or direction for improvements) regarding SBTP compliance. Generally, "a target and means combined can be called a policy" (Akao, 1991, pp. 5–6). Based on the policy, an action plan can be determined with a timetable.

Therefore, this section will present both CLW map and CCLW map to help establish the target profit at the level of module, product, and product families.

3.4.1 Costs of Losses and Waste Map

In order to achieve a continuous decrease in the unit cost of production of the product and to ensure a competitive price level, the basic mechanism of SBTP aims to accurately identify the current state of CLW in each module of each manufacturing flow. Based on the information outputs in Figure 3.3 (the map of causal relationships between losses and waste) the annual CLW map is determined (for the following year and with a projection for 3–5 years).

The evaluation in the CLW map is based on a quantitative analysis, as most of the losses and waste in Figure 3.2 noted with the same score may have different CLWs. Usually, CLW is identified in the proportion of 30–40% of the actual manufacturing costs. This is the evaluation of the work efficiency in Figure 3.2. If 30–40% of the total costs structure is not met for a manufacturing flow or for the entire production company, then the rigor of identifying losses and waste is increased by detailing KPIs related to losses and waste (see Tables 3.1–3.3) and moves to the identification of CLW at the level

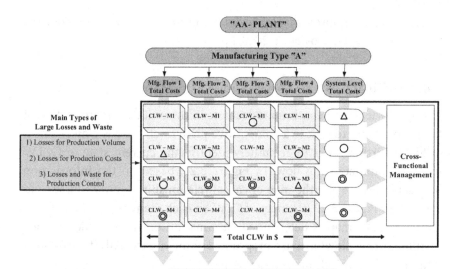

FIGURE 3.20
The map of costs of losses and waste on each manufacturing flow.

of work element and motion (see Figure 2.11 – with the help of MDC; micro-productivity). In order to confirm the percentage of 30–40% it is necessary to transform all losses and waste into costs.

While in Figure 3.2 we looked for the answers to the question where are losses and waste, in the module or in the system, and in Figure 3.3 the answers to the question how losses and waste behave in the module of each manufacturing flow and in the entire manufacturing system were sought; now the CLW map (Figure 3.20) is looking for specific answers to the question what are the total costs behind losses and waste?

As mentioned in this book, the capture of losses and waste is done continuously and is recorded from shift to shift in the *shift report*. The two team leaders from the last and the starting shift are responsible for meeting, about 5–15 minutes, to exchange information and to briefly analyze the shift and business information needed to start the next shift. The goal is to ensure that the start team leader is aware of the past performance and all relevant current issues that may affect the future performance, such as downtime, quality, or changeovers. When establishing the causal relations, the product that was in processing at the time of the occurrence of losses and waste is specified.

Therefore, the improvement priority in Figure 3.2 moves from module 4 to modules 3 and 4 (Posteucă, 2019, pp. 116–127).

3.4.2 Critical Costs of Losses and Waste Map

In order to achieve a continuous decrease in the unit cost of production of the product and to ensure a competitive price level, the basic mechanism of SBTP further seeks to accurately identify the current state of CCLW in each manufacturing flow. In Figure 3.21, based on the information outputs in Figure 3.3 (the map of causal relationships between losses and waste) and Figure 3.20 (the map of CLW on each manufacturing flow) the annual CCLW map is determined (summation on the modules of each manufacturing flow/product or product family; especially for the next year and with projection for 3–5 years).

The CCLW map sets the acceptable future status for the total CCLW of each manufacturing flow (or product/product family) and for the entire company. The aim is to identify the CCLW which amounts to 80% of the CLW identified by the CLW map (representing 30–40% of the total costs). The percentage of 80% represents the observance of the Pareto principle for identifying the causal relationships between losses and waste, the map of causal relationships between losses and waste (Figure 3.3), and the causal relationship between CLW and CCLW map (Figure 3.21).

The questions to be answered by accurately drawing up the CCLW map are: How big is the opportunity to meet the annual and multiannual SBTP mechanism based on the total CCLW level? Where are the most effective and efficient annual and multiannual opportunities to meet the SBTP by addressing the CCLW related to the bottleneck profit module and the CCLW related to the bottleneck capacity module? With the answers to these questions, it will be possible to establish profit policy deployment (targets and means to meet SBTP), both for the next annual year, and especially for the next 3–5 years.

Therefore, the improvement priorities in Figure 3.20 focus on module 3 in Figure 3.21 (bottleneck profit module; the highest level of CCLW that can be prevented for the next year in order to meet the takt profit in particular) and on module 4 (bottleneck capacity module; the highest level of CCLW that can be prevented for the next year in order to meet the takt time in particular). The continuous identification of CCLW that cause other CLW throughout the manufacturing flow and at system level is the

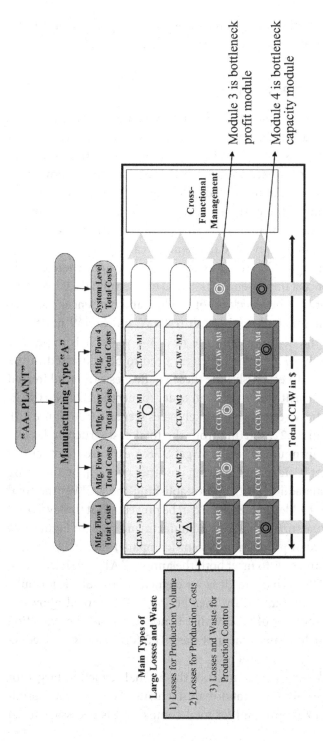

FIGURE 3.21

The map of critical costs of losses and waste on each manufacturing flow.

key to effectively and efficiently address subsequent improvements to prevent probable losses and waste (Posteucă, 2019, pp. 116–127).

3.4.3 Annual Target Profitability

Once the prediction of the possibility of improving productivity has been determined by measuring the current level of CLW and CCLW, it is possible to establish the possible and necessary level of reduction of CCLW for the following year for each module of the manufacturing flow, each product family, or each product. The development of credible hypotheses for the improvement of the current CCLW aims to identify and consistently address the main phenomena, principles, and symptoms of CLW manifestation that can be prevented in the next year.

Having found in Figure 3.21 the answer to how big and where exactly the opportunity for cost improvement is, based on the annual CCLW identification located at the bottleneck profit module and bottleneck capacity module level, the main challenges of future CLW and CCLW must now be established for the next year and the next 3–5 years. It is important to understand deeply why these challenges need to be addressed in the next period and then to establish how these challenges can be addressed as effectively and efficiently as possible in order to meet KAIZENSHIRO.

Again, it is essential to establish the likely sales scenario (see Figure 3.1).

As shown in Figure 3.22, starting from the total cost structure [as elements of the SBTP formula; "E" – the target SG&A expenses (per period) and "C" – the target basic manufacturing cost (per period)], by summing the CLW (non-value-added cost) and establishing the CCLW (the total level of costs without added value which can be prevented) at the level of all modules of a manufacturing flow, of a manufacturing type (in Figure 3.21 of type "A") or on total production system (company) the CCLW reduction targets are set in order to meet both the annual KAIZENSHIRO and, implicitly, the SBTP mechanism [it is an element of the SBTP formula; respectively: "A" – allowable CLW (per period)]. The annual allowable CCLW represents the part of CCLW that is not subject to the reduction process in that year [it is an element of the SBTP formula; "RT" – reduction target for CLW (per period)].

In order to reach the establishment of the annual reduction target for CCLW (KAIZENSHIRO), for total manufacturing flow, for total product, for total product family, and for total company, it is necessary to set

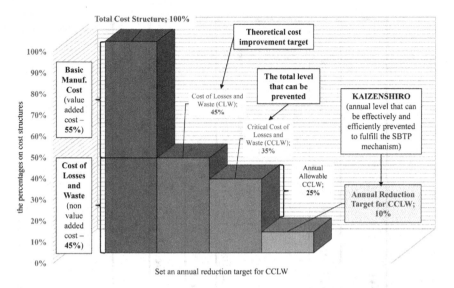

FIGURE 3.22
Uncovering the scientific opportunity to meet the annual reduction target for CCLW (KAIZENSHIRO).

the annual reduction target for CCLW (KAIZENSHIRO) for each type of CLW, for each module that is considered bottleneck profit module (purpose: fulfillment of takt profit) or bottleneck capacity module (purpose: fulfillment of takt time), if it is different from bottleneck profit module.

3.5 SETTING PROFITABLE PRODUCTION FORMULA

The expected effect of the SBTP mechanism is to establish a win-win formula for the production in the next period (e.g., 12 months). Designing the ideal mode of production to accomplish annual planning and developing synchronous profitable operations requires the achievement of a perfect symbiosis between:

1. *the operational expectations* (takt time): it is necessary to review the total plant lead time (see Figure 3.23; L/T is lead time), more precisely:
   • the need to improve the total plant lead time (with all the parameters used);

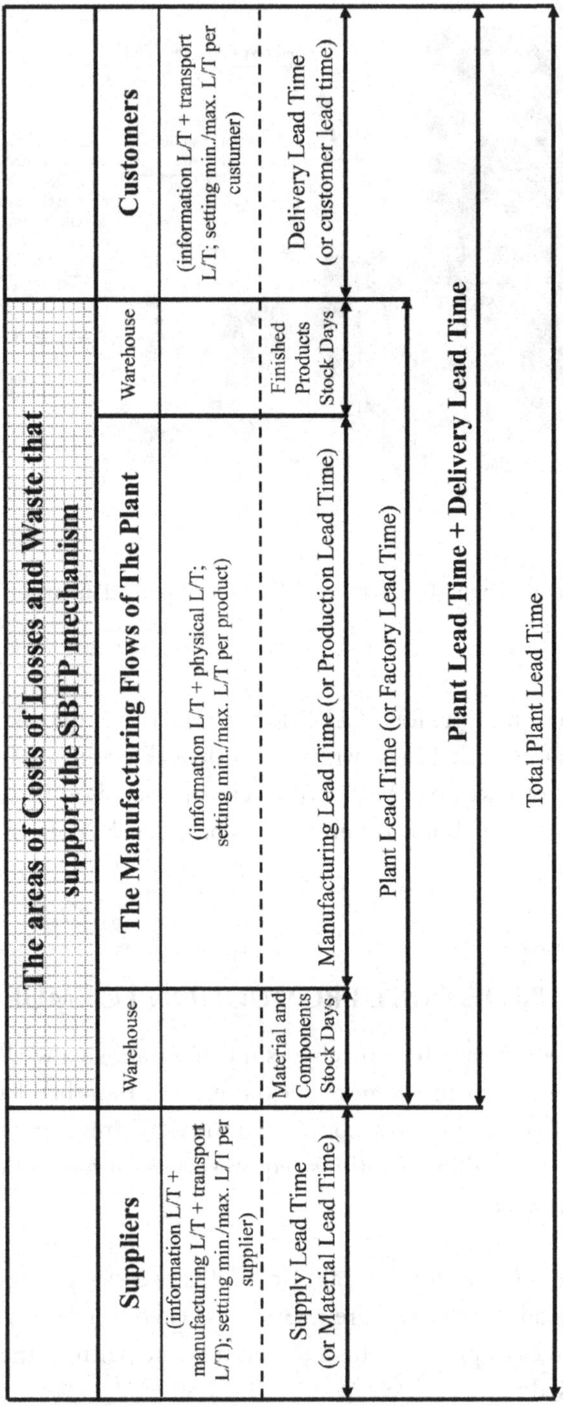

		The areas of Costs of Losses and Waste that support the SBTP mechanism			
Suppliers	Warehouse	**The Manufacturing Flows of The Plant**		Warehouse	**Customers**
(information L/T + manufacturing L/T + transport L/T; setting min./max. L/T per supplier)		(information L/T + physical L/T; setting min./max. L/T per product)			(information L/T + transport L/T; setting min./max. L/T per customer)
	Material and Components Stock Days			Finished Products Stock Days	
Supply Lead Time (or Material Lead Time)		Manufacturing Lead Time (or Production Lead Time)			Delivery Lead Time (or customer lead time)

Plant Lead Time (or Factory Lead Time)

Plant Lead Time + Delivery Lead Time

Total Plant Lead Time

FIGURE 3.23

The holistic approach to total plant lead time to support the SBTP mechanism.

- establishing the locations and size of the buffer points (where inventory must be kept) along the manufacturing lead time (based on the synchronization between the plant lead time and the delivery lead time); the buffer point can be put before the bottleneck capacity module, but there may be cases in which the buffer point is between operations or cases in which the buffer point is in an operation; the locations and sizes of buffer points are determined by the relationship between the delivery lead time (or customer lead time) and the manufacturing lead time (or production lead time) – at least in the case of finished products stock points; in this way the synchronization between the orders received from the customer and the last module (such as, assembly and inspection) can be supported;
- synchronizing manufacturing lead time with customers maximum takt time;
- synchronizing suppliers lead time with manufacturing maximum takt time;
- customers takt time follow up by all the current or future modules (activities, processes, and operations);
- reduction of operations time and "man × hour" for achieving the customers takt time level (against the background of increased sales);
- optimizing the number of operations required by the processes and activities in each module (especially for bottleneck profit module and for bottleneck capacity module);
- reducing the transfer times;
- improving the setup times; and
- establishing the exact production instructions for products on the time axis.

2. *the profitability expectations* (takt profit): it is necessary to establish, understand deeply and continuously improve all areas and modules that attract CLW in order to support SBTP mechanism continuously (see Figure 3.23, top hatch), more exactly:
   - establishing the annual KAIZENSHIRO based on the catchball *process* [the catchball process is the technique that aligns the company's goals, objectives, and *targets* with actions and activities to improve modules (means) at all hierarchical levels, by

creating a two-way flow of information exchange, top-down and bottom-up, until the annual KAIZENSHIRO target of 10% is accepted as achievable by all managers at all levels] starting from the total cost structure (see Figure 3.22) and reaching targets for each type of cost structure of losses and waste depending on the likely scenario of sales, increasing or decreasing (see Figure 3.24). The 10% is budgeted at the time of the annual master budget and is seen as an increase in cost efficiency in the manufacturing area. Depending on the sales scenario, the percentage of 10% can be associated mainly with the improvement of *costs of losses of production volume* on the background of a probable increase in sales volumes or preponderance of the improvement of *costs of losses of production* and *CLW of production control* amid a likely decline in sales volumes. As the SBTP mechanism matures over time, the 10% KAIZENSHIRO percentage tends to decrease with the identification of a lower level of CLW (see Figure 3.24).

- determining the cost-volume-profit relationships before and after KAIZENSHIRO to support the component elements of the SBTP formula (see Figure 3.25); as can be seen, in order to achieve the SBTP mechanism, a transition from the initial break-even point (point "A") to the improved breakeven point (point "B") is planned by establishing after KAIZENSHIRO;

3. *the daily management expectations* (shop floor management expectations): it is necessary to establish a set of agreed principles and structures, processes, and tools to enable accountability for operational performance at all levels of the company, namely:

- appropriate ownership for KPIs and clear scope of decision-making authority defined at each level;
- vertical and horizontal communication loops and alert rules are designed to ensure fast feedback and involvement of all, especially managers;
- SOPs to be updated and communicated in order to achieve a prompt problem-solving process;
- effective visual management to facilitate representing performance against clear targets, touching the process frequently through short-interval monitoring – for each structure of CLW

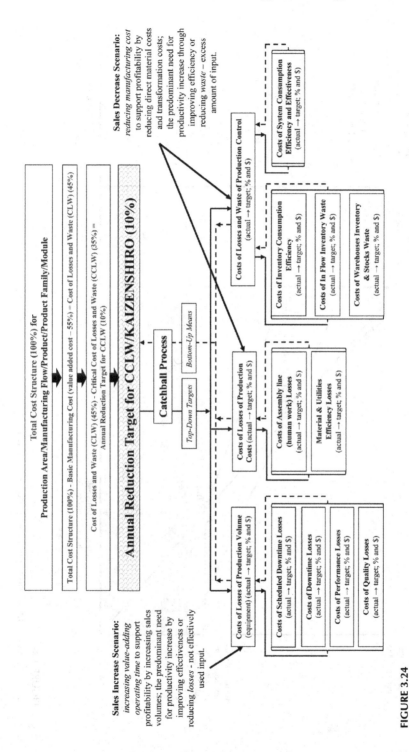

FIGURE 3.24

Catchball process for KAIZENSHIRO annual setting.

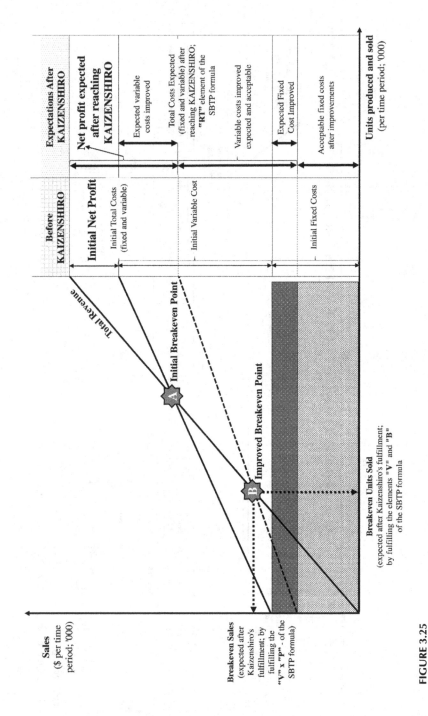

FIGURE 3.25

Cost-volume-profit relationships before and after KAIZENSHIRO.

in order to meet the annual KAIZENSHIRO (see Figure 3.26 in which a segment of CLW transmitted up to the shop floor level is presented);

- continuous promotion of a culture of continuous improvement by empowering shop floor teams and supporting them by a coaching style of leadership, using questions to stimulate initiative rather than giving solutions; and
- improving morale and commitment by encouraging and implementing the ideas and suggestions from all shop floor colleagues to meet the annual KAIZENSHIRO.

Therefore, setting profitable production formula is a very important ingredient of the SBTP mechanism because it is necessary to send a clear, coherent, and consistent message to the company on the direction in which the company expects to go and the level of performance needed to be achieved by SBTP.

3.6 IMPROVEMENT BUDGETS

As shown in Figure 3.26, in order to support the fulfillment of annual and multiannual KAIZENSHIRO and its connection to the vision and productivity mission of the company applying SBTP, the *annual manufacturing improvement budgets* (AMIB) are developed. AMIB is an approach beyond the conventional approach of budget planning and control, an approach that aims to obtain net operating income based exclusively on sales (or annual external profit). AMIB aims at planning and controlling net operating income based on annual internal profit (or operating profit obtained from improving CLW by meeting annual KAIZENSHIRO).

As it is known, the conventional approach to budgeting aims at planning and control for:

- *operating budget* (selling budget/revenues budget, cost of goods sold budget with direct material purchases budget, with direct labor budget, and with manufacturing overhead budget and selling and administrative expenses budget);
- *financial budgets* (capital expenditure budget, cash budget); and

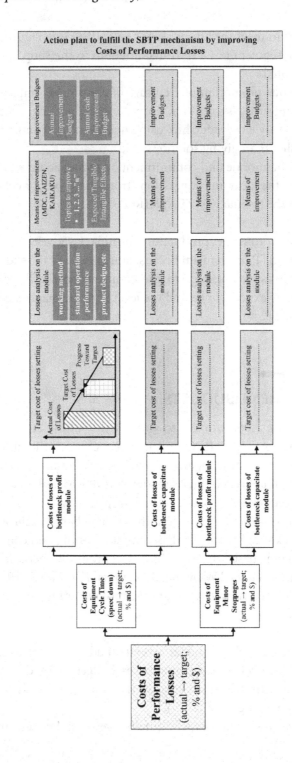

FIGURE 3.26

Example of visual management of the annual KAIZENSHIRO at the shop floor level on a module.

- *pro-forma financial statements* (budgeted income statement and budgeted balance sheet).

According to AMIB, each *operating budget* consists of CLW and CCLW as each cost structure has a part associated with CLW. Therefore, the SBTP mechanism focuses on the *operating budget* (excluding selling and administrative expenses budget), with an extension on the *cash budget*. As presented in Chapter 2 (see Figure 2.19 – Profitability scenarios through productivity), the SBTP mechanism helps to reach the annual and multi-annual target ROI and implicitly the achievement of targets for *financial budgets* (capital expenditure budget).

Therefore, in order to achieve the annual KAIZENSHIRO and, implicitly SBTP mechanism, AMIB are being developed.

3.6.1 KAIZENSHIRO's Financial Visibility in Projected Profit and Loss Statements

The CLW management becomes one means or the purpose of SBTP. From this perspective, two points need to be considered:

1. the need for each module/equipment to be a cost center; and
2. the need for a management of CLW in order to minimize the unnecessary consumption of resources throughout the entire manufacturing system of a company as a whole, continuously capturing all structural changes in dynamics.

So, SBTP deals with the costs: (1) the initial investment, including R&D costs (e.g., new equipment delays installing loss, new equipment inefficiency losses, new products development delay release loss; see Table 3.3); (2) running costs (see Tables 3.1 and 3.2; e.g., losses of production volume); and (3) logistic costs (see Table 3.2; e.g., waste of warehouses inventory and stocks).

Starting from the SBTP principle that any cost structure has incorporated at least one cost structure of losses and waste, the specific planning and budgetary control of SBTP is essential. Figure 3.27 presents in antithesis the projected (pro forma) profit and loss statement for two companies:

Projected SBTP Profit and Loss Statement at "AA-Plant" (with KAIZENSHIRO approach; unit: '000$)		Projected Conventional Profit & Loss Statement at "BB-Plant" (without the KAIZENSHIRO approach; unit: '000$)	
Sales	250,000	Sales	250,000
Annual Target Selling Price (average) - "P" of the SBTP formula	76.6	Annual Target Selling Price (average)	100
Annual Target Number of Units to be Sold - "V" of the SBTP formula	3,264	Annual Target Number of Units to be Sold	2,500
Total Cost Structure for a Plant	72,975	Total Cost Structure for a Plant	72,975
Cost of Losses and Waste (CLW) in Manufacturing (without value added costs; 42%)	30,650	Cost of Losses and Waste (CLW) in Manufacturing (without value added costs)	N/A
Actual Cost of Production Volume and Production Costs Losses	21,455	Actual Cost of Production Volume and Production Costs Losses	N/A
Costs of Production Volume Losses (equipment)	12,873	Costs of Production Volume Losses (equipment)	N/A
Cost of Losses for Production Costs (Costs of Human Work Losses)	5,364	Cost of Losses for Production Costs (Costs of Human Work Losses)	N/A
Cost of Losses for Production Costs (Cost of Material & Utilities Losses)	3,218	Cost of Losses for Production Costs (Cost of Material & Utilities Losses)	N/A
Actual Cost of Production Control Losses and Waste	9,195	Actual Cost of Production Control Losses and Waste	N/A
Cost of Production Control Losses and Waste (In flow inventory)	2,299	Cost of Production Control Losses and Waste (In flow inventory)	N/A
Cost of Production Control Losses and Waste (Warehouses inventory & stocks)	4,138	Cost of Production Control Losses and Waste (Warehouses inventory & stocks)	N/A
Cost of Production Control Losses and Waste (Cost of System Resource Losses)	2,758	Cost of Production Control Losses and Waste (Cost of System Resource Losses)	N/A
Cost of Finished Product (with value added costs; 58%; "C" of the SBTP formula)	42,326	Cost of Finished Product	72,975
Critical Cost of Losses and Waste (CCLW) - Feasible to Improve (36%)	25,541	Critical Cost of Losses and Waste (CCLW)	N/A
Annual Allowable CCLW (25% from Total Costs Structure; "A" of the SBTP formula)	18,244	Annual Allowable CCLW	N/A
Annual Reduction Target of CCLW (KAIZENSHIRO; 10% from Total Costs Structure; "RT of the SBTP formula)	7,298	Annual Reduction Target of CCLW (KAIZENSHIRO)	
KAIZENSHIRO for Production Volume and Production Costs	4,743	KAIZENSHIRO for Production Volume and Production Costs	N/A
KAIZENSHIRO for Production Control Losses and Waste	2,554	KAIZENSHIRO for Production Control Losses and Waste	N/A
Gross Profit in Manufacturing	177,025	Gross Profit in Manufacturing	177,025
Selling, General and Administrative Expenses ("E" of the SBTP formula)	141,168	Selling, General and Administrative Expenses	141,168
Annual Manufacturing External Target Profit	35,857	Annual Operating External Target Profit	35,857
Annual Manufacturing Internal target Profit (reaching KAIZENSHIRO)	7,298	Annual Manufacturing Internal target Profit	N/A
Annual Manufacturing Target Profit (reaching KAIZENSHIRO)	43,155	Annual Manufacturing Target Profit (without KAIZENSHIRO)	35,857

FIGURE 3.27

Projected profit and loss statement (with the KAIZENSHIRO/scientifically improved vs. without approaching KAIZENSHIRO).

- "AA Plant" which adhered to the SBTP mechanism and practices the annual KAIZENSHIRO; with annual manufacturing target profit of $43,155; of which $7,298 related to internal improvements through the subsequent planning and implementation of KAIZENSHIRO; and
- "BB Plant" which has not yet joined the SBTP; with annual manufacturing target profit of only $35,857.

At the same time, "AA Plant" even though it has the same level of sales as "BB-Plant", of $250,000, it practices a much lower average unit price level, of $76.6/unit, compared to those of "BB Plant" of $100/unit.

In conclusion, the use of SBTP and KAIZENSHIRO creates all the premises for the successive decreases of unit prices, ensuring the expected and necessary profitability and competitiveness. It is based on a continuously improved productivity and implicitly on the continuous improvement of the CLW (increase use of current assets, in other words, the visible decrease of fixed costs spent to operate all modules of each manufacturing flow for one hour and increasing the contribution margin generated by an investment/module per hour). That must be the final financial visibility of the SBTP.

3.6.2 The KAIZENSHIRO Budgeting Framework

In SBTP thinking, KAIZENSHIRO's fulfillment is based on a strict and continuously improved standardization of each cost structure of losses and waste. The continuous measurement of losses and waste (see Tables 3.1–3.3) and their transformation into costs, through one of the three methods described above, ensures a continuous standardization of costs (value-added costs and without value-added costs or CLW) and a maximization of the effectiveness and efficiency (productivity) of the entire production system. For example, the transformation cost allocation on bottleneck module (see Figure 3.5; the unique rate method for setting CLW) or on each module (see Figure 3.6; the modules rate method for setting CLW) is in fact the standard transformation cost (running costs) obtained in the previous period as a result. The cost for the next period will be set at a lower level than the transformation cost of the previous period because it relies on the fulfillment of KAIZENSHIRO (necessary to fulfill takt profit and takt time). In this way, the cost restandardization becomes a continuous activity because any improvement in costs must be visible in a lower standard consumption (a lower cost). Even if SBTP is not a method of calculating costs, the SBTP aims at an extreme standardization and improvement of costs.

This means that SBTP aims to reduce or eliminate the CLW to maximize productivity. For example, in modules or equipment centers that are considered bottleneck capacity modules and that have equipment operating time/working time as the main cost driver, improvements are made to meet KAIZENSHIRO. In this context, the main driver cost differs from one module to another. Moreover, the standard cost transformation variation is inevitable, a variation between what was planned and what actually happened in manufacturing and on the market (the cost of purchasing materials, utilities, etc.). These variations must be absorbed by making improvements to ensure KAIZENSHIRO under any conditions. Conventional analysis of cost variation is much less important than analysis of whether or not KAIZENSHIRO is fulfilled. The purpose of costs in any company is to continuously reduce them visibly and not to have justifications over justifications of cost variations. Through SBTP the cost approach is predictive, preventive, proactive, and not reactive. Therefore, when the net standard operating time or the net monthly capacity is constant or decreasing due to the improvement of the working method and the efficiency/performance (with the help of MDC), the loading time becomes long (or the degree of use of the module is higher; using kaizen and kaikaku to reduce/eliminate downtime and speed losses and quality losses; see Figure 2.8). In this way, the standard application rate of the unit cost transformation becomes continuously lower, and the standard unit cost becomes lower and lower.

Figure 3.28 shows the six steps of the KAIZENSHIRO budgeting cycle (manufacturing improvement budgets cycle; AMIB is annual manufacturing improvement budget; AMCIB is annual manufacturing cash improvement budget; the ideal cost is the ideal state of zero costs of losses and waste). As you can see, the six steps follow the PDCA cycle to reach the annual KAIZENSHIRO (Posteucă and Sakamoto, 2017, pp. 157–203; Posteucă, 2018, pp. 188–195; Posteucă, 2019, pp. 142–144).

Based on the six steps of the KAIZENSHIRO budgeting cycle (manufacturing improvement budgets cycle), the five phases of the KAIZENSHIRO budgeting framework are developed (see Figure 3.29).

As you can see, starting from the productivity vision and mission (market share/sales volumes and profitability in the medium and long term),

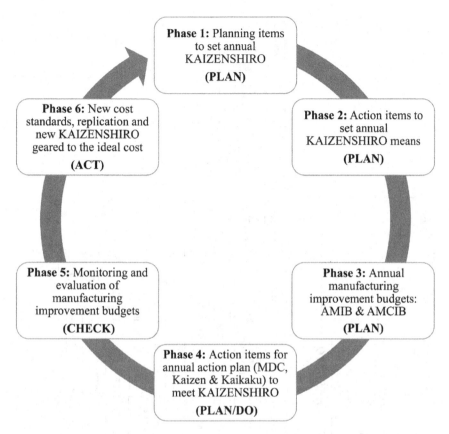

FIGURE 3.28
KAIZENSHIRO budgeting cycle.

the annual KAIZENSHIRO is established by carrying out the catchball process (top-down targets vs. bottom-up means; see Figure 3.24) to reach:

- setting targets for improving annual losses and waste, respectively at the annual KAIZENSHIRO means targets – Phase 2;
- development of three types of budgets: (1) AMIB for existing products; (2) multiannual manufacturing improvement budget for new products; and (3) annual manufacturing cash improvement budget (AMCIB) – Phase 3;
- developing a robust plan for improving the CLW depending on the sales scenarios, respectively at the annual action plan for KAIZENSHIRO means – Phase 4; and

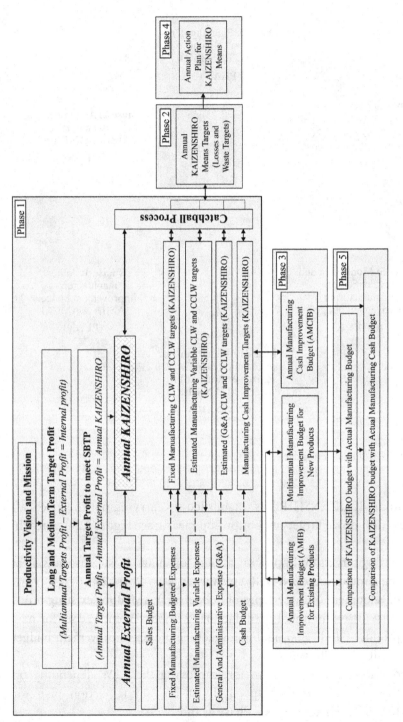

FIGURE 3.29
KAIZENSHIRO budgeting framework.

- at the end to the analysis of the performances obtained by the expected reduction of the annual costs, more precisely to the comparison of the KAIZENSHIRO budget with actual manufacturing budget and comparison of KAIZENSHIRO budget with actual manufacturing cash budget – Phase 5.

In conclusion, the final results of the SBTP should reflect the degree of reduction in costs compared to expectations. If the cost reduction is not clear and visible and does not help to achieve takt time and takt profit, then the SBTP mechanism cannot be considered successful. It is especially important to see in the establishment and fulfillment of KAIZENSHIRO budget all the improvements related to CCLW. If improvement activities are not planned for cost improvement and are not visible in cost improvement, then other cost-increasing factor (CLW) structures must be identified to eliminate them. Therefore, increasing productivity is essential for meeting the KAIZENSHIRO budget, both throughput (efficiency) productivity (TP) and contribution (effectiveness) productivity (CP).

3.7 CONCLUSION: PLANNING OPERATIONS STRICTLY FOR CUSTOMERS' NEEDS IS INEFFICIENT

The practical method of adequately adapting the SBTP mechanism to a production system first of all requires the design of a system for measuring the CLW in order to concurrently fulfill takt time (the pace of customer demand) and takt profit (the pace of profit demand) (see Figure 3.30).

Therefore, the key points to consider when designing and planning SBTP are summarized below.

3.7.1 Continuous Incorporation of Management Needs in the SBTP Mechanism

No matter how accurate the CLW measurements are, the concurrent improvement of takt time and takt profit cannot be achieved. As shown in Figure 3.30, from the perspective of SBTP thinking, the takt time approach alone is insufficient because the takt profit approach is needed at the same

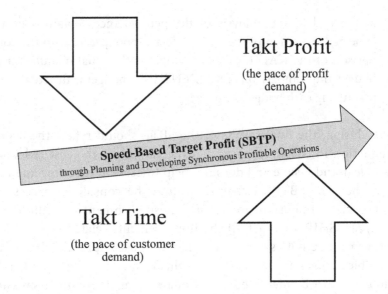

FIGURE 3.30
Insufficient takt time to reach synchronous profitable operations.

time. Measuring the CLW is only a means of sizing past reality. Managers must make appropriate decisions adapted to each current and especially future context. Managers need to be familiar with the SBTP mechanism, know what needs to be achieved and when, and continuously maintain the SBTP mechanism. By doing so, managers and all staff will have the impression that SBTP is their original and valuable system and will gain confidence in its use. Sometimes it may happen that the needs and desires of managers are not necessarily convergent with SBTP. However, the strong opinions of managers must be actively captured in the SBTP mechanism to be useful every day.

3.7.2 Establishment of Several Convergent Measurement Modes

When setting KPIs for losses and waste for a module, one of the challenges is to find a perfect way to measure. It can be said that a single measurement cannot be set for a certain loss or waste. It is necessary to understand the current situation in the module and align it with the SBTP mechanism, so as to gradually exercise an increasingly accurate measurement (see Tables 3.1–3.3).

3.7.3 Establishment of KPIs of Losses and Waste Related to the Expected Results and Possible Actions

This concept is very important when designing KPIs for losses and waste. Assuming that measuring losses and waste and transforming them into costs is easy in a given production system, it is further appropriate to clarify the types of actions and activities that need to be undertaken to visibly improve productivity (losses and waste). Measuring the CLW is not the goal. The aim is to know what effect the improvement actions and activities (MDC, kaizen, and kaikaku) will have in the expected result (KAIZENSHIRO; and also intangible results: teamwork, work satisfaction, the motivation, and real involvement of all people, etc.). Actions and activities to improve productivity are essential component parts of the SBTP mechanism.

3.7.4 The Measurement of Costs of Losses and Waste Is Not Done With a General Purpose

Each company must adapt its own KPIs related to losses and waste. Refining the CLW measurement does not in any way guarantee the improvement of productivity and SBTP compliance. Managers need to think about the specifics of their companies in order to achieve an effective and efficient system of measuring the CLW that suits the current and future real situations, a system of measuring the CLW as a basis for as a basis for future productivity improvement activities, and the design of an original CLW measurement system for each company.

3.7.5 Measuring and Improving the Cost of Losses and Waste Strictly for Customer Needs Is Efficient

In view of the points described above, it is advisable to consider a desirable and practical system for measuring and improving the CLW that corresponds to the real situation of the company and its needs for the concurrent satisfaction of profit needs (takt profit) and customer satisfaction (takt time). If a company tries to make only the products needed by customers, which means that any fluctuation in the quantities ordered by customers will be directly reflected in the company's modules/processes, then control of the company's efficiency will be reduced, including equipment utilization (effectiveness of equipment, and not just equipment). Specifically, because any company is responsible for the efficient coordination of its production, it will not be able to develop a production schedule directly connected to orders received from customers. Moreover, if it is desired to meet all customer needs, the level of stocks of all types tends to increase excessively, implicitly the costs of waste. So, it can be said that this is the real motivation of using SBTP mechanism.

In conclusion, when designing the annual SBTP mechanism, it is necessary to define a realistic and measurable level of KAIZENSHIRO in order to pursue the improvement achieved. The improvement in CLW is endless. The problem is related to the time allocated and the real involvement of the top management and all the people in the company. CLW can be continuously reduced. However, it is necessary to prevent excessive improvements. Consistent standardization of all losses and waste is essential. The thorough search for the best idea, the most effective and efficient idea for improving the cost of losses or waste involves creating a culture of pro-cost improvement. In search of the acceptable level of manufacturing cost for a certain period, the losses and waste converted into costs are deducted from the total manufacturing cost. Therefore, first the KAIZENSHIRO (measured stake of the necessary productivity improvement) is established and then the annual production and the annual strategic improvements are planned.

Forecasting productivity improvement in terms of CLW (or KAIZENSHIRO) involves forecasts in the form of minimizing input and maximizing outputs. Of course, in order to review the results of the improvements, all the planned improvements and the way of profitable production planning will be reviewed in order to reach the state of synchronous profitable operations. Before establishing KAIZENSHIRO, the quantitative data of losses and waste will be sorted and analyzed first. It is often difficult to predict the improvement effect at the beginning of a budget period, as a forecast is made before the start of improvement and production activities, but this forecast can still be made at that time. This is because, not only that the objective data on the CLW and the other elements of the SBTP mechanism are collected, but interviews are conducted with each person concerned, especially experienced managers and practitioners and other surveys. At the same time, a performance system of KAIZENSHIRO fulfillment for each module is being developed. First, what happens when the cost level of losses and waste is improved by 100%

in the bottleneck capacity module (purpose: takt time fulfillment) and/or bottleneck profit module (purpose: takt profit fulfillment) and what happens when it is improved only by 90%? Furthermore, what happens to a lower level of achievement of KAIZENSHIRO? As a result, a continuous analysis of the sensitivity of the improvements to the KAIZENSHIRO level reached is required (see Figure 3.26; progress toward target). It is generally proposed that the level of the value-added costs be 70–80%. Thus, it can be estimated how much the level of costs of losses or waste in a module can be improved. Based on the result of the KAIZENSHIRO calculation, the SBTP team members and the top managers will perform an analysis to predict the level of CLW possible to reduce. Also, as specified in Figure 3.26, an improvement action plan to fulfill the SBTP mechanism is established in detail.

4

Feedforward Control for Production Planning and Scheduling

As presented in previous chapters, speed-based target profit (SBTP) allows profitable production management targeted to achieve synchronous profitable operations based on reaching the target profit per minute in the bottleneck module by planning and improving both the capacity of the bottleneck module and the costs of losses and waste (CLW) for all operations, especially in bottleneck profit module.

Starting from the need to improve productivity from the production planning and scheduling phase, in this chapter we present a global image of the feedforward control architecture for production planning and scheduling of SBTP. To establish an SBTP profitable production management, a company has to build up the following key elements from the feedforward control perspective: production planning, production scheduling and planning for manufacturing costs improvement (MCI) by setting targets and means for improvement depending on the probable sales scenario from next period (increasing or decreasing). An important feature of SBTP is that MCI is done concurrently with the planning and scheduling of the profitable production system. Synchronized and profitable scheduling involves scheduling of MCI in the modules that cause drifting and unprofitable production schedule.

4.1 PRODUCTIVITY IMPROVEMENT IN PRODUCTION PLANNING AND SCHEDULING

In order to successfully promote and implement the productivity improvement and innovations in manufacturing systems, a symbiosis between people, machines, and materials is needed in order to achieve the value expected by both shareholders and customers. The losses and waste are often caused by the technical instability of the manufacturing system. This condition can be the result of a poor level of equipment, supply of materials and components unsynchronized with the production takt time (PTT), a lack or misuse of the standard operating procedures (SOP), or a lack or inconsistency of the appropriate working method. These phenomena are made visible by the lack of balancing of the modules and/or variations of the production volume, because the production volume has not been distributed equally at all workstations of the manufacturing flow.

To limit the amplitude of CLW, the strictest possible planning and scheduling of production, a robust and consistent maintenance system, and adequate quality control are needed to provide the highest possible use of available assets. In this way, the continuous planning and improvement of CLW contributes to increasing productivity from the production planning and scheduling phase. The production planning in the SBTP logic aims to improve productivity through objective and profitable production planning, taking into account the bottleneck capacity module and the bottleneck profit module and not just the acceptance and planning of orders to be delivered on time. In other words, the prevalence of profitability over the customer (ensuring profitability to support the continuity and development of the company with dignity is more important than just customer satisfaction).

4.1.1 From Method and Performance to Production Planning and Scheduling

Before performing production planning and scheduling it is necessary to finalize the working methods (level of standard; innovative design of a standard time as short as possible) and the level of performance (valiance of standard time; maintain level of set standard time). In other words, methods and performance are actually the ingredients of a consistent standard time (such as, minimum man × hour per product; minimum machine or facility hour or operating time; minimum setup; minimum material handling hour; minimum blocking of jigs and fixtures; minimum motions, etc.). Without a consistent standard time (with SOP) production planning and scheduling for synchronous profitable operations is difficult to achieve.

Therefore, method improvement is the most important dimension of productivity improvement (Sakamoto, 2010; Posteucă and Sakamoto, 2017). The application of working methods leads to a more pleasant and motivating work environment, more rigorous and stable production planning and scheduling, and lower CLW level, against the background of preventing the occurrence of losses and waste (less disturbances).

Therefore, improving productivity must start with the design of effective and efficient working methods, then with the limitation of the variation of standard times, and finally with a planning and scheduling to ensure the best possible use of assets. A good design of working methods should be found in minimum cycles time (without unnecessary time included), in equipment movements in parallel with human work, in minimum distances of movements (especially empty movements), and in maximum speeds of equipment (logical and reasonable speed).

Performance includes real-time lost compared to the standard level and is found in time-related losses and waste (TRLW). Specifically, the level of performance refers to the difference between standard time and actual time (see Table 3.1; equipment cycle time loss or speed down and equipment minor stoppages loss; see Table 3.2; line organization/balancing loss and non-digitalization loss or losses resulting from failure of digitalization).

In fact, in many companies, the speed of people and equipment often differs greatly from standard time. The potential for improvement to eliminate these variations and the possibility of increasing speed is high. The effect of improving performance on the level of availability and quality is a multiplier effect. After eliminating the variations of performance, it is possible to proceed to increase the speeds in a consistent and safe way, in other words, to move again to the innovative design of the working methods.

Therefore, to achieve production planning and scheduling, it is first necessary to define a time standard without significant deviations. Standard time variations determine the occurrence of losses and waste in a systemic way (see Table 3.3). Improving productivity from the perspective of production planning and scheduling means improving the allocation of people, equipment, and materials to concurrently achieve the necessary production for customers and profitable production for the company.

4.1.2 The Main Factors for Production Planning Improvement

The objectives of improving production planning and scheduling in the SBTP logic (to achieve synchronous profitable operations) are clear, respectively: (1) reducing production lead time; (2) synchronization of modules to takt time (through bottleneck capacity modules); (3) synchronization of modules to takt profit (especially through bottleneck profit modules); (4) reducing work-in-progress (WIP) inventory; (5) creating and continuously supporting the one-piece flow (OPF) state and/or small lots; (6) reducing material inventory; (7) reducing/eliminating overtime; (8) reduction/elimination of handling; (9) reducing setup time for fulfilling product volumes (fulfilling of takt time); (10) reduction of setup time to meet the profitability of products (fulfillment of takt profit); and (11) reducing CLW, etc.

In order to achieve these objectives of improving production planning and scheduling, it is essential to address three major factors (see Figure 4.1).

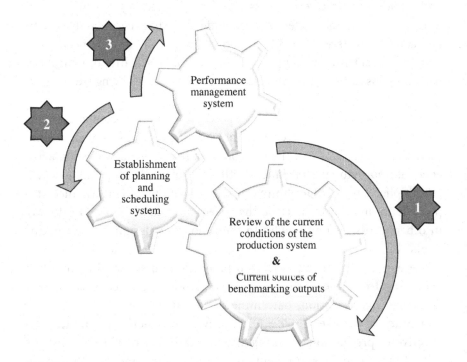

FIGURE 4.1

The three factors for production planning improvement for synchronous profitable operations.

> What are the most critical costs of losses and waste?
>   ✓ Cost of Production Volume Losses?
>   ✓ Costs of Production Costs Losses?
>   ✓ Costs of Production Control Losses and Waste?
> What are the modules that cause the most trouble?
> What are the outputs of the modules that cause the biggest trouble?
> How do these modules affect the expected synchronization and profitability?
> What are the factors (losses and/or waste) that determine the most important critical cost of losses and waste now and in the future?
> What are the phenomena and principles that cause critical costs of losses and waste now and in the future?
> How can costs of losses and waste be measured in the current production system?
> How are the cost structures that tend to increase or have unexplained fluctuations in the company?

FIGURE 4.2
Questions that may indicate the need for benchmark outputs.

For the SBTP planning, the current conditions of the company will always be reviewed from the perspective of improving working methods and measuring and evaluating the efficiency of manufacturing modules. The organization of production planning and scheduling, in order to meet the expected outputs, can be done only after the revision of the production system (the level of CLW, the status of the bottleneck capacity modules, and the status of the bottleneck profit modules) and improvements of the manufacturing flow have been planned. At the same time, the analysis of current sources of benchmarking outputs is done. More precisely, the answers to the questions in Figure 4.2 are sought.

Regarding the establishment of planning and scheduling system, there are two levels of thinking related to the SBTP:

1. *Planning the distribution of activities in modules* (vertical planning; defines WHAT and HOW); is the plan of distribution of activities appropriate for each module to meet the required workload and profitability? In order to do this, it is necessary to take into account the type of activities to be done, the workload to be submitted, and to allocate all the necessary resources at the right time. To support this planning, scheduling is needed.

2. *Scheduling capacity and profitability in each module* (horizontal planning; defines WHEN and WHO); which, depending on the evolution of production volumes, aims at the need to increase the allocation of

weekly and daily resources or not. It is necessary to develop an effective and efficient system for the correct allocation of the necessary resources. The scheduling capacity and profitability in each module is the state in which specific planning is assigned data, a chronological order of tasks (so that planning can be put into action), and considers the potential variations from planning.

Furthermore, from the perspective of a performance management system, it is important to see the real performance between what was planned and what was achieved, between planned and achieved KAIZENSHIRO. By comparing the plan with the real result, the result can be reflected in the next plan, which must be much more accurate in order to meet KAIZENSHIRO (see improvement budgets; Figures 3.27–3.29). The continuous improvement of productivity facilitates a planning and scheduling of the modules with a higher accuracy and, implicitly, the fulfillment of the annual and especially multiannual KAIZENSHIRO. It must always be considered whether the relationship between the planned volume and profitability and the allocated resources was adequate.

4.2 WHY AN SBTP CONTROL TRILOGY?

The control systems have been recognized a long time ago as a tool used by managers to achieve corporate goals by monitoring the implementation of the strategy, evaluating results, and strengthening the ability to meet business expectations.

The term of *control* is widely used in many disciplines. Generally speaking, control is when the variation of a target system is kept within the desired limits. A situation under control requires two components: a control system and a target system that needs to be controlled (manufacturing system). A simple example of a situation under control is that of a thermostat that is designed to maintain the temperature in a storage of raw materials at 20 degrees Celsius. Normally, the thermostat is attached to the device that can change the temperature of the storage. The thermostat needs information about the current temperature in the storage, so that it can turn on/off the heat source according to the desired temperature. If the storage temperature exceeds the standard 20 degrees Celsius, then the thermostat will turn off the heat source. If the temperature in the warehouse drops below the standard level of 20 degrees Celsius, then the thermometer in the warehouse will trigger the heat source to raise the temperature. This is a simple example of output regulation based on *feedback control* (in case of business, performance management system at the end of the period). A completely feedforward-driven system approach could provide the heat source with output signals according to a model of typical indoor storage temperatures over a typical period (e.g., a calendar year or winter), and a temperature of approximately 20 degrees Celsius is expected to be achieved continuously. Therefore, the *feedforward control* may exist without the feedback control and vice versa. However, most systemic approaches have both feedforward control and feedback control. The motivation is obvious. A system based only on feedback control (such as the one with the thermostat above) will only work if a deviation from the standard occurs. A completely feedforward-driven system approach would be able to take the necessary measures in advance, but it would not be able to adjust its performance in relation to the system it operates. The feedback control investigates the difference between a current state and an expected state and adjusts the output of a system according to a standard. A completely feedforward-driven system control approach uses the knowledge about the system to be controlled to act directly on it, anticipating changes. Therefore, the SBTP needs both a completely feedforward control and a feedback control (it will be detailed in Chapter 5). Moreover, SBTP needs a concurrent-driven system approach to exercise a *concurrent control* over the modules when the transformation is performed (it will be detailed in Chapter 5 as well).

Generally speaking, in order to have something to control, the control presupposes having a well-defined goal (KAZIENSHIRO) and a desired state that must be achieved by a target system (achieving synchronous profitable operations in all manufacturing modules). The control actions must produce a feedback from the target system. These feedback points are feedback to the controller (KAZIENSHIRO). KAZIENSHIRO will maintain or change its target depending on the feedback and will take additional action. The three control phases required by SBTP are successful if production planning and scheduling succeeds in achieving synchronous profitable operations in all manufacturing modules in accordance with an objective (KAZIENSHIRO). When the three control phases fail, then we say we have a deviation. But what is a deviation? A deviation is a departure from a standard of a manufacturing system variable.

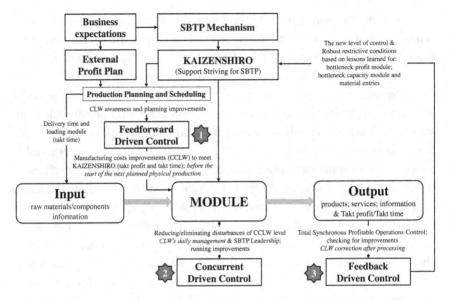

FIGURE 4.3
Control trilogy for KAIZENSHIRO.

Therefore, from the perspective of the three phases of the control or the control trilogy for KAIZENSHIRO, as shown in Figure 4.3, it can focus on events before a module (or *feedforward controls*), on events during processing in a module (work in process; or *concurrent controls*), and on events after processing from a module (or *feedback controls*).

In the real life of companies, the nature of the activities to be performed includes various things, such as urgent orders, orders that are difficult to carry out, and orders that can be postponed for a period of time. Prior planning is done to balance load and capacity, including schedule and number of people required. In reality, there are many cases where there is a lot of free space (inactive time), excessive extensions of activities, and so on.

This requires the accurate capture of losses and waste continuously in each module to provide the necessary standards for the three phases of the control. The real and clear situation is just that time has been used efficiently or not (see especially at *feedback controls*). The only way to prevent this loss of opportunity for production and profit is to schedule the activities to be performed in advance in each module (especially in bottleneck capacity modules and bottleneck profit modules; *feedforward controls*) and carry out and control activities in accordance with this planning (any deviation being subject to *concurrent controls*). Moreover, since planning is determined only for static conditions for a certain period, it is indispensable to take actions to correct the deviation between planning and the actual state of scheduling (in a short cycle based on this scheduling/*concurrent controls*, and finally by the *feedback controls*).

Therefore, the gap between what was planned and what was scheduled must be reduced or eliminated in order to fully fulfill the KAIZENSHIRO. This is the reason for the need for the three phases of control.

So, the answer to the question *Why an SBTP Control Trilogy?* is: The SBTP uses knowledge about the manufacturing system it needs to control (current and required level of: CLW, CCLW, bottleneck capacity module, bottleneck profit module, etc.) to act directly on it (through production planning and scheduling and through cost manufacturing improvement based on productivity improvement – strategic kaizen and kaikaku projects to prevent the occurrence of probable and preventable; by *feedforward controls*) anticipating the problems in the modules to obtain the expected managerial outputs (especially the annual and multiannual fulfillment of KAIZENSHIRO by total company, by product families, by individual products, and by modules; by *feedback controls*). Continuous measurement of productivity and non-productivity (of losses and waste) and continuous determination of CLW and CCLW is essential to capture the phenomena, principles, and parameters of non-productivity that can be effectively and efficiently improved during processing (by *concurrent controls;* or daily management/shop floor management for KAIZENSHIRO).

Continuously measuring and increasing productivity is an eternal concern for manufacturing companies, regardless of sales scenarios, rising or falling. The roles of the three phases of control are essential parts of carrying out synchronous profitable operations through SBTP.

4.3 FEEDFORWARD CONTROL: PRODUCTION PLANNING

The synchronized and profitable production planning process is standardized and is focused both on the capacity of the bottleneck mode (to support the synchronization of modules at takt time) and on the level of critical costs of losses and waste (CCLW; to support the profitability of modules at takt profit).

As shown in Figure 4.3, after defining business expectations and SBTP mechanism to establish external profit plan (based on sales plan) and internal profit plan (based on KAIZENSHIRO) we move on to production planning and then to production scheduling.

Several departments are involved in the production planning process. These are as follows:

1. *Sales and after-sales services*: forecast; collecting demand, both for sales and for buffer stock.

2. *Production planning*: (processing modules means bottleneck module capacity); the production order and times are planned starting from the shipment term, the assembly term and CLW backwards; the production plan is made for 30 days to establish the general production framework. Production planning in the SBTP logic has restrictions in terms of accepting orders. The compliance with delivery deadlines and loading and balancing bottleneck capacity module are not enough in the SBTP logic. Accepting orders that fall within the level of takt profit (contribution profit per unit/minute) is a cardinal restriction (in fact, production planning is free to refuse an order that does not fall within takt profit). In trying to cope with the changes of production plan, sometimes frequent, different algorithms and tools are developed. The production planning software archives all the changes made to the production plan in time in order to be able to periodically follow the typology of the causes that determined the changes of the production plan and to take measures to increase the stability of the synchronous and profitable production plan. The changes to the production plan due to internal problems of the company must be on a downward trend. An important role is played by the standardization of profitable target products (see Figure 2.6). At the same time, it ensures the timely release of all material orders to suppliers (considering the standard lead time for each type of supplier; minimum and maximum lead time is continuously improved for each supplier). Production planning also takes into account the material constraints and procurement and production constraints. After several revisions of the draft production plan, the final production plan and critical materials list are reached.

3. *Production engineering*: Its main role is to ensure that equipment and tools constraints are under control. The report of critical equipment and tools is presented and activities and actions necessary to reduce and/or eliminate their critical condition are proposed and carried out. It ensures that takt time is met by all modules (including new operations and processes) and for all products (including new products). It knows and does everything necessary to fulfill the future takt time (together with all the departments involved).

4. *Cost management*: Presents the report of the updated unit cost level of each individual order (updated after the successful implementation of all cost improvements) and the types of CCLW that are planned to be improved during the order period (especially for orders that are made over a longer period). It presents the report of the target profitability on products and modules.

5. *Suppliers*: Must provide a prompt feedback to the possibility of timely delivery of orders for raw materials, materials, and components. It must continuously ensure the synchronization of delivery lead time from the suppliers with PTT.

The future conditions for synchronized and profitable planning take place in four stages (see Figure 4.4).

So, only on-time delivery of the necessary products to customers is no longer enough – the manufacturing profit must be continuously secured. Figure 4.5 shows production planning and scheduling for synchronized and profitable operations. As you can see, starting from the four stages in Figure 4.4, it shows how to move from production planning to production scheduling to meet the objectives of takt profit and takt time concurrently.

The goals and foreseeable effects of synchronized and profitable planning are:

- fulfilling takt profit and takt time (improving bottleneck profit module and bottleneck capacity module);
- reducing the unnecessary cash-out;
- reduction of the level of stocks (money stuck in stocks in deposits and on flow; more precisely, reduction of waiting days for material and components stock days, WIP and finished products stock days);
- reducing the total plant lead time (TPLT) (see Figure 3.23);

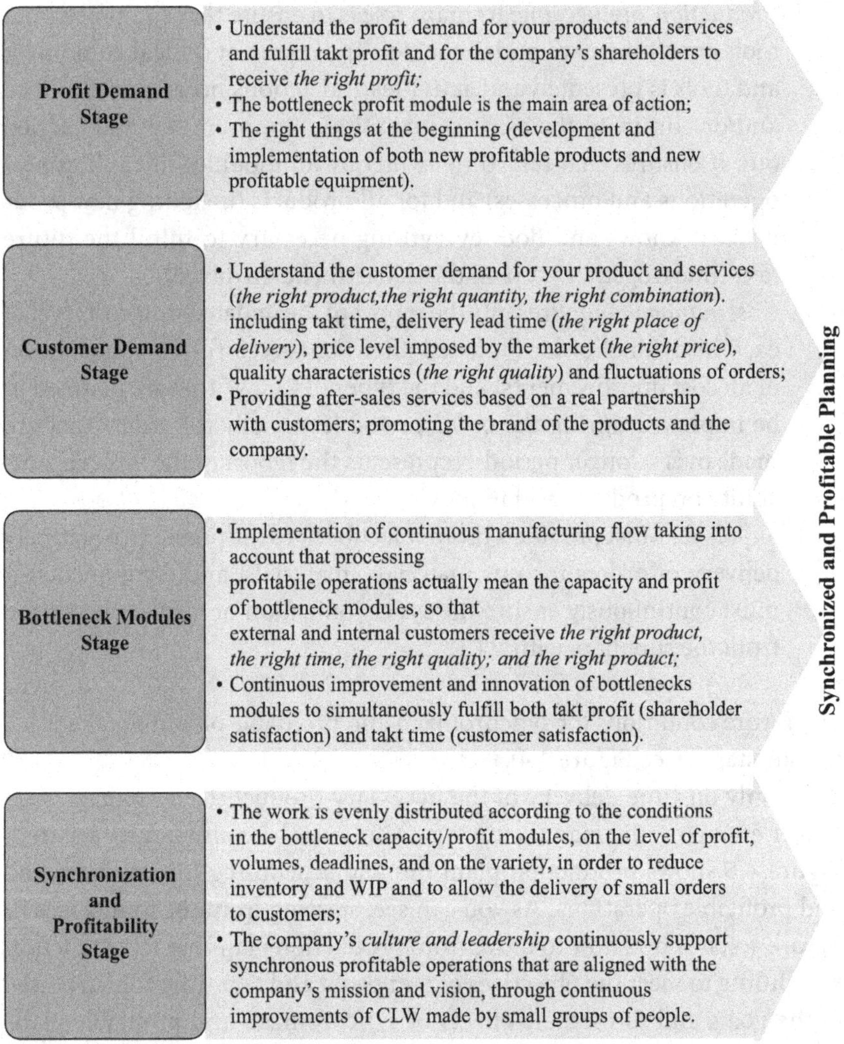

Profit Demand Stage	• Understand the profit demand for your products and services and fulfill takt profit and for the company's shareholders to receive *the right profit;* • The bottleneck profit module is the main area of action; • The right things at the beginning (development and implementation of both new profitable products and new profitable equipment).
Customer Demand Stage	• Understand the customer demand for your product and services (*the right product,the right quantity, the right combination*). including takt time, delivery lead time (*the right place of delivery*), price level imposed by the market (*the right price*), quality characteristics (*the right quality*) and fluctuations of orders; • Providing after-sales services based on a real partnership with customers; promoting the brand of the products and the company.
Bottleneck Modules Stage	• Implementation of continuous manufacturing flow taking into account that processing profitabile operations actually mean the capacity and profit of bottleneck modules, so that external and internal customers receive *the right product, the right time, the right quality; and the right product;* • Continuous improvement and innovation of bottlenecks modules to simultaneously fulfill both takt profit (shareholder satisfaction) and takt time (customer satisfaction).
Synchronization and Profitability Stage	• The work is evenly distributed according to the conditions in the bottleneck capacity/profit modules, on the level of profit, volumes, deadlines, and on the variety, in order to reduce inventory and WIP and to allow the delivery of small orders to customers; • The company's *culture and leadership* continuously support synchronous profitable operations that are aligned with the company's mission and vision, through continuous improvements of CLW made by small groups of people.

Synchronized and Profitable Planning

FIGURE 4.4
The four steps for synchronized and profitable planning.

- continuous improvement of the reconciliation between the delivery L/T and manufacturing L/T based on the reconciliation of the real capacity needed in production (a bottleneck capacity module);
- maximizing compliance with delivery deadlines to customers; and
- fulfilling the man × hour established in the planning phase.

We will detail each of the four stages in the following sections.

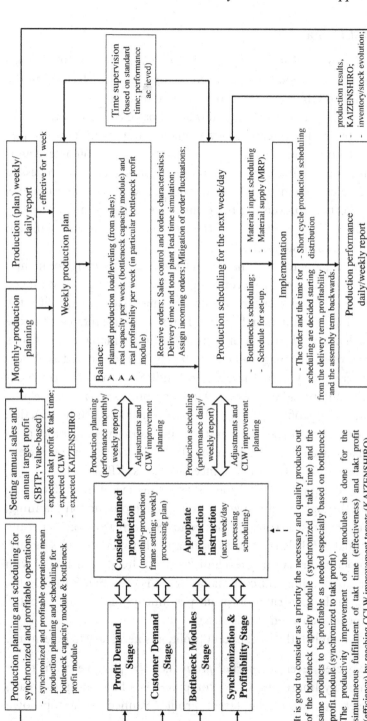

FIGURE 4.5

The cycle of converting production planning into production scheduling to achieve synchronized and profitable operations.

4.3.1 Profit Demand Stage

In this section we will focus on the profit demand stage of future conditions. We will describe the associated techniques for determining the profit demand and the tools that can be used to meet it.

From the beginning it must be said that the basic concern of the profit demand stage is the research, development, and continuous implementation of both new profitable products and new profitable equipment. Continuous innovation, by creating new products, new processes, new technologies, new materials or any innovative idea in any module, must have effects in preventing the occurrence of losses and waste and implicitly CLW. CLW prevention is the key to an effective and efficient feedforward-driven system approach.

As it is known, any team of managers from manufacturing companies is evaluated at the end of the accounting period according to several criteria. Regardless of which criteria are chosen, manufacturing profit is the central criterion of evaluation, because shareholders are interested in the level of dividends paid to each of them. Even if the management teams develop other overall management indicators (OMI) considered as important as manufacturing profit, these are only indicators that help to achieve annual and multiannual target manufacturing profit. Such OMI helping the manufacturing profit are: total lead time, production costs, production number, sales factory turnover, manufacturing capacity, scrap ratio, market share, major accidents, etc. Then the OMIs are detailed in tree style at the level of operational key performance indicators (KPIs).

As presented in previous chapters, ensuring target manufacturing profitability, through synchronized and profitable production planning, regardless of future scenarios of sales volumes, decreasing or increasing is the basic goal of SBTP. For this, coordination between the sales department and production planning (excluding orders already concluded) with production engineering and cost management is essential. Ensuring the level of takt profit (contribution profit per unit/minute) is the essential point that must be ensured at this stage.

In order to establish the level of takt profit, it is necessary to determine:

- the expected level of *internal profit* (i.e., the possible profit to be obtained by improving CLW; computed as a bottom-up estimate) to meet manufacturing target profit (planned by a top-down approach); and

- the expected level of *external manufacturing profit* (i.e., the possible profit to be obtained through sales requested by customers – planned by a top-down approach; sales based on an anticipated level of net processing production per unit in bottleneck operation optim – computed as a bottom-up estimate).

The takt profit level is established according to the two possible scenarios of the sales evolution, respectively:

- Expected increase in sales: aims at focusing on fulfilling the multi-annual and annual manufacturing target profit, especially through external manufacturing profit through maximizing outputs of bottleneck capacity operation (productivity growth through improving effectiveness – reducing losses or not effectively used input); and
- Expected decrease in sales: aims at focusing on fulfilling the multi-annual and annual manufacturing target profit, especially through internal manufacturing profit through minimizing inputs (productivity increase through improving efficiency – waste reduction or excess amount of input).

Therefore, the expected level of takt profit can only be obtained by increasing the level of productivity regardless of the expected volume of sales. Increasing productivity is essential regardless of whether sales increase or decrease.

The techniques that support takt profit from the design and development phase of new products and new equipment are:

- *Product life cycle/sales vs. profit:* describes the sales and profit plan of each product for all five phases of their life cycle with their specific forms of expected evolution of revenue vs. profit shape, respectively:
  - Product development: There are no sales yet; investments are made in the development of the new product; time-to-market is established; target cost is set based on the target costing process (target price – target profit = target cost); product life cycle costs are determined as follows:

$$LCC = BC + RC \qquad (4.1)$$

where:
LCC is life cycle costs
BC is basic/initial cost
RC is running costs

- Introduction: The product is tested and then goes into production and sale; usually, for many industries the level of profit is low (except for the drug, electronics, or cosmetics industries where the novelty effect can lead to an irrational behavior accepted by buyers, which can lead to consistent sales and profits in the product introduction phase); one can anticipate a certain level of CLW with some specific CLW.
- Growth: The product tends to become mature and customers know its value; sales and profit must maintain an upward trend, both in terms of increasing sales (emphasis is on maximizing outputs of bottleneck capacity operation), and in conditions of temporary reduction of sales (emphasis is on minimizing inputs); again a certain level of CLW can be anticipated with some specific CLW.
- Maturity: The product has become mature; sales and profits reach maximum values and begin to need minimizing inputs (productivity increase through improving efficiency) to support the level of target profit and takt profit; again a certain level of CLW can be anticipated with some specific CLW.
- Decline: Sales are declining sharply, but the level of profit must be maintained by minimizing inputs (extreme productivity increase through improving efficiency) until the profit plan of the product is fulfilled throughout its life cycle, if it has not already been fulfilled in previous phases and until the release of another type of new product of the company to take over part of the profit of the product that ended its life cycle; again a certain level of CLW can be anticipated with some specific CLW.
- *Equipment life cycle cost/manufacturing capacity vs. manufacturing number*: describes the optimal and balanced load plan of the current and future equipment capacity (adjusted by the setup time); the expected evolution of the capacity vs. the possible contracting volume of the products is determined. The elements related to equipment life

cycle cost that are analyzed when purchasing new equipment that would later contribute to the fulfillment of the annual and multiannual profit plan and implicitly to KAIZENSHIRO are:

- General information: current working days/year; number of shifts/day; working time/day (net standard operating time per unit in bottleneck capacity operation in minutes per day); expected life of the equipment; depreciation method and cost of losses of the equipment (cost with depreciation not covered by production – in a state of overcapacity); the average weight of a product; cost of materials and current cost of waste with materials; staff cost and cost of current staff losses and waste; cost of utilities and cost of waste of utilities;
- Specific details (for comparative analysis between different equipment suppliers): percentage of scrap; expected overall equipment effectiveness (OEE) level; number of operators per equipment; consumption of utilities per product; cycle time standard (seconds); expected annual production capacity;
- Basic/initial cost: the value of the equipment; the cost of transport; installation and reception cost; the cost of preparing the production – technological tests, etc.
- Operating/running cost: based on the planned production volume; certain specific CLWs can be anticipated; (see Figure 4.6);
- Life cycle cost on product: based on the planned production volume, the probable annual cost structure is established for basic manufacturing costs, for annual CLW, for annual allowable CCLW, and for annual reduction target for CCLW (KAIZENSHIRO) (see Figures 3.11 and 3.17).

Turning to annual planning, as presented in Chapter 2 (see Section 2.2), in profit demand stage is:

- depth understanding of current state of the previous period:
  - profit per product in last period;
  - takt profit established in the last period (the pace of profit demand) based on takt time established in the last period (per month on a shift; in bottleneck; the pace of customer demand); and
  - the SBTP in last period;

Cost elements		Basic manufacturing costs (transformation costs and material costs)	Expected level of annual CLW	Annual allowable CCLW	Annual reduction target for CCLW
Equipment Running Costs	Material	Material cost	$ Cost of material waste	$	$
	Labour	Labour cost	$ Cost of personnel losses and waste	$	$
	Utility	Utility costs	$ Cost of energy waste	$	$
	Maintenance	Maintenance cost	$ Cost of maintenance losses and waste	$	$
	Spare parts	Spare parts cost	$ Cost of spare parts waste	$	$
	Tools and fixture inventory	Tools and fixture inventory cost	$ Cost of tools and fixture inventory losses and waste	$	$
	Training	Training cost	$ Cost of training losses and waste	$	$
	Others	Others cost	$ -	$	$
				ANNUAL KAIZENSHIRO ($)	

FIGURE 4.6

Equipment running costs expected and KAIZENSHIRO.

- the future state of the this period (future period):
  - profit per product in this period;
  - setting the takt profit for this period (in bottleneck capacity module and bottleneck profit module), based on takt time established for this period (per month on a shift; in bottleneck capacity module); and
  - the SBTP for this period (future period).

The standard for profitable target products classification (A-B-C analysis) (see Figure 2.6) begins to be determined at this stage for the next period. The determination of the takt profit is done before or concurrently with the development of the master budget and KAIZENSHIRO budgeting (see Figures 3.28 and 3.29). Based on the takt profit, the order of the products in the production planning is determined. Decisions of profitable production planning are made according to the takt profit (contribution profit per unit/minute). We seek the excellence of profitability through productivity in bottleneck capacity/profit modules based on the excellence of operations. The throughput is assessed by cash generated at the pace of sold. The profit demand stage focuses more on the proactive fulfillment of takt profit and less reactive and corrective. The bottleneck profit module is the main area of action. *Feedforward control* (profitable design of new innovative products, innovative design of new working methods, use of new efficient innovative materials, and use of new equipment/technologies that are innovative and productive, and especially efficient) being essential for fulfilling both the contribution profit per unit and the net standard operating time per unit in bottleneck capacity operation (*the right things at the beginning*).

The successive fulfillment of KAIZENSHIRO for the fulfillment of takt profit will determine a continuous improvement of CLW which will concurrently generate both the satisfaction of stakeholders (by securing the expected level of dividends and development of the company) and customers (products with acceptable prices, quality level, and delivery times). The takt profit design goes hand in hand with designing the required and expected ROI level. By synchronizing takt profit to ROI, the bridge between the expectations at the level of the headquarters of the companies and the opportunities at the level of the shop floor are ensured (see Figure 2.20). The takt profit ensures peace between external productivity (acquisitions of equipment and more productive technologies) and internal productivity (maximizing the use of current assets). So, *fulfilling the takt profit comes first.*

4.3.2 Customer Demand Stage

Takt profit is inseparable from takt time. There are two facets of the same currency called productivity for profitability.

The purpose of the customer demand stage is to design future conditions that satisfy and illustrate the customer demand. Unfortunately, even though in many companies there are concerns of top managers for the satisfaction of external customers, often these concerns are only declarative and remain in the stage of good intentions. In fact, the measurable improvement in customer satisfaction is often poor. An essential element of customer satisfaction is the selling price (in relation to the functions of the product).

In order to design the future conditions of custom demand, it is necessary to create a system for synchronizing all current and future resources of the company and all modules in the factory and the processes beyond it at the current and especially future level of takt time.

At this stage of customer demand, the following dimensions are designed:

- Takt time, to answer the question: What is the demand? (see Section 2.2 for answer).
- The characteristics of the products coming from customer demand, to answer the questions: What will be the trend of the products (or product groups)? Depending on this answer, the target products that will support the SBTP mechanism will be established. To answer this question, three projections are required: (1) product-quantity design (volumes and frequency to determine high-volume products from total production volume and sales and low-volume products); (2) product-buyers/customers design (designing the relationship between target products and final companies; designing the amounts of products to be produced and delivered); and (3) product routing design (designing product volumes and frequencies on module paths to identify target products that have similar paths in order to establish a common KAIZENSHIRO on products and bottleneck capacity module and bottleneck profit module); most of the time, in order to do product routing design, the factory gates are passed and it is up to each supplier who contributes in one way or another to the product. All possible risks are analyzed here. Only three/four target product categories will be selected to fit into the SBTP mechanism and planning and scheduling (see Figure 2.6).
- The required capacity of bottleneck modules, based on sales evolution scenarios (increasing or decreasing), to answer the question: Is

the company in a state of overcapacity, undercapacity, or meeting demand? (see Figure 2.9 for answer).

- The need to increase internal productivity (improving the use of current assets) to answer the question: Is the current or improved capacity of bottleneck modules sufficient for the next period? (see Figure 2.20 for answer).
- The need to increase external productivity (improving capacity through the purchase of new equipment, new technologies, etc.) to answer the question: What capacity increase requested by demand cannot be ensured by the current or improved capacity of bottleneck capacity modules? (see Figure 2.20 for answer).
- The real need for stock for each product/the target products selected in Figure 2.6 (warehouse – material and components stock days and warehouse – finished products stock days; see Figure 3.23), to answer the questions: What stocks are needed? How much? Where are they located? Inventory data must be projected at the level of the map of stocks and storage area in monetary value, in terms of volume and value in total sales.
- Delivery timing, to answer the question: How well is the delivery of orders on time to customers? For this it is necessary to design the future conditions to reach the state of zero missing items (any product that did not reach the customer on time is considered missing item).
- Improvements needed to meet the optimization of material and finished products lead time and flow, to answer the questions: What improvement methods, techniques, and tools are needed to be used to fully ensure customer demand? (see Section 4.5 for details).

Therefore, the purpose of the customer demand stage is to design, in order to implement, the necessary ingredients for a flexible and profitable planning that satisfies the needs of customers (in takt time) and the needs of profit (takt profit) by optimally loading the modules (without missing items or under capacity of production and without overcapacity of production).

4.3.3 Bottleneck Modules Stage

After profit demand stage and customer demand stage were designed, now we move to the investigation and design of manufacturing flow so as to reduce and/or eliminate regular interruptions and factors that determine the occurrence of both bottleneck capacity module and bottleneck profit module to ensure the satisfaction of shareholders and customers at the same time. We recommend the implementation of methods design concept (MDC) for innovative redesign of production processes in order to have the best cycle time of various SOPs, without investments and 5S for workplace standardization and organization to prevent the occurrence and manifestation of losses and waste and implicitly CLW.

This stage investigates and designs the modules to ensure that production management plans and controls:

1. all necessary production times and material inputs throughout manufacturing flow, especially in bottleneck capacity modules; and
2. all CLW and CCLW throughout manufacturing flow, especially in bottleneck profit modules.

4.3.3.1 The Management Tasks Design

The design of management tasks aims at investigating and designing the modules through which the products will be made, especially target products, more precisely the investigation and design of lead time related to each module and CLW related to each module. This can clarify the detailed characteristics of the bottleneck capacity module (cycle time > takt time; at an acceptable level), of the bottleneck profit module (module with the highest CCLW) and the problems associated with manufacturing methods.

Through a *feedforward control*, the basic goals are to implement continuous flow, to tend toward the OPF state (between two operations there is only one part/product) and/or toward small batches. The following questions are often asked (SBTP guidelines): Where can you apply or extend continuous flow? What flow level can you implement (OPF/small lots)? Did you eliminate parallel activities? Is the distance between two operations/modules minimal? Where can you apply or extend digitization and/or automation? How will you control upstream production planning (in-process supermarket, Kanban, material requirement planning, first in first out lanes)? What level of flexibility is required for customer demand (setup)? What level of flexibility is required for profit demand (setup)?

This investigation that considers the design of the modules aims at three steps:

- *Investigating and planning lead time on modules*: Investigation of modules according to the types of products to be manufactured aims at establishing the target manufacturing lead time (see Figure 4.7);

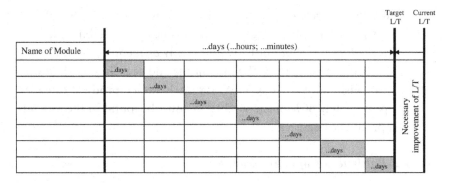

FIGURE 4.7
From current to target lead time on modules.

only 3–4 major categories of target products will be investigated (see Figure 2.6).

Lead time investigation targets both information and physical flows, both inside and outside the production area (see Figure 3.23). Examples of lead time investigations with distinct perimeters can be: (1) *in manufacturing areas* (processing, assembly, release of new products, maintenance, health and safety, manufacturing information management, etc.); (2) *in R&D* (new product design, time to market, etc.); (3) *in material management* (production planning, supply planning, outside logistic, inside logistic, etc.); (4) *in quality assurance* (supply improvement, increase customer satisfaction, incoming quality assurance, quality information management, etc.); (5) *in human resources* (employment, training, dismissal, human resources information management, etc.).

• *Investigating and planning TPLT* (see Figure 3.23): Production planning needs to plan the delivery of orders requested by customers: (1) deliveries of products from the finished product warehouse or safety stock (planning as a percentage of total deliveries; TPLT is equal to delivery lead time); (2) deliveries of products that are not in the warehouse of finished products, but for which all raw materials are in the warehouse of raw materials (planning as a percentage of total deliveries; TPLT is equal to plant lead time plus delivery lead time); and (3) deliveries of products that are not in the warehouse of finished products, there is no raw material (or not all necessary raw materials) for them in the warehouse of raw materials [planning as a percentage of total deliveries; TPLT is equal to supply lead time (SLT) plus plant lead time plus delivery lead time]. Depending on the specifics of each company, the TPLT planning for the next period is established.

- *Investigating and planning CLW and CCLW on modules*: Investigating the modules according to the magnitude and causality of CLW aims to establish targets for CCLW for each target product category. Approximately 80% of the total CLW must be found in the 3–4 target product categories.

4.3.3.2 Bottleneck Capacity Module

After investigating lead time in the previous section (the management tasks design) on modules, now is the time to investigate and design the capacity (losses) of manufacturing flow, which actually means bottleneck capacity module, in order to rethink production framework and to identify opportunities to increase effectiveness and efficiency and shorten lead time.

The investigation and design of the production, in order to prevent the potential problems creating losses and waste and implicitly CLW, aims at four types of topics:

- *Bottleneck capacity module*: This means the planned hourly capacity for the bottleneck capacity module. Balancing the entire manufacturing flow based on the bottleneck capacity module is essential. Since there are often differences between the designed and actual capacity of the bottleneck capacity module, it is important to clarify the actual capacity of the bottleneck capacity module which is actually the capacity of the entire manufacturing flow. Moreover, as bottleneck capacity module is often influenced by human labor, especially if it is an assembly and inspection module (if it is a manufacturing and assembly company) it is necessary to clarify human labor capacity (see Table 3.3; assembly line/human work, with downtime human losses). Clarifying the planned capacity implies increased attention to improving the work of each person and the capacity of each team/line. Moreover, any unfavorable variation of the bottleneck capacity module (a lower capacity than planned) is found in the increase in the level of stocks of all types.
- *Net capacity of modules loading (or OEE required)*: The measurement of the real capacity was presented in Figure 2.9. An example of feed-forward controls for planning a bottleneck capacity module (OEE for "E10" equipment) is shown in Figure 4.8. The OEE planning for the

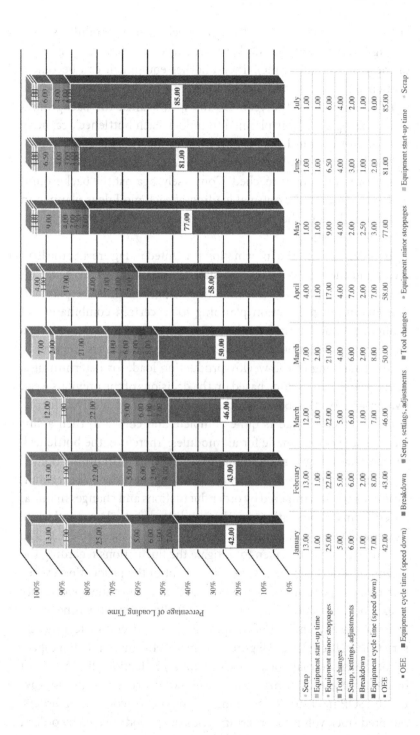

	January	February	March	March	April	May	June	July
Scrap	13.00	13.00	12.00	7.00	4.00	1.00	1.00	1.00
Equipment start-up time	1.00	1.00	1.00	2.00	1.00	1.00	1.00	1.00
Equipment minor stoppages	25.00	22.00	22.00	21.00	17.00	9.00	6.50	6.00
Tool changes	5.00	5.00	5.00	4.00	4.00	4.00	4.00	4.00
Setup, settings, adjustments	6.00	6.00	6.00	6.00	7.00	2.00	3.00	2.00
Breakdown	1.00	2.00	1.00	2.00	2.00	2.50	1.00	1.00
Equipment cycle time (speed down)	7.00	8.00	7.00	8.00	7.00	3.00	2.00	0.00
OEE	42.00	43.00	46.00	50.00	58.00	77.00	81.00	85.00

■ OEE ■ Equipment cycle time (speed down) ■ Breakdown ■ Setup, settings, adjustments ■ Tool changes ▫ Equipment minor stoppages ■ Equipment start-up time ▫ Scrap

FIGURE 4.8

Example of planning feedforward controls for a bottleneck capacity module (OEE equipment).

"E10" equipment, considered as bottleneck capacity module, is done taking into account the market demand for the first eight months of the year (the takt time). Then another equipment can become a bottleneck capacity module compared to market demand for the last four months of the year. In this way, against the background of increasing sales, it is planned to unlock each bottleneck capacity module in turn until the synchronization of the bottleneck capacity module (net standard operating time or net capacity and cycle time) with takt time is reached. Conversely, against the background of declining sales, the optimal loading of each module is planned in order to reduce to the point of elimination the load of certain dispensable equipment.

In order to reach the information presented in Figure 4.8, the load levels and the necessary and possible/feasible improvements for all the modules related to each manufacturing flow must be planned. The loading of production planning for a certain combination of profitable product targets tends to focus on certain modules and thus the dynamic evolution of bottleneck capacity modules is identified.

The balancing of the weekly production load, for determining a loading standard, is done based on the decisions of the previous week (which are fixed) – based on the profitable orders received firmly. If the production load is quite complete and constant, then a single schedule can be made for all modules. Therefore, the bottleneck capacity module gives the annual pace and volume of production.

- *Fluctuating and unconfirmed orders*: Planning the order and execution time of orders is hampered by order fluctuations and changes in initial orders from customers/buyers. This condition creates losses and waste (losses and waste for production control are special; see Table 3.3). The measures that can be taken to mitigate the fluctuations regarding the receipt of orders can be: (1) the adjustment of the production execution terms at intervals of 2–3–4 hours; (2) analysis of the opportunity to expand production subcontracting; (3) allocating more time for an order; (4) careful analysis of equipment capacity to eliminate unnecessary time in the SOP (see Figure 2.9) and careful analysis of the capacity of the entire manufacturing system; (5) reduction/elimination of quality problems that may cause customer distrust; and (6) improving the SOP in customer relations (taking orders, confirming orders, required stock volumes, ordering cycles/the period covered by orders, ordering amounts/at the beginning of the month, at the end of the week. Regarding the order confirmation, it is necessary to establish in the SOP the time required between the initial receipt of an order from a customer/buyer (including the deadline for delivery of the order) and the release of the order in production. It is necessary to investigate and predict the behavior of each customer/buyer in order to reduce the inconveniences of production planning (see Table 3.3; production changes/adjustments plan loss).

• *Order-based load balancing*: Stabilization and synchronization of the bottleneck capacity module at the level of customer orders is the goal of consistent production planning and the entire factory. Decisions on the loading level of the bottleneck capacity module are taken in the previous week (fixed part) and as few orders as possible are added in the following week when production takes place. Based on a firm order level, a weekly loading standard can be established taking into account the profitability of the target products (see Figure 2.6), the minimum and profitable size of a batch, and the setup time for takt profit. The purpose of the order-based load balancing is to seek to achieve the state of continuous flow to optimize the use of labor and balance the workload to achieve a smoother flow. Measures that can be taken to achieve order-based load balancing can be: (1) innovative redesign of modules to achieve a shorter cycle time (using MDC); (2) balancing cycle time using the operator balance chart to achieve takt time and to determine the number of operators required (using Yamazumi chart); (3) standardizing setup time (using MDC); (4) using work cells to facilitate OPF, etc.

Therefore, in this stage the planning for the bottleneck capacity module is clarified, which in fact represents the planning of the entire production, balancing the number of units necessary to produce, and the necessary capacity. The role of the *feedforward control* is to prevent potential problems generating losses and waste caused by the bottleneck capacity modules with an impact on the achievement of KAIZENSHIRO (see Figure 4.3).

4.3.3.3 Bottleneck Profit Module

After investigating in order to plan the manufacturing flow (losses), which actually means bottleneck capacity module, in order to rethink the production framework and to identify the possibilities to increase the effectiveness and efficiency and shorten lead times, this section will present investigation mode for planning on bottleneck profit module.

Starting from the previous investigation and planning of the bottleneck capacity module, the investigation and production design for the bottleneck profit module, to prevent CLW and to contribute to the fulfillment of KAIZENSHIRO for the following year, is presented in Figure 4.9. In order to establish KAIZENSHIRO for the next year, it is necessary to investigate the performance of the last three years and make projections for the next five years.

Apart from the last step in Figure 4.9 (production planning for KAIZENSHIRO; a step that will be addressed in the following sections), most of the elements in Figure 4.9 have already been presented. Exceptions are:

- *The key inputs/outputs* that refer to: Takt profit, takt time, production volumes, volumes on each type of target product, actual machine running hours per year, assembly line speed (products per minute), production expectations on each production phase, planned operating hours (percentage of utilization; percentage of availability), number of direct production labor hours, number of direct maintenance labor hours, number of operators per shift, direct and indirect labor hours, yield targets, manufacturing target cost per product (raw material cost plus cost of conversion), target cost of transport and loading, non-quality target costs per target product (or family products), marginal cost of labor per hour per person for each target product (or family products), target cost of utilities, percent of time sold out (of total time; time without losses and waste), etc.
- *CLW structures under study:* These are established based on the results from improvement budgets and the results of the annual feedforward, concurrent and feedback control and taking into account the CLW of each module who will be responsible for achieving KAIZENSHIRO for the next period. Particular attention will be paid to the costs of WIP between modules.
- *Assumptions for bottleneck capacity modules and for future CLW structures/modules:* SBTP requires dynamic evaluation (usually as accurately as possible for the next 12 months) of both losses and waste related to bottleneck capacity modules and CLW structures related to bottleneck profit modules using references set by benchmarking,

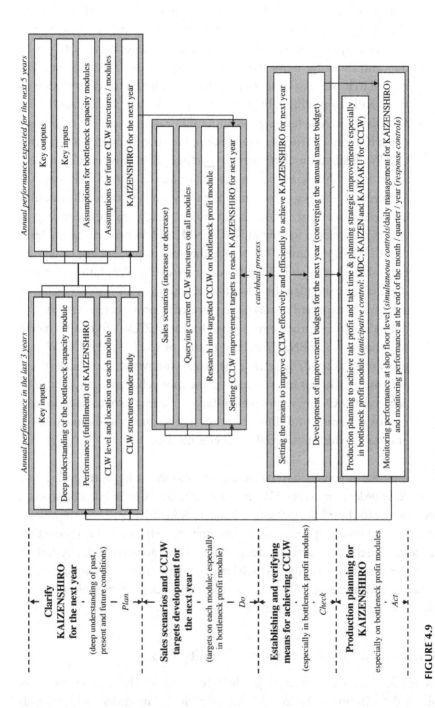

FIGURE 4.9
Production planning on bottleneck profit modules to meet KAIZENSHIRO for the next year.

best practice, or an ideal/zero CLW reference. These references are chosen for the next five years and are references that are part of the long-term plan. Both assumptions for bottleneck capacity modules and those for CLW structures/modules take into account KPIs related to losses and waste (see Tables 3.1–3.3) and the distribution of these KPIs by modules, by target products, by cost structures.

- *Catchball process* (among setting CCLW improvement targets to reach KAIZENSHIRO for next year and setting the means to improve CCLW effectively and efficiently to achieve KAIZENSHIRO for next year): It involves creating and maintaining open feedback loops at all levels of the organizational hierarchy and between all modules by creating a two-way flow of information exchange between targets and means related to annual KAIZENSHIRO. When setting the level of CCLW improvement targets (or the annual preventable CCLW of bottleneck profit modules) it is necessary to establish how to achieve these targets and plan the allocation of resources for improvements to achieve the expected results (at the level of improvement budgets). The annual catchball process ends when for each CCLW target, that meets the annual KAIZENSHIRO, the means of reaching the CCLW targets are associated, by setting the targets for systematic (kaizen) and systemic (kaikaku) improvements. The more challenging (difficult to achieve) the CCLW improvement target, the more robust a definition of means, greater and timely allocation of resources and more intense and real/visible managerial support is needed.

Therefore, the investigation and design of production for bottleneck profit module, in order to prevent CLW and especially CCLW from bottleneck profit module and to contribute to the fulfillment of KAIZENSHIRO for the following year, requires a *feedforward control* to support the fulfillment of production requests (especially for target products) – based on customer orders. Depending on the product requests expected to be requested by customers, it is planned to improve CLW and especially CCLW in the bottleneck profit module to ensure takt profit concurrently with takt time.

4.3.4 Synchronization and Profitability Stage

Depending on the expected product requests of the customers, it is planned to improve the synchronization of the modules (a bottleneck capacity module with takt time) and the CLW/CCLW level in the modules (especially a bottleneck profit module with takt profit) in order to ensure takt profit concurrently with takt time.

Production planning dictates the timing and magnitude of these improvements to ensure on-time deliveries, to optimally load equipment, and to ensure the target profit level. For example, against the background of increased sales, if production planning has the information from the sales department that starting from August next year it will need a 30% increase in bottleneck capacity module in order to achieve the volume of products requested by customers and that this increase in volume will be maintained in the coming periods, then it will be analyzed whether this increase in capacity is possible and feasible to be ensured through systematic improvements (kaizen projects for bottleneck capacity module) or through systemic improvements (kaikaku – a new equipment for increasing the capacity in the bottleneck capacity module; external improvement). Improvement planning must ensure a 30% increase before August by unlocking bottleneck capacity modules (within takt time, see Table 3.1). Another example, against the background of declining sales, if production planning knows that in the middle of next year the level of manufacturing profit will not be satisfactory, then it will require the planning of systematic and systemic improvements in all modules, and especially in bottleneck profit module to achieve MCI (CLW/CCLW; see Tables 3.2 and 3.3). Moreover, production planning will require the marketing department to more intensively promote the target products considered more profitable. In this way, the usefulness of a *feedforward control* in production planning is essential.

In general, in order to achieve the annual KAIZENSHIRO, regardless of the evolution of sales scenarios, increasing or decreasing, this last stage of synchronous and profitable planning of SBTP modules seeks to achieve the expected improvement targets before production actually begins for:

1. CCLW reduction for framing in the takt profit;
2. reduction of the TPLT (see Figure 3.23) for framing in the takt time (synchronization of each module to takt time – especially a bottleneck capacity module);
3. reducing WIP stocks;
4. reducing the physical transport of materials by determining and analyzing the movements of materials;

5. creating OPF/small lots to increase the flexibility imposed by the expected profitability and by the clients;
6. early planning of the two forms of setup (for takt time and for takt profit) – excluded from the available time left to achieve the production volume;
7. promoting a daily management focused on CLW and CCW;
8. promoting a culture of consistent improvement (MDC; kaizen and kaikaku) approach among all the people in the company and beyond;
9. increasing the visible productivity of all modules and simplification of the working method; and
10. increasing the visible productivity of all modules in tandem with the likely evolution of sales.

In conclusion, the entire production planning materializes on obtaining synchronous (takt time) and profitable (takt profit) modules. Systematic (kaizen) and systemic (kaikaku) improvements are planned and implemented to fulfill the profitable production planning in each module and implicitly the KAIZENSHIRO level. At the same time, some improvements will target improvements in the production support areas (such as, supplier planning, outside logistics, incoming quality assurance, etc.).

4.4 FEEDFORWARD CONTROL: PRODUCTION SCHEDULING

Continuing the approach of the control trilogy (see Figure 4.3) to achieve the annual KAIZENSHIRO, it was the turn of the presentation of the *feedforward control* for production scheduling (see Figure 4.5). There are two types of production scheduling periods: a week and a day. Production planning is at a high level, for a month, then it is detailed weekly and daily (for each shift).

4.4.1 Scheduling Practice: Freedom

In the SBTP scheduling cycle, every Friday or Saturday, a daily work plan for the next week is drawn up. Moreover, from one day to the next, the plan for the next day is drawn up, including all the profitable and hot orders. Moreover, the expected daily production report is used for planning, because the plan and the real results must be clear. This daily work report is prepared for one week.

Why freedom? From an SBTP perspective, any order must be profitable. Practitioners of the production planning department are free to accept only productive orders (which fall within the takt profit). This type of production planning is the opposite of production planning in which the practitioners of the production planning department do not have the freedom to choose the orders, the delivery term, and the balanced loading of the production being a priority. Free production planning can only be achieved if the annual and multiannual KAIZENSHIRO level is reached and its visibility is found at the level of product prices perceived as acceptable. In this way, the demand for quality and cheap products is ensured; it is possible to sort the orders according to their profitability. Production planning for SBTP has as a priority the fulfillment of takt profit.

The free scheduling procedure is presented in Figure 4.10.

$$PLF = \frac{TPL\ (plan)}{NWH\ (plan)} / PF \tag{4.2}$$

where:
  PLF is daily production load factor;
  TPL is total production loaded on bottleneck capacity module (equipment × hours);
  NWH is number of working hours on bottleneck capacity module;
  PF is performance forecast;
  Note: production scheduling usually collapses with the passage of time (daily scheduling is required; or on shifts; or every 2/3/4 hours; daily scheduling is required for setup).

Production scheduling is freely established by practitioners in the production planning department to concurrently meet takt profit and takt time weekly and daily. But the most important thing is that managers have a strong interest in production scheduling. At the same time, it is necessary to consider the fact that special unplanned orders may appear (see Table 3.3; production changes/adjustments plan loss).

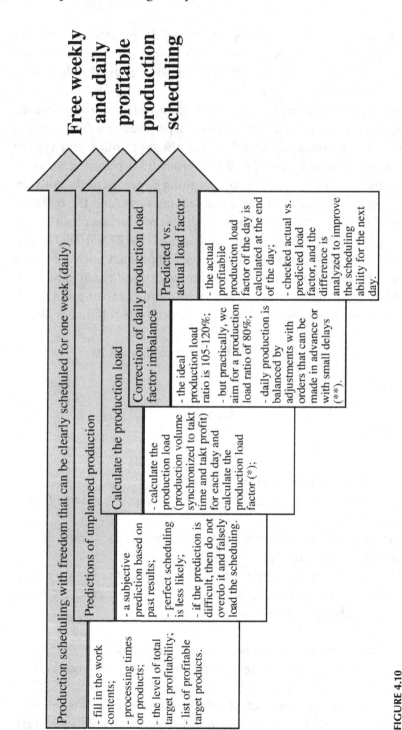

FIGURE 4.10

Free weekly and daily procedure for profitable production scheduling.

4.4.2 Synchronization of Supply Lead Time With Production Takt Time

From a production scheduling perspective, a focal point of many manufacturing companies that generate unnecessary stocks of raw materials and components is the poor timing between sending orders to suppliers and receiving materials (SLT or material lead time: information L/T + manufacturing L/T + transport L/T; see Figure 3.23) which are required in production at the level of the takt time of production scheduling. Moreover, when production scheduling is done, deficiencies are often found in the rhythm of the purchasing period for materials and in the volume of a profitable order [economic order quantity (EOQ)]. When a certain type of material has a major impact on production scheduling then the min-max L/T per supplier and alternative suppliers must be established precisely. When late deliveries from suppliers occur, the SLT is longer than the maximum allowable (the maximum allowable time level is synchronized with the SLT of other materials according to production scheduling) or when the batch size is too large, a standardization of the min-max SLT levels and profitable order volumes (EOQ) are needed. The identification of standardization needs is in fact the identification of the needs for systematic improvement (kaizen for improving relationships with existing suppliers) or systemic (kaikaku for identifying and choosing other suppliers for the necessary materials).

PTT (the pace of production demand) is set per month on a shift, in bottleneck this is shown as follows.

$$\text{Production takt time} = \frac{\substack{\text{Net available processing production} \\ \text{time in bottleneck (minutes)}}}{\substack{\text{Total monthly quantity required} \\ \text{to be supplied on a material (units)}}} \quad (4.3)$$

PTT has an impact on the level of raw material stocks. At the same time, the current level of raw material stocks adjusts the demand on material suppliers compared to the PTT level.

PTT is actually the extension of takt time coming from the client. Takt time coming from customers is absorbed at the production level by leveling all modules and operations (including assembly lines if applicable), both for existing products and for new products and then takt time from the customer is "delivered" to material suppliers. The continuous reduction of cycle time for all bottleneck operations in order for them to fit in takt time of the clients (man × hour reduction; equipment × hour reduction) has the effect of modifying the PTT and implicitly the rhythmicity and volume of sending orders to suppliers (SLT must be improved continuously to bring only the necessary raw materials and components at the right time, in the right quantity, and in the right combination). Otherwise, the phenomenon of waste generation occurs systemically (see Table 3.3; inventory consumption efficiency).

Therefore, in accordance with production planning and scheduling, it is necessary to deliver materials to production modules on time in full (OTIF).

4.4.3 Load Balancing in Profitable Order-Based Production

In order to reach the synchronization state of all modules (or continuous flow) for the production of a product or product families, an identical takt time is needed for all modules and operations. The overall line effectiveness (OLE) is often calculated as a product of the OEE indicators in each module of a product family or individual product.

The lack of material brought to the modules on time or too much stock of materials and components in the modules causes systemic losses and waste. The profitable order-based production requires a balanced and profitable loading of production capacities decided one week before the start of physical production. The lack of this optimal load of module capacities is found at the level of nonproductive hours (engaged on production, but nonproducing) and not at the level of OEE (see Figure 2.9; waiting for materials).

Production scheduling one week in advance avoids production based on orders for the current thus avoiding statements such as: "How good it would be for us to get an order by Thursday, but…" and avoid delayed deliveries caused by equipment defects, product defects, and lack of staff.

Practicing production scheduling one week in advance and observing it as much as possible offers the possibility to standardize the profitable loading of the modules with the profitable target products (see Figure 2.6) as the orders from customers are firm and stable. In this way, production scheduling can become stable. Moreover, practicing production scheduling one week in advance offers the possibility to:

- carry out the rigorous planning of the work on shifts;
- strictly monitor the operational performance (difference between standard cycle time and real cycle time);
- plan the buffer times between batches (5–30 minutes);
- carry out the planned maintenance on time and well;
- carry out the autonomous maintenance activities on time and well;
- staff to participate in thinking, implementation, and monitoring of improvements;
- staff to participate in training;
- set the buffer size;
- establish the necessary quantities of materials and components (if applicable) for the bottleneck operation (taking into account the level of scrap and rework);
- set the standard level of WIP;
- plan the setup activities for the fulfillment of both takt time and takt profit; and
- have time for analysis and choice of the most profitable products for production, etc.

In this way a capacity control can be made, an optimal rhythm of production can be chosen to ensure the maintenance, and continuous improvement of the manufacturing system and the precision of the control regarding the production progress can be continuously improved.

In conclusion, the practice of production scheduling one week in advance offers the necessary time to collect data related to losses and waste and to transform them into costs in order to be able to follow in real time the level of productivity and non-productivity found in CLW. In this way, timely knowledge and awareness of the results of weekly (sometimes daily) profitability provides time for reflection and action (concurrent control; daily management for CLW). Reporting the CLW level once a month no longer makes sense for improvement because significant percentages of CLW are no longer affordable in real time (such as exceeding standard consumption of consumables in production to place an order within 12 days of the month already completed). Practicing production scheduling one week in advance leads to the decrease of stocks, decrease of TPLT by smoothing the passage through the bottleneck capacity module and by approaching the bottleneck profit module.

4.5 FEEDFORWARD CONTROL: MANUFACTURING COSTS IMPROVEMENT

Continuing the approach of the control trilogy (see Figure 4.3) to achieve the annual KAIZENSHIRO, it was the turn of the last step of *feedforward control* and the establishment of targets and means for MCI, more precisely for CCLW, to meet KAIZENSHIRO (by fulfilling takt profit and takt time), before the start of the next planned physical production.

Reducing or removing each CLW from each module to meet the target CCLW (or KAIZENSHIRO) in the production system requires different enhancement techniques appropriate to each type of CLW. The aim is to reduce or eliminate CLW by addressing losses and waste, especially from the bottleneck capacity module and the bottleneck profit module.

In general, there are two types of approaches for reducing/eradicating CLW (Figure 4.11). A first type of approach is the one based on the time of realization of the improvements and their magnitude, respectively:

- *Individual improvements*: They focus on the short-term reduction or elimination (maximum 3 months) of a CLW that has appeared in the past and has a high chance of occurring in the near future; for example, improving setup costs, settings, adjustments time losses; cost of tool changes time losses; cost of rework losses; cost of motion losses, etc. In general, the individual improvements are mainly adopted in man/machine/material associated losses improvement activities.
- *Systemic improvements*: They focus on reducing or eliminating CLW that occur at the production system level and require continuous and long-term activities; for example, operative maintenance, preventive

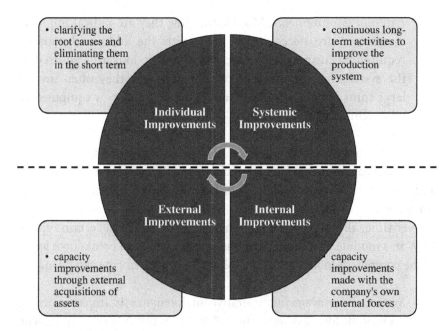

FIGURE 4.11
The improvements cycles.

maintenance, predictive maintenance, quality assurance, education, and training for people, etc.

Usually individual improvements are addressed first and then systemic improvements.

A second type of approach is the one that is based or not based on the improvement with own internal forces, respectively:

- *Internal improvements:* These are the improvements made on their own by small groups of people tasked with achieving a CLW target, without involving large sums of money; these improvements can be both individual improvement and systemic improvement; these improvements can be both systematic (kaizen; with small steps) and systemic (kaikaku; with big and/or radical steps), and innovative (MDC – redesign of working methods in an innovative way; the use of new technologies developed within the company, development of new innovative products within the company); and

- *External improvements*: Most of the time they are radical improvements and are necessary to cope with the additional capacity required by customers, a capacity that can no longer be ensured by the systematic improvement of current assets; they often involve large sums of money for investment; for example, new equipment, a new technology, etc.

Normally, internal improvements should be addressed first, to make the most of the capabilities available to achieve the ROI target (see Figure 2.20) and then external improvements to ensure the natural development of the company.

Over time, all four types of enhancements can target a certain type of CLW in a module. For example, in the case of the cost of breakdown losses of the equipment in a module, the following improvements can be made:

- *Systemic improvements:* operative maintenance is implemented to prevent the forced deterioration of each component of the equipment; planning improvement in skill of maintenance workers to reduce breakdown through education and training for people is implemented;
- *Individual improvements:* analysis of processing points to eliminate the root causes of breakdown;
- *Internal improvements:* preventive maintenance to repair the components of the installation on a regular basis; predictive maintenance by using different diagnostic technologies of the equipment; and
- *External improvements:* replacement of a subassembly of equipment that is worn out or with a subassembly that is more efficient (purchase from the equipment manufacturer – with or without special technical specifications from the company making the purchase).

Going further, as mentioned in Chapter 3 (see Figures 3.1 and 3.12), the scenarios for MCI develop according to the sales trend, respectively for the trend of increasing sales and the manifestation of the predominant need to maximize outputs or for the trend of declining sales and the overriding need to minimize inputs.

The basic logic of the scenarios for achieving MCI is: product unit cost of manufacturing tends to decrease proportionally with the decrease of CLW and especially of CCLW from bottleneck capacity module and from

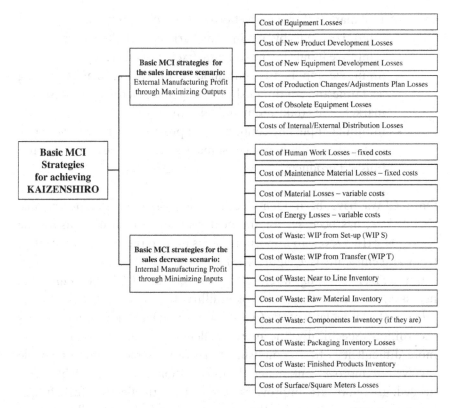

FIGURE 4.12
Framework for the development of MCI's core strategies for achieving KAIZENSHIRO.

bottleneck profit module. The more CCLWs are identified and improved, the more feasible KAIZENSHIRO is, and the feedforward-driven control mechanism fulfills its purpose (see Figure 4.3).

MCI core strategy aims to (see Figure 4.12) (Posteucă, 2019, pp. 41–74):

- external manufacturing target profit through maximizing outputs:
  - maximize outputs of the entire manufacturing system by continuously improving the effectiveness of the current equipment;
  - maximize outputs of future equipment to meet the demands of current and future products; and
  - maximizing the load of current and future equipment through the continuous development of new profitable products.

- internal manufacturing target profit through minimizing inputs:
  - minimize inputs by maximizing variable cost efficiency;
  - minimize inputs by maximizing fixed cost efficiency;
  - minimize inputs by continuously improving manufacturing lead time and continuously aligning manufacturing processes to market needs (takt profit and takt time); and
  - minimize inputs by continually improving inventory levels: raw materials, components, consumables, near to line inventory, and finished products.

Once CLWs have been identified in the past, once the preventable CCLW level has been set for the next year and which can ensure the KAIZENSHIRO level, an important step is to set targets and means effectively and efficiently (see Figure 4.13).

In the SBTP thinking, when setting a target for a CCLW (*What?*), it is necessary to specify the means of fulfilling the target or CCLW means (*How?*). The target level of the CCLW means involves allocating resources accordingly. Specifically, the more challenging a CCLW means is, the more difficult it is to accomplish, the more resources (time for people involved in improvement, materials, information, etc.) are available when needed. Therefore, any improvement must be both effective (fully fulfilling its improvement target by the set deadline) and efficient (falling within the default resource level). Therefore, a performance improvement must

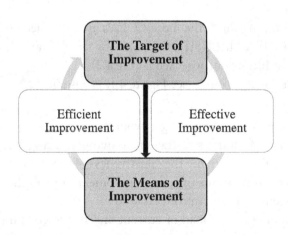

FIGURE 4.13
From the improvement target to effective and efficient means.

fall within the predetermined level of effectiveness and efficiency. This is the purpose of improvement budgets (see Figures 3.27–3.29). Once the improvement target has been met for a relevant period of time, it becomes standard. The transition to a new improvement of the standard is made after the standard no longer has significant variations or if there are business needs for the improvement of the standard.

In conclusion, production planning and scheduling must continuously take into account the planning, implementation, and results of MCI and the degree of annual and multiannual fulfillment of KAIZENSHIRO. In this sense, in order to continuously support the uncovering hidden reserves of profitability through SBTP, the multiannual productivity master plan is planned and developed for implementation.

4.6 CONCLUSION: PRODUCTION PLANNING IS USELESS IF IT DOESN'T TAKE INTO ACCOUNT IMPROVEMENTS AND THE TAKT PROFIT

Therefore, for the SBTP approach to provide a profitable management of production targeted to achieve synchronous profitable operations based on reaching the target profit per minute in the bottleneck module by planning and improving both the capacity of the bottleneck module and the CLW for all operations, especially in bottleneck profit module, a three-phase control is needed to start with production planning and scheduling in order to achieve visible productivity improvement.

To establish a SBTP profitable production management, a company has to build up the following key elements from a *feedforward control* perspective: production planning, production scheduling and planning for MCI by setting targets and means for improvement depending on the probable sales scenario from the next period (increasing or decreasing).

The planning and development of CCLW improvement projects may not reach the planned KAIZENSHIRO level. It is necessary to go through the three phases of the specific control of SBTP (see Figure 4.14).

The improvement projects must be carried out correctly and completely to fulfill the purpose of the *feedforward control*. At the same time, the CLW level in each period is limited to the number and extent of losses and waste. The probable level of future CLW that can be

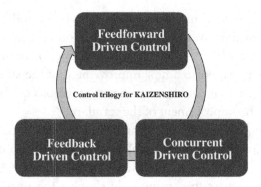

FIGURE 4.14
Control trilogy for KAIZENSHIRO by planning and scheduling production.

prevented is an estimate of the dynamics behaviors of losses and waste associated with the types of products planned to be achieved. During the development and implementation of improvements, the level of CLW and implicitly of losses and/or waste will not improve; the effect of reducing CLW will appear only after completion of improvement and after a period of validation of improvement – this is the role of improvement budgets (tracking the effectiveness and efficiency of each improvement relative to the initial target; or the *feedforward control* of MCI). In order to have the visibility of CLW improvements over a period of 12 months or more in terms of improvement budgets, it is necessary to calculate the value of the real benefit of CLW improvement by multiplying the MCI by the amount of production in each period. Furthermore, it should be borne in mind that often a solution of an improvement can be applied horizontally in several modules (e.g., solutions to reduce setup time from one module can be applied in other modules which have identical or similar equipment). Prioritization of improvements is based on their feasibility.

Therefore, the exercise of a *feedforward control* in the production planning and scheduling phase of manufacturing plants is not sufficient to fulfill the purpose of the SBTP mechanism, even if the improvements have been successfully implemented, as each improvement may not be successfully promoted at shop floor level to carry out a *concurrent control* and to find the links between losses and waste and MCI possible to be achieved by approaching the CCLW. Moreover, during the activities of the modules there are many opportunities to address certain losses and waste that could not be planned to be improved (*feedforward control*) because they are either very specific or too small to be collected (e.g., cost of auxiliary consumables losses; cost of manual work losses, etc.). The development of a robust daily management (*CLW's daily management*) to achieve the *concurrent control* is essential (it will be detailed in Chapter 5). To conclude the control trilogy, some CLWs can appear only after the processing activity in the modules is completed (e.g., costs of scrap and rework losses; cost of performance losses; cost of material yield losses; cost of utilities losses, etc.). For these it is necessary to perform the *feedback control*.

In conclusion, especially production planning must consider the takt profit when accepting production orders. Accepting and planning production orders to load production capacity and meet delivery deadlines is no longer enough. The more dependent a company is on a customer/buyer and does not take into account the takt profit, the greater the risk of business continuity with that customer. Avoiding excess stock entries and accepting delivery deadlines over the capacity of the module considered bottleneck are essential.

Section III

Developing Synchronous Profitable Operations

5

Concurrent and Feedback Controls

As presented in previous chapters, the speed-based target profit (SBTP) allows a profitable management of production targeted for achieving synchronous profitable operations by developing and implementing the concept of *control trilogy* (feedforward controls, concurrent controls, and feedback controls). The feedforward controls approach was presented in Chapter 4. We will now present the concepts of concurrent controls and feedback controls to highlight an important feature of SBTP, i.e., the manufacturing staff participate in cost of losses and waste (CLW)'s daily management. The importance of day-to-day activities on mastering CLW has become necessary for the survival of manufacturing companies in a competitive world. The review of the role of manufacturing operators, supervisors, and managers, and of the control of the CLW level has become necessary. The workshop staff needs to be aware of the types, level, and trend of each CLW category in their area in order to approach them continuously and consistently. For example, it is nothing spectacular if an operator knows and continuously addresses, together with his colleagues, the top five types of losses and waste in his area (managers setting this top by knowing the level of costs associated with each type of losses and waste in each area covered). From the SBTP perspective, statements such as: "the high level of costs is the fault of managers and those in offices" or "this high cost is caused by ... (someone else, from another department/module)" must be corrected. Many of the CLWs can be addressed at the time of production (concurrent controls) and many can be prevented (from feedback controls to feedforward controls) if the workshop staff had performed timely problem-solving activities related to production planning and sales plan. Therefore, in this chapter we will present the concepts of concurrent and feedback controls, tasks, instruments, and behaviors of leadership necessary to achieve the objective of synchronous profitable operations, phases, and main steps of implementation of SBTP, critical success factors for implementation, and the main directions for creating and supporting the culture for SBTP. All this is necessary to support the work of individual workers to carry out routine inspections of losses and waste, to detect consumption above the standard as early as possible, to participate in setting cost standards, to participate in the investigation, and reduction or eradication of CLW from their area, etc.

5.1 CONCURRENT CONTROL: CLW'S DAILY MANAGEMENT

Concurrent control, through CLW's daily management, is the approach to controlling CLW performance during production that aims to monitor the performance at the shop floor level of CLW (especially the KAIZENSHIRO support), comparing parameters [key performance indicators (KPIs) related to losses and waste; see Tables 3.1–3.3], and the action stages in case of deviations.

In other words, the concurrent control through CLW's daily management means supporting the achievement of KAIZENSHIRO and get the best possible results in terms of safety, quality, and deliveries (their current conditions being collected continuously at the level of losses and waste and transformed into costs) through fast loops shop floor level feedback, with high problem-solving skills from the entire workshop staff, in a standardized way, supported and led by a robust leadership (coach; mentor; leading by questioning and inspiring others, etc.) at all levels of the manufacturing plant. In this way, the entire workshop staff can take responsibility for the results of each module, while the work is in progress, as opposed to a feedback control, in which the results of each module and the entire manufacturing flow will not be queried until the completion of the transformation process.

The concurrent control aims to address all CLW structures and especially critical cost of losses and waste (CCLW; those responsible for achieving KAIZENSHIRO). Each module will have its own CLW depending on the specifics of the activity. Moreover, the structures and magnitude of CLW at the level of each module change over time with the need to capture and improve the constantly changing non-productivity.

The basic values of the concurrent control through CLW's daily management, as an improved management on the way to a learning organization, are: *respect* (open mind; deep understanding; acceptance of personalities, abilities, ideas, opinions, and values of other colleagues and anyone; continuous mutual respect), *confidence* (saying what I think and doing what I say; learning by insight), *communication and empathy* (sharing thoughts and feelings openly; understanding others; addressing the right people all the time; clear messages based on real events and data; giving others time to communicate; actively listening to others), and *teamwork and fellowship* (the objectives are ours; teamwork is a pleasure; learning organization).

5.1.1 The Goals of Concurrent Control of CLW

The mission of each production department is to produce goods as cheaply as possible, as quickly as possible, and with an acceptable level of quality. The continuous determination of CLW determines the possible extent of improvements in production speed and quality. The concurrent control of CLW (while production takes place) covers any activity carried out by the production department that aims to identify, standardize, and resolve deviations from the CLW standard in order to effectively and efficiently maintain plant operating and fulfill the production plans (including the annual KAIZENSHIRO – annual internal profit through manufacturing cost improvement to support SBTP).

To implement the concurrent control of CLW, the workshop staff must become "experts in CLW". The workshop staff must be able to perform routine inspections of standard levels of losses and waste in their area to detect abnormal losses and waste behaviors as early as possible and must acquire the skills necessary to understand the root causes of losses and waste.

In this context, the workshop staff must be able to:

- establish criteria for the abnormality of the losses and waste behavior in each module;
- observe the abnormal behavior of losses and waste in each module;
- solve the problems generated by losses and waste (with visibility in CLW) or in other words to maintain the standard level of CLW in each module;

- understand the phenomena, principles, and parameters of the module in which he/she works in order to easily identify the causes of the appearance of any CLW in each module; and
- understand the relationships between the level of production and the level of losses and waste and to predict the potential for capacity growth by reducing/eradicating losses and waste (supervisors and managers will continuously know the CLW level in each module).

Therefore, the goals of concurrent control of CLW program are:

- preventing CLW for each module by setting CLW standards and maintaining them;
- daily collecting the level of losses and waste and establishing the daily/weekly/monthly level of CLW;
- determining the root causes of losses and waste and determining the daily/weekly/monthly CCLW level; and
- determining the ideal level of CLW for each module (first acceptance of the zero concept: zero above the current standard level of CLW; second acceptance of the zero concept/ideal state: zero CLW).

Another goal is to teach the entire workshop staff a new way of thinking and working at the shop floor level, in order to perceive that reducing costs and implicitly CLW is as important as safety, quality, and delivery.

5.1.2 The Need of Concurrent Control of CLW

In the past, the workshop staff was expected to carry out the production and to keep the equipment in normal working conditions by carrying out specific autonomous maintenance activities.

Even if reducing costs by increasing productivity is a perennial necessity, lately, manufacturing companies have felt an increasing need to control costs amid increasing global competitiveness in terms of prices and profit level. In this context, for the real mastery of manufacturing costs it is necessary to go to the place where they are made (at the shop floor level; at the modules/cost centers level) and to fully understand them and to identify, monitor, and continuously improve the CLW level. Thirty to 40% of CLW-associated costs cannot be left unaddressed consistently and scientifically as manufacturing cost policy deployment (MCPD) and SBTP do.

The standardization and improvement of the conditions of occurrence and manifestation of losses and waste and implicitly of CLW represents the vital need of using the concurrent control of CLW. Although CLWs need to be addressed continuously in all three phases of control (feedforward controls, concurrent controls, and feedback controls), some CLWs can be better addressed by planning strategic projects for manufacturing cost improvement (feedforward controls; e.g., improving and standardizing the setup time level to reduce costs of setup, settings, adjustments cost or reducing breakdown time to reduce or eradicate costs of breakdown losses), other CLWs can be better addressed after processing is complete (feedback controls; e.g., planning for improvements/problem-solving for scrap losses or rework losses to reduce costs of scrap losses or costs of rework losses), while other CLWs can be better addressed while production is taking place (concurrent controls; e.g., solving problems of deviation from the standard time of a setup time; standardization and approach of deviations for costs of auxiliary consumables losses, costs of die, jig and tool losses, costs of energy and other utilities; cost of maintenance materials losses – including those specific to autonomous maintenance/cleaning-oiling-inspections).

The future is uncertain; many manufacturing companies hope to be able to survive with dignity in a global market by mastering and reducing costs based on continuously increased productivity. The concurrent control of CLWs becomes indispensable to reduce/eradicate losses and waste and their associated costs.

The benefits of digitalization are obvious and tend to extend to most manufacturing plants. However, in such digitized production environments, the CLW level can only be reduced but cannot be eliminated completely by implementing Industry 4.0 specific elements. The need to use concurrent control of CLWs is increasing with increasing opportunities to accurately collect losses and waste and turn them into costs in a timely manner. Therefore, the concurrent control of CLWs refers to activities designed to involve the entire workshop staff and all losses and waste data collection systems to measure and continuously improve and/or eliminate all CLW structures from manufacturing costs. In this way, the direction of improvement ideas coming from the workshop staff level to achieve KAIZENSHIRO will be endless as long as losses and waste are continuously collected, as long as the most feasible and affordable CLWs are established, and as long as the management team offers total support. CLW's culture of continuous improvement can be developed and consolidated at the shop floor level in a more consistent way and is more directed toward the necessary results.

By the concurrent control of CLW program, the connection of SBTP mechanism with synchronous profitable operations at shop floor level is made. The workshop staff and the concept of manufacturing cost improvement become inseparable.

5.1.3 Roles for Supporting Synchronous Profitable Operations

In many cases, the relationship between manufacturing and cost and budgeting departments are often adverse, even conflicting. There are often statements in manufacturing areas, such as: "We have been trying to achieve cost reductions for some time, but we feel that we have reached the maximum limit of reducing them". or "We are concerned about the cost reduction target in module 'x' this year. We do not know how we will achieve it because the failures of cost reductions from previous years have accumulated". or "Managers really can't understand that nothing can be done to reduce costs in module 'x' this year". By measuring, raising awareness, and continuously improving the level of CLWs and CCLWs the mentalities present in the above statements are changed.

When the cost and budgeting department together with the continuous improvement department was not able to reach the annual KAIZENSHIRO, they complain that the manufacturing department is more interested in achieving the annual production volumes and less in reducing costs. It is obvious what statements they make: "Manufacturing doesn't know its cost improvement job". Workshop staff say they are too busy to do manufacturing cost improvement activities. At the same time, the continuous improvement department criticizes the manufacturing department: "We have planned to make improvements and solve problems but they do not allocate time for people to participate in thinking and implementing improvements on CLWs". Moreover, "Collecting data on losses and waste and identifying the daily root cause of losses and waste does not often capture reality". The manufacturing department apologizes and motivates this state by the fact that people are very busy. In discussions with the continuous improvement department, those in the manufacturing department make statements, such as: "We are manufacturers, and you are the one from continuous improvement who has to reduce costs among other things".

With such attitudes on the part of those involved in manufacturing cost improvement, the annual KAIZENSHIRO level cannot be met. The congruence of objectives at interdepartmental level and the assumption of ownership for manufacturing cost improvement are essential especially for:

- *manufacturing department*: detection of losses and waste with honesty; dealing with CLWs; accurate identification of CCLWs; promptness in approaching CLWs at the shop floor level; compliance with the deadlines for approaching CLWs;
- *cost and budgeting department*: continuous and accurate delivery of the CLW level; establishing an effective and efficient annual KAIZENSHIRO; last but not least, the planning and control of improvement budgets;
- *continuous improvement department*: planning and timely development of all improvements (feedforward controls based on feedback points from feedback controls) and problem-solving (concurrent controls) so that production planning and scheduling to be done according to profit (takt profit) and deliveries (takt time) planning; and
- *HR and training department*: providing an annual updated training plan for all people to gain the knowledge needed to identify sources of losses and waste, such as teaching about bottleneck takt time and bottleneck takt profit importance or the cycle time and lead time reduction.

All departments in manufacturing plants must clearly define and agree on interconnected roles and remove any barriers to meet the annual and multiannual KAIZENSHIRO's consistently. This is the only way to create a pro SBTP culture.

5.1.4 The Basic Tools

CLW's daily management is an agreed set of principles, processes, and tools that allow everyone to be responsible for meeting CLW's operational performance at all levels of the manufacturing plant. The vertical and horizontal communication and the alert system are the basic ingredients of concurrent control of CLWs to ensure a fast feedback. SOPs are developed to promptly address problem-solving related to CLWs. The standardization tools and methods are used to stabilize and continuously improve the performance of losses and waste and of CLWs. A visual management and a visual control are used to represent the current performance against the CLW targets, practicing a process of monitoring losses and waste at short intervals (e.g., every 2 hours on each shift), and a process of daily transformation of losses and waste into costs (with some adjustments at the end of the week or month). At each shift, the losses and waste are interrogated in order to establish critical losses and waste at the level of modules (those that generate other losses and waste in other modules).

An excellent CLW problem-solving process that guarantees a fast and correct feedback to deviations from standards and targets related to losses and waste (shop floor KPI's of losses and waste) with short control intervals needs to ensure an efficient information flow. The problem-solving skills [by plan-do-check-act (PDCA) cycle; usually using the A3 problem-solving technique] at the level of each module, by working in teams, as close as possible to the modules and operations, must be present at all hierarchical levels of manufacturing plants. Moreover, the responsibility for key figures and results must be clear and visible at all levels. In this way, the work teams may be able to understand the principles and evolution of the observed process parameters and to report and address CLW issues (which already include safety, quality, and delivery). The transfer of information between all levels must be accurate and visible continuously. The person who communicated, what, when, how, and to whom; all this must be monitored. In the event of significant deviations of KPIs related not only to losses and waste, the alert rules must be followed by the entire workshop without delay.

A culture of continuous improvement of CLWs is consistently promoted at the shop floor level. Increasing everyone's level of motivation and interest is based on a deep understanding of the problems and how to approach them. Everyone knows how to escalate exceptional problems. This transparent approach improves employee morale and engagement by encouraging the implementation of the most effective and efficient ideas. When addressing a CLW issue, just like any other shop floor issue, anyone knows how to answer questions like: What are we going to do? (theme); Why will we do it? (necessity and vision); How far will we go? (goals and targets); How will we do it? (method of approaching the problem); What are the phases of the activities and their scheduling in time? (problem-solving planning); Who and what does he do? (roles and responsibilities); What results are expected? (evaluation).

FIGURE 5.1
The basic tools of CLW's daily management.

To answer the above questions, it is necessary to develop the basic tools of concurrent control of CLW, respectively (see Figure 5.1).

We will address, in turn, the basic tools of concurrent control of CLW in the following paragraphs, as follows:

- *Visual management (CLW information center and module activity panel):* An effective CLW's daily management needs primarily to develop, implement, and especially maintain the CLW information center and module activity panel to view, to allow quick and easy recognition of deviations from KPIs targets, and to continuously provide the correct direction of activities. Specifically, the purpose of a CLW information center is: (1) to continuously and accurately capture the current state of non-productivity by displaying all KPIs related to losses and waste (see Tables 3.1–3.3) and CLWs, both at the centralized level on total manufacturing plant and at the level of each module – as well as other relevant KPIs; (2) provide a system for the rapid recognition of deviations from KPIs' losses and waste and CLW targets and provide a way to investigate and eliminate these deviations – including all other important KPIs of the company; (3) provide clear visibility to support the setting of priorities in addressing deviations; (4) view all important KPIs of the organization (e.g., safety, quality, workforce, production status, problem-solving, and other relevant KPIs) that help to control the day-to-day business and recognize deviations from the target state; (5) the losses and waste KPIs are updated by workshop staff or managers (hourly/two hours/shift/day, etc.) and are designed to be easy to understand and to complete; (6) the trends of losses and waste, of CLWs and especially of CCLWs are presented, investigated, and analyzed (on each shift/daily/weekly/monthly) using clear dynamics charts; and (7) all presentations of activities at the level of modules from the perspective of concurrent control (CLW daily management) are centralized at the level of the plant CLW information center where it is analyzed together with the information related to feedforward controls and feedback controls. A CLW module activity panel is a guide to the activities of a module's team (sometimes there may be multiple modules). For this reason it must contain the following information: (1) the name of the team, the name of the module (specify whether it is a bottleneck capacity module or a bottleneck profit module), the name of the leader and team members and also the required level of KPIs for losses and waste; (2) the past team results (weekly and monthly graphs of losses and waste KPIs); (3) the current team issues to be addressed – based on setting priorities to eliminate deviations from KPIs' standards of losses and waste; (4) the current status of losses and waste KPIs and their causes (expressed as quantitatively as possible); (5) the current and future actions to address the causes and effects of losses and waste in support of KAIZENSHIRO – annotation charts are often used to present the relationship between team activities and results; (6) the objectives achieved, the remaining issues and the future actions planned to address deviations from KPIs related to losses and waste. For each of the above information at the level of

CLW module activity panel, the problems encountered at each step and their alerting/escalation mode are presented. As already mentioned, at the end and beginning of each shift, the losses and waste are interrogated to establish critical losses and waste at the module level (those that generate other losses and waste in other modules) and the preliminary structure of CLWs and of CCLWs is established (by preparing the *shift handover report of CLW/CCLW*). The two team leaders from the last and the starting shift must meet for 5–15 minutes to discuss the shift and business information required for team briefs and shift start up. The goal is to ensure that the starting team leader knows the past performance from the previous shift and all relevant current issues that may affect the performance of the next shift, such as risks for downtime, quality, or changeovers. All these risks are assessed based on the level of losses and waste from the previous shift specific to the respective modules. The team leader of the previous shift presents the structure of collected losses and waste and makes the production settlement from his shift – motivating the production level according to the real time available for production. At the same time, he presents in shift handover report of CLWs/ CCLWs and the interconnection relations between losses and waste from the modules supervised by him and the first draft of the CCLW level (cost information is available in real time in the system). The line boards and the team board contain all the details regarding the production made and the level of losses and waste and the interdependence relations between losses and waste. For example, a lack of materials at module loss will attract all losses and waste generated by this unplanned event. Consequently, the cost of lack of materials at module losses will attract all other CLW generated by the event of lack of materials at module (see Figure 3.11). A shop floor cost practitioner is often assigned to determine the level of CLW and CCLW based on losses and waste and based on critical losses and waste (those that cause other losses and waste throughout the entire manufacturing flow) assumed by the team leader of the previous shift. It is not an easy job. It seeks to have the highest possible accuracy of the CCLW. In fact, the shift handover report of CLW/CCLW shows the production achieved and the level of unnecessary costs achieved (CLW and CCLW), with the risk of extension to the next exchange. The centralization of all shift handover report of CLW/CCLW at the level of the CLW information center offers the possibility to inform and understand in depth the production made by each shift and the level of CLW and CCLW generated by each shift. The identification of CCLW and implicitly of critical losses and waste provides the management team with a clear picture of the needs to improve CLW. The managerial decisions for effective and efficient planning of projects to solve problems (concurrent controls) and/or systematic (kaizen) and/or systemic (kaikaku) improvement (feedforward controls) are much easier when losses and waste are visible in terms of money. In this way, the journey of continuous improvement is endless and with clear and continuous financial visibility (from shop floor level, from shift level to balance sheet level, income statement level, and master budget with improvement budgets included level). The continuous improvement gets a money stake from the start to accomplish SBTP and synchronous profitable operations.

- *Communication – horizontal and vertical*: In the manufacturing plant, the workshop staff are the heart of the company. They are the ones who turn the company's strategy into results. Despite their key role, some workshop staff are not fully connected to the company's objectives (sometimes up to 80% of employees). A clear and consistent communication at and between all hierarchical levels (level 1 – plant manager; level 2 – production manager; level 3 – department head; level 4 – subsection supervisor; level 5 – workshop staff) regarding the current and necessary future state of CLWs (of losses and waste; together with other relevant KPIs) and the effective meetings are essential. This requires: (1) detailing the previous performance of CLW for each module; (2) CLW production diary standardized and updated from shift to shift (shift handover report of CLW/CCLW); (3) for each meeting regarding the discussion of the results and targets of CLW KPIs, the exact interval of the discussion, the importance of the discussion, the place, the participants (production, cost management, maintenance, etc.), the periodicity, etc. are known; CLW's daily management uses an easy escalation model (e.g., in a maximum of 45–60 minutes the plant manager is informed if a problem has passed the filters of the entire organization and did not have a clear and consistent answer and approach; different means of warning are used: sound, light, messages on the phone, email, etc.).

- *Top CLW challenges* (focusing on the main challenges of CLW that contribute to the annual fulfillment of KAIZENSHIRO): Based on the information available at the level of CLW information center (target/actual CLW/CCLW deviation measure), the needs regarding CLW at the level of each module (available on module activity panel) are distributed through an effective and efficient communication, both vertically and horizontally; then the main deviations of the losses and waste indicators of each module are investigated in order to select the most necessary and accessible projects to solve the problems of losses and waste of that moment the polar star that directs the priority level of the approach to the problems of losses and waste is the level of CLW, or more precisely of CCLW; moreover, the setting of priorities is made taking into account the specifications of manufacturing improvement budgets; the module leader/team leader identifies the top issues, the impact of which must be constantly monitored and addressed with problem-solving techniques (usually with the A3 technique); in this way, anyone working in the area of a module or anyone passing through the area of the *module activity panel* can see and understand which are the top three or five main problems of CLW in different stages of approach.
- *On the spot investigation* (Go & See – Gemba; real place): It means understanding what is really going on at the module and manufacturing flow level, so that CLW investigation decisions are made based on information obtained directly from Gemba – decisions based on actually going, seeing, and understanding the real situation. To get to the root cause of a problem investigated on the spot, the *5 why* technique is usually used (observation of phenomena, principles, and parameters is essential). The time allocated for observing the real problems at Gemba level differs depending on the hierarchical level in the company. For example, the plant manager can allocate 10–20% of his time for direct observation of modules and operations and to understand in dynamics the behavior of CLWs and CCLWs (along with any other relevant KPIs of the company). Instead, a team leader can allocate between 80% and 100% of his or her time daily to directly observe the module(s) under observation to understand the dynamics of losses and waste and CLWs/CCLWs behavior (along with any other relevant KPIs of the company).

- *CLW problem-solving:* Addressing deviations from losses and waste standards need a structured approach, teaching the entire workshop staff about how to approach a problem and about teamwork to facilitate creativity to find effective and efficient solutions; a process for resolving deviations from CLW standards must be able to provide a fast and consistent feedback to deviations (CLW KPIs at shop floor level) using short intervals of concurrent controls and problem-solving as close to the modules as possible [5G: *Gemba* – actual place or the place where losses and waste creation events occur and where they are visible; *Gembutsu* – actual things or current losses and losses that are affected by losses and considered root causes; *Genjitsu* – actual facts or the phenomenon that causes the occurrence of losses and considered root causes; *Genri* – principles or the theoretical and practical principles that determine the occurrence of losses and waste considered to be the root causes, and *Gensoku* – standards and parameters or current standards and operational parameters (SOP) that facilitate the emergence of losses and waste considered to be root causes] (Posteucă, 2019, p. 115). The main tool for solving CLW problems is A3. However, other dedicated tools can be used to solve problems, such as: root cause analysis, Ishikawa, 8D, quick response quality control (QRQC), caused by, before/after kaizen, fault tree analysis or Six Sigma. One feature that can be considered delicate is the seemingly antagonistic relationship between the approach to the subject of shop floor costs and the need to use a transparent system to solve CLW problems. In fact, it is not an antagonistic relationship. At the level of the modules (shop floor) detailed and complete information on KPIs related to losses and waste (see Tables 3.1–3.3) specific to the monitored module and their conversion into costs for each structure and for short time intervals is provided. Only the supervisors (at their level) and the managers have the overall image of CLW and CCLW. They perform KAIZENSHIRO deployment at the module level and they also set priorities in addressing CLW issues.
- *CLW standards confirmation check on modules:* It is, in fact, the area where most concurrent controls are manifested; here the observance of the work processes within the standard limits and of the standards related to losses and waste is continuously monitored;

the daily level of KPIs related to losses and waste and of CLW is collected and displayed at the level of each module, together with other relevant KPIs; the individual daily tasks regarding the work of eliminating the problems are displayed; special attention is paid to modules that are declared as bottleneck capacity module or bottleneck profit module; this is a good time to remember what was learned in previous trainings; this is the time when the analysis of the daily causality of losses and waste is made at the level of all the modules of a manufacturing flow in order to determine later CCLWs at the level of shift/days/weeks/months (or at 3, 6, 9, 12 months); the transversal causal relations between losses and waste can be established only by the workshop staff at the moment when losses and waste occur; the concurrent controls at the process level and at the level of losses and waste show the current status of the daily tasks related to CLW's daily management and is designed for team leaders; the time of specific tasks (e.g., attendance at meetings; planned maintenance; hourly process controls that include the level of losses and waste) must be brought to the level of a standardized daily routine; one of the standardized tasks is the *standardized weekly audit of losses and waste*, by all levels of the organization, which verifies compliance with operational standards and constantly strengthens the approaches to losses and waste and implicitly CLW (the goal is to ensure consistent application and execution of monitoring losses and waste, raising awareness of the entire workshop staff on losses and waste, etc.); it is the time when managers justify weekly the level of production achieved and the lost opportunities for production and cost reduction; for example, for production times, total contracted hours is 100% justified – time-related losses and waste (TRLW) (see Figure 2.9); for physical losses and waste (PLW) separate reports are prepared; the responsibility for standardized weekly audit of losses and waste is that of manufacturing leadership.

- *Team support*: Continuous, consistent, and visible managerial support is the key to CLW's daily management; the desirable behavioral identity of the entire management team [management branding (MB)] (Posteucă, 2011) is essential; each level of leadership has a mentoring attitude for the next level; leaders are the real examples for everyone continuously.

Therefore, the purpose of the basic tools of CLW's daily management is to improve the level of knowledge of CLW operators and to provide the information needed to solve CLW-related problems through training programs. CLW's daily management activities are integrated with other daily management. Particular attention is paid to both the bottleneck capacity module and the bottleneck profit module.

5.1.5 Step-by-Step Implementation

The purpose of concurrent control of CLW is to check the conditions of manifestation of losses and waste and of CLW at the level of each module and to direct each module toward the ideal state of CLW (zero CLW). It is not easy for workshop staff to move from the "I make – you improve" mentality.

The implementation steps of concurrent control of CLW are presented in Figure 5.2.

In order to support the annual achievement of KAIZENSHIRO and the evolution toward zero CLW, this step-by-step approach facilitates the understanding by everyone of the activities necessary to implement a concurrent control of CLW and ensures the preservation of the gains obtained in each step. The priority in the first three steps is to identify and reduce and/or initially eliminate the root causes of the occurrence of losses and waste and implicitly CLWs. The objective of these first three steps is for the entire workshop staff to become interested in identifying, investigating, and improving losses and waste at the source of their generation. In steps 4 and 5, team leaders present and teach their team members ways to develop standards for losses and waste and inspection procedures for each module and for all manufacturing flow. The objective of these two steps is to reduce the level of losses and waste, especially those in the bottleneck capacity module and bottleneck profit module, and to facilitate the in-depth understanding of the modules and the entire manufacturing flow by the entire workshop staff. The last two steps, steps 6 and 7, are designed to encourage and update concurrent control of CLWs, to support problem-solving activities, and to support improvement activities by developing instructions for CLW's expected performance, by standardizing the system and methods of concurrent control of CLWs, and by conducting periodic audits to verify the level of understanding of the purpose of each step and implementation. The ultimate goal of these last two steps is to support a robust approach to concurrent control of CLW at the shop floor level and

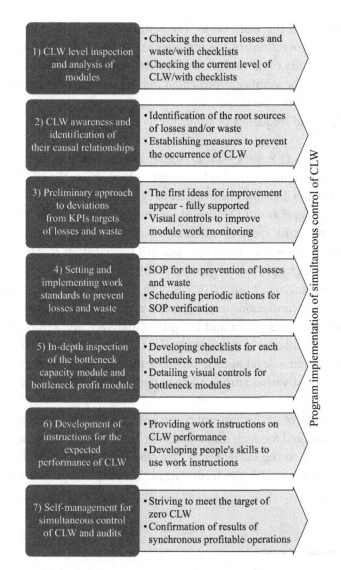

FIGURE 5.2
Basic steps of the concurrent control of cost of losses and waste implementation program.

to develop and sustain a culture in which people in every module or area of the company are capable of full self CLW's daily management.

The only success factor in the step-by-step implementation of concurrent control of CLW is to conduct periodic audits for each step to confirm the results achieved and to provide directions for future activities. The audits provide guidance where needed and give the entire workshop staff satisfaction with the work done. The results of each audit must be confirmed if the operations of the modules are in line with the CLW targets and if the severity of the auditor is objective (not too much or not enough). The results of the audits are presented publicly where they are freely discussed between the participants.

The types and frequency of audits are as follows:

1. *Self-audits* (1 × week → team leader, production members, and continuous improvement leader; its role is to promote the effective monitoring of CLW and the evaluation of progress);
2. *Section-level audits* (2 × month → production specialist, continuous improvement specialist, maintenance specialist, quality specialist, cost and budgeting specialist, and HR specialist; its role is to address hot topics by providing guidance and assistance); and
3. *Top-management audits* (1 × month → plant manager, production manager, continuous improvement manager, maintenance manager, quality manager, cost and budgeting manager, and HR manager; its role is to discuss in detail the topics presented by the participants in the section – level audits, provides guidance and advice, and promotes motivation among all by recognizing the work done).

The seven steps of the concurrent control of the CLW implementation program are adjusted for each manufacturing plant according to the industry and according to the current and expected conditions. They are in continuous symbiosis with the feedforward controls and with the feedback controls.

5.2 FEEDBACK CONTROL: TOTAL SYNCHRONOUS PROFITABLE OPERATIONS CONTROL

Feedback control of CLW aims to monitor the control of CLW performance at the level of the effect (outputs) of the production system/of a manufacturing flow/of a module. The aim is to monitor the performance of production outputs on the level of CLW (especially those necessary to support KAIZENSHIRO) and compare the parameters of CLW to achieve total synchronous profitable operations control in order to provide the new level of control and robust restrictive conditions based on lessons learned from bottleneck profit module, bottleneck capacity module, and material entries.

The basic purpose of the feedback control of CLW is to verify that the production has achieved only what is necessary for the customers and profitable for the company. The reduction of the plant lead time (or factory lead time; see Figure 3.23), the reduction of stocks, the control of bottleneck capacity modules (to increase efficiency), and the control of bottleneck profit modules (to increase efficiency) are the expected results of fulfilling synchronous profitable operations and implicitly fulfilling SBTP. Consequently, it is necessary to evaluate the degree of compliance with the established rules of production planning and scheduling, starting from the control of production volumes and continuing with the validity of KPIs of losses and waste and all production parameters, placing the SBTP mechanism in general production management. In other words, the feedback control of CLW verifies whether the PDCA cycle is followed to obtain synchronous profitable operations after the production has been performed.

Therefore, the control trilogy for KAIZENSHIRO ends with a feedback control that provides the data needed to restart the control cycle, for feedforward controls (see Figure 4.3). The feedback control for total synchronous profitable operations control means supporting the achievement of KAIZENSHIRO by going through the cycle of continuous improvement (see Figure 5.3), respectively:

- *complete flow control based on five PULLs*: material inputs (pull 5), accumulation (pull 4), make (pull 3), delivery (pull 2), profit (pull 1);
- *control of profitability of production volumes and future directions* (or leveling bottleneck capacity modules by synchronizing them to takt time and leveling bottleneck profit modules by synchronizing them to takt profit): the control of the effectiveness and efficiency of the production volumes on the time axis and of the production instructions in the order of their development; control of the effectiveness and efficiency of orders on the time axis and their order of processing and execution; necessary future corrective actions;
- *result reports of synchronous profitable operations*: evaluation of results on profitability and synchronization of operations;
- *development and implementation of robust restrictive conditions*: control of the effectiveness and efficiency of production volumes

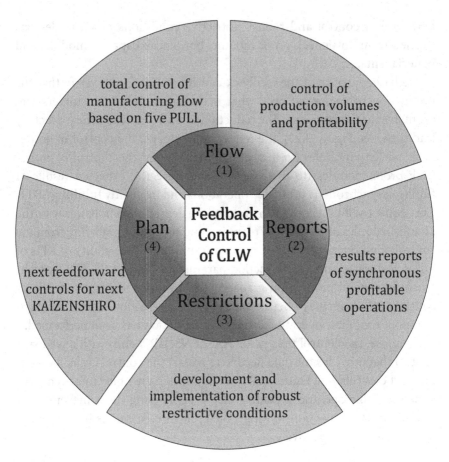

FIGURE 5.3
Feedback control in control trilogy for KAIZENSHIRO.

for type A, B, and C target products; improving setups and cycle time; checking all restrictions in bottleneck capacity modules and bottleneck profit modules in order to improve them systematically (kaizen) and systemically (kaikaku); and

- *control of the anticipatory approach* (feedforward controls): planning foreseeable CCLW improvements and eliminations for the next period in order to meet next year's KAIZENSHIRO.

Each of the five elements of the feedback control will be detailed in the following sections.

5.2.1 Total Manufacturing Flow Control Based on Five PULL

The complete flow control based on five PULL aims to verify the making of profitable and synchronous production by checking the production mode in bottleneck capacity module and bottleneck profit module (monthly, weekly, daily, on each shift, every 4 hours, and every 2 hours). Confirmation of information and things is done by checking the manufacturing flow as follows: material inputs (pull 5) – accumulation (pull 4) – make (pull 3) – delivery (pull 2) – profit (pull 1), respectively (see Figure 5.4):

- *connecting the bottleneck profit module to pulling rhythm of necessary profit* (Pull 1: takt profit – the pace of profit demand; synchronization bottleneck profit module to the necessary rate of profit generation per minute); bottleneck profit module can be the same as bottleneck capacity module;
- *connecting the bottleneck capacity module to pulling rhythm of clients* (Pull 2: customer takt time; the pace of customer demand; synchronization production takt time to delivery lead time/customer lead time);
- *connecting the size of the buffer inventory to pulling rhythm of the bottleneck capacity module* (Pull 3: production takt time; the pace of production demand; synchronizing the buffer inventory size to production takt time from the bottleneck capacity module);
- *connecting the standard WIP with the buffer inventory size* (Pull 4: buffer inventory takt time; the pace of buffer inventory demand; synchronization between standard WIP to buffer inventory takt time; buffer inventory is temporary inventory before bottleneck capacity module); and
- *connecting the material supply of the first module with daily work instructions of the first module* – internal logistics task (Pull 5: the first module takt time; the pace of the first module demand; synchronization between material supply of the first module according to takt time of the first module – in accordance with the working instructions; this synchronization is ensured in any module that requires materials, components and consumables).

Therefore, the purpose of feedback control through the total manufacturing flow control based on five PULL is to support the basic purpose of SBTP, respectively, the fulfillment of synchronous profitable operations

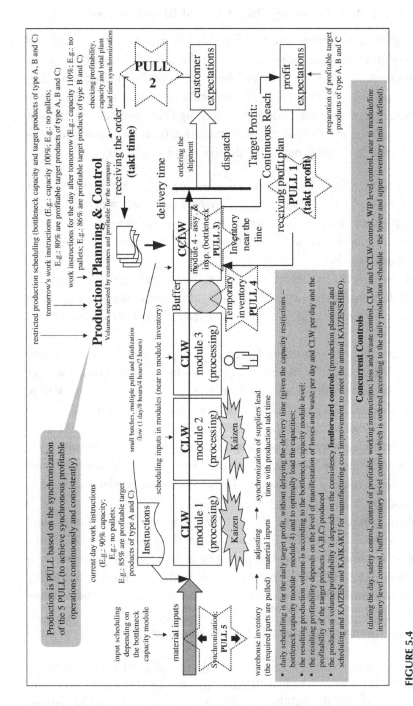

FIGURE 5.4

Feedback control: Example of applying total manufacturing flow control based on five PULL to achieve synchronous profitable operations continuously and consistently.

continuously and consistently. The daily work instructions and the ordering of the activities of the five PULLs are essential in order to fulfill KAIZENSHIRO and implicitly the monthly/annual production and profit plan.

5.2.2 Control of Production Volumes and Profitability

The control of production volumes and profitability considers the control of all aspects of production, including scheduling target product profitability, scheduling machines and people considering the bottleneck capacity module, managing materials, and coordinating suppliers and key customers. As these elements change over time, in order to respond to different customer orders and different needs of the company's profitability, production control is essential to ensure the success of any manufacturing company. Moreover, the truly effective control of production volumes and profitability coordinates the supply chains – joint efforts across company boundaries. The control of the production volumes and profitability must constantly adapt and respond to the environmental changes, the company strategies, the company's profit needs, the customer requirements, and the specific supply chain problems and opportunities.

More specifically, the control of production volumes is done by controlling the work instructions according to the planned capacity of the bottleneck capacity module and the profitability of the bottleneck profit module. Clear work instructions are required for both bottleneck capacity module and other non-bottleneck capacity modules.

The work instructions on the production volume aim at controlling the pull-type synchronization at the capacity level of the bottleneck capacity module. The verification of material inputs is done in correlation with the pull information together with the orders from the clients and with the need for profit. The material inputs, the production volumes, and the method of adjusting the inputs according to the need of the materials on the time axis are controlled. Controlling the volume of materials is essential to avoid unnecessary investment in stocks. The launch times of orders for materials to the warehouse, the minimum stock at the time of launching the order, the volumes ordered according to the daily production scheduling in bottleneck capacity module and especially the time of physical flow of material supply of modules are checked. All stocks are reviewed from the perspective of minimum and maximum levels to see if there is a need to change the minimum and/or maximum level for certain categories of materials and/or components. The behavior of fluctuating customer orders is especially controlled and analyzed as some CLWs tend to increase depending on the irregular times generated by fluctuating orders. In conclusion, the verification of the production scheduling mode according to the bottleneck capacity module is done as detailed as possible to ensure that the production load was optimal and was based on profitable orders.

The work instructions regarding the production volume from the non-bottleneck capacity module aim at verifying the order of processing the orders according to the capacity from the bottleneck capacity module and the setup time for fulfilling the takt time. An essential role is played by the flexibility provided by the short times regarding the setup activities. Setting a SOP for setup is essential (as is setting a SOP for all items that involve time spent). In order to achieve a SOP as effective and efficient as possible, it is recommended to use methods design concept (MDC). Single minute exchange of die (SMED) or kaizen for setup techniques can be used to improve the setup time.

The control of the profitability of the performed volumes has as special purpose the control of the production from the bottleneck profit module. Specifically, the dynamic evolution of each loss and waste, of each CLW and of the CCLW structures that were designated in the phase of feedforward controls to contribute to the fulfillment of the annual KAIZENSHIRO. Particular attention is paid to checking and improving the standard consumption of materials, consumables, utilities, die, jig, and tool. If necessary, it is proposed to restore consumption standards (often through kaizen projects in the phase of feedforward controls).

Therefore, the control of the profitability of the performed volumes concerns both the production management part at shop floor level and the office management.

5.2.3 Results Reports of Synchronous Profitable Operations

The control of the production results, from the perspective of synchronous profitable operations, aims at annual performance results reports and monthly performance results reports and goes to the level of detail to identify the factors that directly or indirectly contributed to a possible non-fulfillment of KAIZENSHIRO, of planned production volume and of successful profitability.

The main purpose of the results reports is to compare the company's annual objectives with the results obtained by production planning and scheduling. Often the annual objectives of production companies that underlie the feedforward and concurrent controls and that converge with the company's values, mission and vision and on the basis of which targets are set for KPIs, including for losses and waste KPIs (see Tables 3.1–3.3) are of the following type: (1) reduction of material stock days; (2) reduction of work in progress (WIP); (3) reduction of overtime; (4) reduction of handling; (5) reduction of rework; (6) reduction of manufacturing cost by reducing CLWs; (7) increase of sales turnover; (8) reduction of setup times; (9) reduction of total plant lead time (TPLT) and/or its components (see Figure 3.23); (10) zero accidents; (11) increase of employee satisfaction; (12) reduction of man × hour by product; (13) increase of maintenance effectiveness; (14) increase of efficient utilization of the factory floor (value-added usage); (15) increase in manpower flexibility, etc.

Annual and monthly performance results reports include detailed reports on the achievement of the above objectives at the level of overall management indicators (OMI) and further at the level of KPIs for each type of OMI. For example, to verify the achievement of the objective of reducing TPLT (measured in days) the level reached by the related KPIs is reported: production numbers (number of products), production capacity (number of products), overall equipment effectiveness (OEE; measured as %), man × hour by product (measured as man × hour/product), setup time (measured as minutes), production tempo (measured as products/shift). Another example: To meet the objective of reducing manufacturing costs (OMI), the level reached by the related KPIs is reported for: transformation cost (measured by index; reducing TRLW and their associated costs – see Tables 3.1–3.3), work in process inventory (measured as hours; reducing PLW and their associated costs – see Tables 3.1–3.3), material cost reduction (measured as %; reducing PLW and their associated costs – see Tables 3.1–3.3), utilities cost reduction, etc.

Controlling the fulfillment of the KPIs targets starts from the control on months, weeks, days, and continues up to the level of shifts and hours. The production results are verified based on the production planning and scheduling at the level of:

- input vs. output for each module – especially for the bottleneck capacity module;
- temporary inventory and buffer inventory;

- the stability of net standard operating time or net capacity for good parts (see Figure 2.9) form the bottleneck capacity module compared to production planning and scheduling (was it standard or not);
- the relationship between profitable production scheduling vs. requests received from customers;
- complete daily orders (then follow the ones completed on the next day/days);
- CLW for each module – especially for the bottleneck profit module (CLWs were in standard or not? Where they could not keep the standard? What was done? What remained to be done?); and
- the flows gone through and the parameters and basic principles of achieving profitable target products (A, B, and C) (see Figure 2.6).

Therefore, the control of the quantitative and value results of the production aims at verifying if what was requested by the customers and if what was profitable for the company was produced.

5.2.4 Robust Restrictive Conditions

Increasing the robustness of the restrictive conditions means the extension and stability of the standardization, both of time and material consumptions that are found in the company's final products, as well as of the losses and waste and implicitly of CLWs. Restrictive conditions apply to all material and time consumption for target products, materials, bottleneck capacity module, and bottleneck profit module. Some material and time consumptions are daily (daily cleaning by 5S, daily lubrication of equipment, daily inspection of equipment, etc.), others are occasional (setup, scrap, breakdown, etc.). Daily cleaning of equipment is an example of both material and time consumption.

The equipment cleaning standard will specify:

- cleaning points and areas;
- normal condition: required level of cleanliness;
- cleaning method: manual or not;
- types of materials: with a standard weekly or monthly consumption; equipment dedicated to cleaning;
- duration of daily cleaning: for example, 5 minutes a day for a cleaning point or area; the time in which production can be scheduled or

not; this is an element of non-productive hours – engaged on production, but non-producing; a part of the cost of non-productive
hours losses (see Figure 2.9); and
• cleaning frequency: the total daily minutes allocated to the cleaning
of the respective equipment.

Deviations from this standard, such as insufficient time to perform normal cleaning of a point in the equipment that has caused a quality problem
(dirty part), are subject to concurrent controls or problem-solving projects
(or reset of the standard).

Standardization and standardization through feedforward improvements (feedforward controls) and through daily improvements (concurrent
controls) must continuously reduce unnecessary consumption found at the
level of CLW and meet the annual and multiannual level of KAIZENSHIRO
moving toward the ideal state of zero CLW. The basic premise of standardization is to ensure the stability of manufacturing flow, of all modules, by
ensuring a continuous flow based on effective concurrent controls (profitable work instructions and strict control and at low production intervals)
and effective feedback controls (control of the information from the five
PULL). The challenge is to ensure the stability and continuity of the flow in
the event of the movement of the necessary restrictions during the planned
period (e.g., some manifestations specific to the seasons – winter or sum-
mer; or fluctuations in demand from certain customers).

Restrictions on target products must ensure the profitability of products
considered in class A, B, or C. It is time to review the classification of target products for the next period (see Figure 2.6). Usually class A products,
considered the most profitable, are those that are associated with special
orders and usually have a short life cycle. Special orders often have a multitude of hidden costs, of CLW, which must be predetermined from the
beginning of the period and for which it is necessary to plan both feedforward controls (kaizen and kaikaku projects) and concurrent controls
(A3 to resolve deviations from the standard or small improvements to the
shop floor level). At the same time, orders with small batches require bear-
ing setup time and implicitly a cost of setup time losses. Setting the SOP
for setup time as innovative and efficient as possible can be the goal of a
feedforward control project.

Therefore, the early identification of all restrictive conditions contributes
to the substantiation of the objectives of the next period and implicitly to

the substantiation of feedforward controls and concurrent controls. The consistent verification of the primary factors that generated differences between the established and the achieved targets are the ones that are investigated first. The purpose of developing robust restrictive conditions is to achieve production planning and scheduling for the next period so as to ensure the fulfillment of synchronous profitable operations by planning manufacturing costs improvements (CCLW) to meet KAIZENSHIRO (takt profit and takt time), before the start of the next planned physical production and by identifying all consumption standards that require re-standardization so that the CLW level is acceptable for the next period.

5.2.5 Control of the Anticipatory Approach

This type of feedback control aims to establish manufacturing cost improvement (CCLW) projects to meet KAIZENSHIRO (takt profit and takt time) for the next period. The targets needed to be met by future kaizen and kaikaku projects are set to meet both the production volume by unlocking the capacity of the bottleneck capacity modules and setting future work instructions, as well as the fulfillment of KAIZENSHIRO. These projects are allocated to each department and are centralized at the level of the manufacturing plant (or the SBTP steering committee).

For the annual planning of all kaizen and kaikaku projects considered strategic for the next year, the following are detailed:

- *Annual type of improvement* (kaizen and kaikaku);
- *Annual total manufacturing cost improvements (CCLW) targets (%);*
- *Annual individual CLW targets (%)* (from current status to target);
- *Defining/preparing improvements:* type of losses or waste; code of process/operation; responsible department; responsible manager; location for improvement; defining loss, waste, and costs; project sponsor; leader of project; improvement team; workforce training; type of training (internal/external); type of workshops required; on the job training;
- *Solutions, resources, and expected benefits:* solution for improvement; possible obstacles; material resources needed; man × hours needed; estimated benefits; investment needed; activities for implementation; start date; interim data for reporting; end date; the expected benefits, the size and the moment of their fulfillment are in accordance with the production planning and with the need to fulfill

KAIZENSHIRO – this is how their efficiency and effectiveness are evaluated;

- *Evaluation stage:* stage 20%; stage 40%; stage 60%; stage 80%; stage 100%; actual resources consumed $; planned resources consumed $; public presentations; delays/review deadlines; reasons for delays; impact delay in CLW and unrealized production – lost profit opportunity;
- *Gains:* time; production capacity; distances; motion; direct and indirect labor; stocks: materials, WIP, finished product; intangible effects; investment avoided; and last but not least the reduction or eradication of CLW by reaching the CCLW targets in order to reach KAIZENSHIRO for the next year; and
- *Project evaluation:* benefits vs. MCI targets; MCI targets vs. actual costs; benefits vs. time; team evaluation – gains; team leader evaluation – gains; total actual benefits $; total planned benefits $; *CapEx* spend on MCI projects; benefits/costs for 12 months (%); payback: MCI projects (years); solution validity over time, etc.

Therefore, based on the development of the restrictive conditions of the next period, the detailed development of the specific activities of feedforward controls is carried out in order to conclude the control trilogy for KAIZENSHIRO (feedforward controls, concurrent controls, and feedback controls; see Figure 4.3).

All the people in the manufacturing plant and beyond are continuously aligned to fulfill the control trilogy for KAIZENSHIRO and implicitly SBTP mechanism. This requires effective leadership. Leadership continuously supports the productivity and innovation targets of the manufacturing plant.

5.3 SYNCHRONOUS PROFITABLE OPERATIONS LEADERSHIP

The implementation of the SBTP mechanism involves the continuous transformation of manufacturing plants, which means that leaders need to change in terms of their leadership. At the beginning, the implementation of the SBTP mechanism is sought in order to obtain tangible results necessary for the dignified development of the company. But once these goals are achieved, only a consistent approach to leadership can ensure consistency in SBTP results. The transition to SBTP is not easy. Leaders need a deep understanding of what they have to do and what behavioral changes they need to make in order to continually focus on themselves. Moreover, resistance to change is often more pronounced at the level of leaders. Transforming leadership into a pro-manufacturing cost improvement culture is challenging. But without this, a manufacturing plant risks losing the desire to continuously improve CLW and fulfill the status of synchronous profitable operations. Synchronous profitable operations are the cardinal reason for making the change. The basic goal is to develop a new organizational culture and an ethos with a high level of motivation for the continuous fulfillment of KAIZENSHIRO. This requires the full involvement of all people in the company and beyond in kaizen and kaikaku programs aimed at directing the manufacturing plant to the ideal state of zero CLW. The implementation of KPIs for losses and waste and for CLW are essential to continuously evaluate the performance of the SBTP mechanism.

So, what tasks do leaders have to perform? What tools can they use? What behaviors do they need to change?

We will answer these questions one by one in the following sections.

5.3.1 Leadership Tasks

Five essential and fundamental basic tasks contribute to building an everyday leadership that supports the control trilogy for KAIZENSHIRO. These are as follows:

- *Effective communication* (CLW information center and module activity panel): The daily flow of information is fluent at all levels of the manufacturing plant (hierarchical levels); all levels are informed about the current target of CCLW and the real situation of CLW regarding the achievement of KAIZENSHIRO; the preparation of the *shift handover report of CLW/CCLW* is done continuously, completely, and on time; problem analysis sessions are conducted in an effective manner, that is, according to an agenda; deviations from KPIs' targets are addressed with short-term corrective action; action plans are clear to all participants in order to make changes in a timely and consistent manner; the tasks of all people at the shop floor level and not only on improvements and problem-solving are mutually agreed and respected; the communication style is clear;

the atmosphere is trustworthy and cooperative, and the information is based on 5G principles (Gemba, Gembutsu, Genjitsu, Genri, Gensoku) which are easily verifiable; anyone knows the levels of escalation; at the level of annual manufacturing improvement budgets (AMIB) and annual manufacturing cash improvement budgets (AMCIB) all the necessary resources to support improvements and problem-solving are specified, and one week before the resource plan for the following week is finalized and communicated effectively.

- *Monitoring modules at short intervals*: Leaders have a proactive behavior and continuously attract everyone in this style of behavior; the consumption standards regarding TRLW and PLW are defined for each module and continuously visually describe the state of the work done; leaders check compliance with standards regularly and at short intervals; all the leaders' comments are visible at the activity panel module and the most relevant at the CLW information center level; all deviations from CLW standards are discussed, monitored, and visually exposed; current CLW standards are continuously improved to meet KAIZENSHIRO; module monitoring is used as an active element for identifying and validating issues related to CLW or other current topics; bottleneck capacity modules and bottleneck profit modules are strictly monitored.

- *Supporting autonomy and self-determination*: Developing workforce flexibility in addressing improvements and issues requires the development of employee methodological, technical, and social skills that are often improved through active questioning by leaders to move toward continuous learning organization; leaders move from providing the right answer to asking the right questions; the roles and tasks of each are unequivocally described; qualification needs are derived from daily work and systematically documented (the matrix of individual skills to achieve excellence by highly skilled people); feedback is given regularly and the role of leaders is to ensure the continued readiness of people to address issues and improvements; the continuous development of people and the creation of the learning environment is the main duty of leaders to ensure the empowerment of employees to achieve the expected performance.

- *KAIZENSHIRO*: Polar star of continuous improvements at the module level: Leaders actively promote and continuously support the fulfillment of KAIZENSHIRO by improving CCLW and by solving problems at shop level (especially those regarding CLW); the continuous (daily) interrogation of the current situation of CLW and of the efforts to improve and solve the problems is the responsibility of the leaders; continuous encouragement and enhancing the creativity of all people to generate valuable and innovative ideas for improvement is channeled to all levels of the company (the internal feedback system is functional and continuously directed to the most challenging problems at the module level – the top 3–5 problems of a module are continuously known by anyone working in that module and available to those who are passing through).

- *structured processes to address both problem-solving and the achievement of systematic (kaizen) and systemic (kaikaku) improvement targets:* leaders encourage and verify the use of structured problem-solving and structured improvements; all deviations from CLW standards and CLW KPIs targets are systematically captured, prioritized, and addressed; the most important deviations are analyzed systematically and methodically in order to identify the main root causes in order to reduce or eliminate their effects in a consistent way; leaders check the use of structured problem-solving processes to solve a simple problem (e.g., before and after kaizen – according to PDCA), for structured problem-solving (e.g., A3) and to approach kaizen and kaikaku projects; the leader continually supports team members in recognizing problems and initiating the appropriate problem-solving and improvement process; leaders allocate sufficient time to participate in consistently reducing or eliminating CLW issues.

Therefore, from the perspective of the leaders' tasks, in order to support the control trilogy for KAIZENSHIRO, they must provide the vision of the manufacturing plant and set the direction, continuously transmit the company's values, set high standards and expectations for achieving KAIZENSHIRO by providing their full support continuously and really motivate people in the fight to meet business expectations, involve all people in the decision-making process, be a model, a mentor, and a coach, actively listen and explain what he thinks and guide the followers.

5.3.2 Leadership Instruments

The leadership instruments have been largely described in Section 5.1.4 – the basic tools of concurrent control (CLW's daily management) (see

Figure 5.1). Therefore, in addition to the purposes related to concurrent controls (visual management – CLW information center and module activity panel; communication – horizontal and vertical; top CLW challenges; on the spot investigation – Go & See/Gemba; CLW problem-solving; CLW standards confirmation check on modules and team support), the leadership instruments aim to present the detailed and planned approach of the projects for the continuous improvement of CLW and the achievement of objectives (feedforward controls), and to visualize the current state of the stages of implementation of individual and systemic improvement projects (feedback controls). The leaders must display and monitor deadlines and responsibilities and request details in case of deviations and validate the proposed measures.

5.3.3 Leadership Behaviors

The continuous and deep understanding of the conditions around him and the development of a personal conviction is an individual journey for each leader. The personal experiences and the availability for flexibility can help leaders imagine their future and capitalize on their will and skills to achieve and sustain change continuously. The leaders need to understand how and why they need to change their own behavior to consistently support the change they want and see as necessary.

Without confidence in what needs to be done, there is no leadership. Very few managers are leaders. A leader is someone that people will follow and feel they can trust. A leader is a respected man. When a leader continually inspires trust in the team, it truly shows that it is a team, and people freely share their views without fear of judgment of the leader. Often the most innovative ideas for change come in such environments. Workforce and teamwork become stronger, more motivated, and more productive. A leader is as effective and efficient as his team. Building trust requires time and a conscious effort directed toward a clearly expressed vision and mission, based on a set of real and visible values.

Continuous promotion of contextually desirable managerial behavior – MB – to maintain the creative and innovative state of spirit and people's desire to continually make systemic and systematic changes for the better is the goal of a leader in SBTP thinking. (Posteucă, 2011; Posteucă and Sakamoto, 2017, pp. 240–244; Posteucă, 2018, pp. 227–230; Posteucă, 2019). Management branding "is a managerial system that, by an integrated approach, creates and synchronizes, for the application, contextual managerial behavioral identities in order to increase organizational productivity and/or economic growth" (Posteucă, 2011).

We will present seven key elements of everyday leadership behaviors in supporting the KAIZENSHIRO culture, as follows:

- *Lead by example:* You can't ask someone for something if you don't know how to do it; for example, if you expect your team to come up with innovative ideas for solving problems or making improvements without making investments, then you should provide such examples first; in this way the leader becomes a member of the team; the leader thinks before he speaks and what he says is short and complete; the leader does not make long monologues and is focused on action rather than words – the dynamics of CLWs manifestation does not allow time for inaction; the transparency of CLWs creates trust and the perception of control over the production system, while hiding problems with CLWs destroys transparency and trust in the production system; true leaders are direct and honest and communicate all the time; a leader wants to understand in depth the reasons for possible resistance, to personally observe their manifestation and not to break these resistances by force – he wants to dissolve the resistance in a lasting way.

- *Admitting one's own mistakes and those of others in learning situations:* Leaders publicly acknowledge their own mistakes when they occur; leaders admit that they can be wrong, it is not a sign of weakness; leaders always propose a new framework for action when error occurs; they are aware that no one knows everything and we all have our limits; the leader tolerates the mistakes of others in learning situations and favors the experiments of those around him so that they learn; if an employee makes a mistake in a learning situation, the leader asks what the employee's hypothesis was and what was the result of testing his hypothesis; he always tries to understand the cause-effect connections.

- *Keeping the promises it can keep and keeping its commitments:* No one trusts those who do not keep their word; however, there are circumstances beyond his control that could manifest, and the leader will make his team understand his behavior, information, reasoning and decisions; the congruence between words and action must be maintained continuously.

- *Trust your team:* If a leader does not trust his team, then the team will not trust him either; the success of the team is before the success of the leader; the leader leaves no one behind and he never forgets that his whole team is made up of people; leaders do not practice micromanagement; leaders do not want employees to develop solutions on their own and therefore do not get stuck in micromanagement, but provide support where needed; if the leader notices that an employee is struggling with a task, then he observes the task together with the employee and allows the employee to explain the difficulties he is experiencing; the leader keeps the overview of CLWs and does not unnecessarily add individual details for some employees;
- *Providing and receiving feedback*: Nobody is perfect; leaders ask for feedback from the team to see how he can help the team to be more productive and how to improve the work environment to see how KAIZENSHIRO can perform better; leaders see feedback as an opportunity for growth, so they ask for and provide feedback to their employees; the leader observes and reports on specific situations of each feedback, whether it is positive or negative.
- *Not looking for culprits ... but the root cause*: Leaders treat all people correctly, with the same set of expectations, according to a set of team rules – already known (e.g., the "do not gossip" rule); leaders are more interested in identifying the root cause than in identifying the culprits; he seeks the consistent approach of CLWs and not to show his own strength in front of others; leaders want to understand the problem and work on the solution with the people involved; the tone of a leader's voice remains respectful and in critical situations; the leader has the ability to proactively discuss facts and data to identify the best solutions with the team.
- *Acts consistently all the time:* Consistency is indispensable for great leadership; leaders recognize all loss and waste structures and know how to turn them into costs and the evolution of CLWs for each module; during audits, leaders focus on CLW and CCLW in the bottleneck capacity module and bottleneck profit module; leaders provide all necessary resources and continuously involve employees in reducing or eliminating CLWs; leaders create their own image of the current state of KAIZENSHIRO's performance at any time; leaders conduct Go & See sessions to show employees that the issues they have highlighted are being addressed; leaders observe and understand issues

before seeking support to address different structures of CLWs; leaders continuously comply with standards (clothing, punctuality, order and cleanliness, etc.); leaders use interrogation techniques intentionally (open or closed questions) to generate a common understanding of CLWs and KAIZENSHIRO.

In conclusion, trust and respect for people provide the prerequisites for gaining team loyalty. The loyalty of the teams can contribute to the fulfillment of the expected performances of the manufacturing plant and of the entire SBTP mechanism and implicitly of KAIZENSHIRO. To gain trust and respect, trust and respect must be given.

5.4 PHASES AND MAIN STEPS OF IMPLEMENTATION OF SPEED-BASED TARGET PROFIT

The implementation of SBTP is done in three phases (establishment, introduction, and implementation) which are composed of several steps (see Figure 5.5). A decisive role in the successful implementation of the SBTP mechanism is played by the implementation and practice of effective leadership on the background of a consistent KAIZENSHIRO culture.

In the first phase (*establishment*), the first activities of joining the SBTP are done. The phase begins with a review of the current state of the production system and past levels of productivity and profitability and future expectations. An important moment is the sensitivity analysis on profitability scenarios through productivity (ROI; see Figure 2.20). It is essential to set carefully an in-depth SBTP goals and policy (targets and means) so as not to require repeated changes and corrections in the introduction phase. At the same time, establishing the KAIZENSHIRO level for 3–5 years and for the next one must be done scientifically and convergently with the company's vision and mission (often the connection is made with the MCPD system). All employees in the company must understand why it was chosen to introduce SBTP and MCPD in their company, in order to be aware of the need for these approaches to achieve the company's goals effectively and efficiently.

The second phase (*introduction*) begins with the development of the SBTP mechanism, the establishment of CLW deployment maps and the

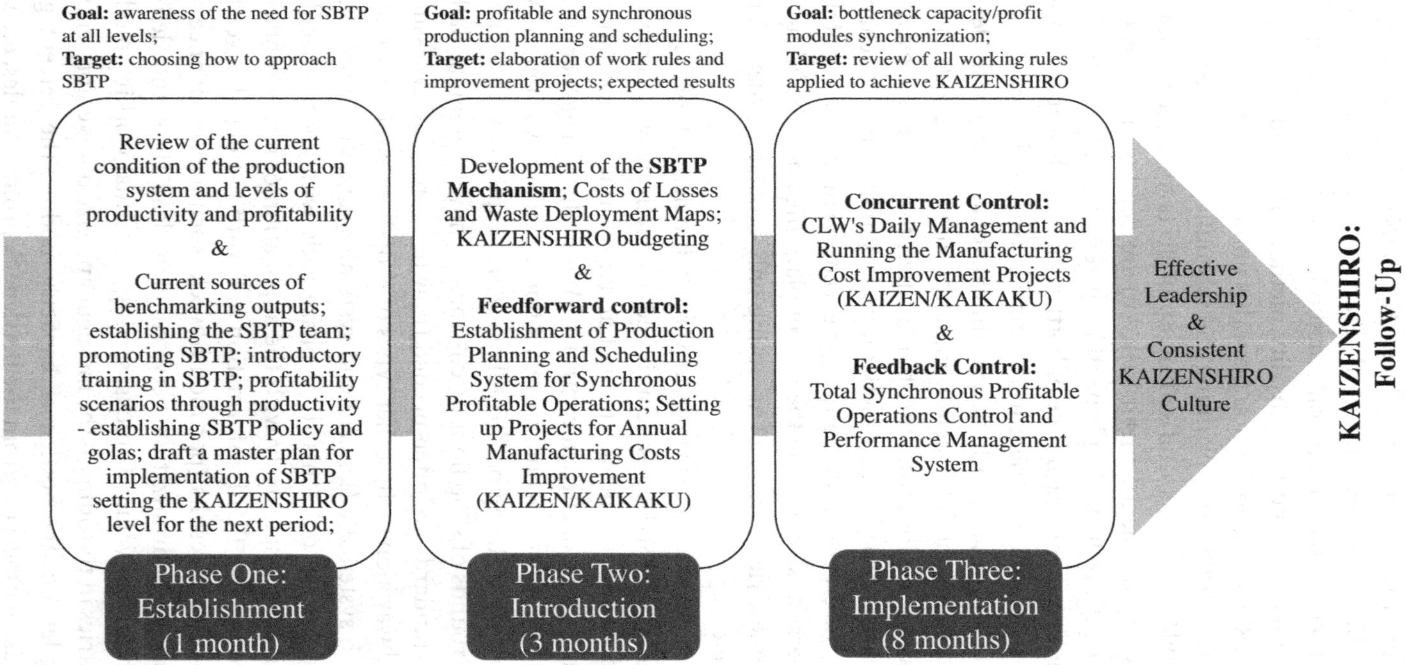

KAIZENSHIRO:
Follow-Up

Effective Leadership & Consistent KAIZENSHIRO Culture

Goal: bottleneck capacity/profit modules synchronization;
Target: review of all working rules applied to achieve KAIZENSHIRO

Concurrent Control:
CLW's Daily Management and Running the Manufacturing Cost Improvement Projects (KAIZEN/KAIKAKU)
&
Feedback Control:
Total Synchronous Profitable Operations Control and Performance Management System

Phase Three: Implementation (8 months)

Goal: profitable and synchronous production planning and scheduling;
Target: elaboration of work rules and improvement projects; expected results

Development of the **SBTP Mechanism**; Costs of Losses and Waste Deployment Maps; KAIZENSHIRO budgeting
&
Feedforward control:
Establishment of Production Planning and Scheduling System for Synchronous Profitable Operations; Setting up Projects for Annual Manufacturing Costs Improvement (KAIZEN/KAIKAKU)

Phase Two: Introduction (3 months)

Goal: awareness of the need for SBTP at all levels;
Target: choosing how to approach SBTP

Review of the current condition of the production system and levels of productivity and profitability
&
Current sources of benchmarking outputs; establishing the SBTP team; promoting SBTP; introductory training in SBTP; profitability scenarios through productivity - establishing SBTP policy and golas; draft a master plan for implementation of SBTP setting the KAIZENSHIRO level for the next period;

Phase One: Establishment (1 month)

FIGURE 5.5
Overview of the three phases of SBTP master plan implementation.

establishment of improvement budgets (KAIZENSHIRO budgeting). To determine CLWs, we often start with the first method of sizing losses and waste in costs (the unique rate method), and then move on to the modules rate method and the causality method. The control trilogy for KAIZENSHIRO begins to develop from this phase. Feedforward control, establishment of production planning and scheduling system for synchronous profitable operations, and setting up projects for annual manufacturing costs improvement (kaizen/kaikaku) are developed in this phase. Choosing target products, implementing losses and waste KPIs, understanding the specifics of each type of bottleneck module (capacity and/or profit) and synchronizing them to the market (shareholders: takt profit; customers: takt time), strengthening maintenance activities at the level of bottleneck capacity modules, determining the foreseeable effects of SBTP implementation, establishing the buffer inventory volume, establishing the materials procurement method, understanding market changes, establishing the order of orders and their execution time (leveling of modules and operations), changing the way of planning and scheduling production in free style in terms of accepting only profitable orders (for the most part), etc.

In the third phase (*implementation*), the specific elements of the control trilogy for KAIZENSHIRO are continued, respectively with concurrent control and feedback control. The first activities aim at developing the specific elements of concurrent control, CLW's daily management (activity every 24 hours, every 8 hours, every 4 hours, and every 2 hours). After the introductory training on SBTP has been completed for all employees, several rounds of shop floor discussions on how to organize daily to meet CLW standards are often needed (how to approach CLW issues in a structured way along with other types of shop floor issues) and for the way in which systematic (kaizen) and systemic (kaikaku) improvement projects are carried out. This third phase ends with specific feedback control activities, respectively with the application of total profitability control through five PULL information and with the detailed verification of production results (per month/week, such as: compliance with delivery time; synchronization between plant lead time and delivery lead time, financial value of stocks, setting the actual working mode of material entries in the buffer – the moment and size of inventory entries, the loading level of the bottleneck capacity module, the percentage of CLW decrease – especially from the bottleneck profit modules, etc.).

All these activities of the SBTP master plan are adapted to the specifics and needs of each company, plant, or modules. At the same time, some activities are done concurrently.

5.5 CRITICAL SUCCESS FACTORS OF SPEED-BASED TARGET PROFIT PROGRAM

The critical success factors of the SBTP application are closely related to those of the visible increase of productivity (decreasing input and increasing output). Decreasing input refers to the reduction of inputs of all means of production that can be dispensed in one module and often moved to other modules where needed (raw materials, auxiliary materials, WIP, number of people, utilities, production spaces, and/or offices, etc.). Increasing output refers to increasing the use of capacities to obtain new quality outputs. Therefore, the basic purpose of SBTP is decreasing input and increasing output at the same time, or in other words the improvement of CLWs according to the probable sales scenarios, increasing or decreasing for the annual and especially multiannual KAIZENSHIRO fulfilment.

In the following discussion, we will summarize the points for the successful implementation of SBTP:

- *Real management commitment:* Real and strong managerial commitment, the active and visible participation of the top management team in establishing and supporting the SBTP program and maintaining a continuous desire for change toward achieving synchronous profitable operations with the help of a continuously improved production method are essential. Without the implementation of SBTP, managerial support for improvements often remains only declarative. With the help of SBTP, opportunities for improvement are visible at the money level and continuously provide the team of top managers with the opportunity to understand and be aware of the cash stakes of possible improvements. This continuous monetary sizing of non-productivity (CLW) helps managers be patient in thinking and effectively and efficiently improving CLWs and meeting their business expectations, including KAIZENSHIRO.

We often hear the statement that continuous productivity improvement is a primary need in manufacturing plants, but at the same time it is a difficult challenge. How can this difficult challenge be solved through the activities of all people who do not specialize in improving productivity? It is effective to use an experienced external consultant, and it is important for the consultant to state clearly and in detail what needs to be done to achieve the expected objectives. With extensive experience in addressing problems and productivity improvements, a consultant may propose productivity improvement advice and specific measures to visibly improve productivity. In fact, the experience of the consultant gained in going through many companies over the years is capitalized. By doing this, the company and managers will more easily accept the implementation of new things and the implementation of SBTP will run smoothly. Technically speaking, it is easy to understand how CLWs are sized and how the required level of KAIZENSHIRO is set, even people in the company can do this without problems, but it is more difficult to reach the full implementation of the control trilogy for KAIZENSHIRO. Therefore, without a real management commitment, possibly supported by a consultant, it is quite difficult to achieve organizational change and meet other success factors of SBTP (see Figure 5.6).

- *Clarification of purpose:* The implementation and consolidation of SBTP and the improvement of productivity will not be completed in a year or two. Therefore, it is essential that the team of managers understand what they are looking for. Objectives must be clear, narrow, and in order of priority. As mentioned above, the annual and multiannual fulfillment of KAIZENSHIRO is a very important goal. However, the purpose of improving productivity is often unclear. It should aim to consistently improve profit margin and ROI as a whole (see Figure 2.2). All people in the company and beyond must remain continuously focused on the annual objectives of the SBTP until they are met; then this focus remains valid year after year.

- *Choosing and implementing an effective promotion organization:* In retrospect, without the use of SBTP, productivity improvement was not based on the continuous quantification of CLWs and the continued visibility of non-productivity at the budget level (see Figures 3.27–3.29). Therefore, it is important to focus on the full implementation of the SBTP program so that the program is found

FIGURE 5.6
Critical success factors of speed-based target profit program.

in the daily tasks of each person in the company. The establishment of the control trilogy for KAIZENSHIRO provides a continuous targeting system for achieving the state of synchronous profitable operations. For these reasons, it is important to choose and implement a promotion and organization program so that small groups of people overlap, and small group leaders at each level of the manufacturing plant are members of other small groups of people from the next higher level. The top managers are such a small group. This approach to SBTP promotion and organization is very effective for deployment of manufacturing plant policy and goals throughout at every hierarchical level. At the same time, a person (or a group of 2–3 people) is designated responsible for the continuous internal visual communication of the SBTP program (tasks are: preparation of SBTP master plan, coordination of all activities and promotion actions, keeping track of all activities regarding implementation and development SBTP, dissemination of information, updating of information from CLW information center, keeping track of all Kaizen/Kaikaku projects to achieve annual KAIZENSHIRO, etc.).

- *Continuous measurement of CLW and CCLW:* When establishing the annual and multiannual level of KAIZENSHIRO, it is necessary to confirm the current level of CLWs and CCLWs or how much it is possible to effectively and efficiently improve productivity, in which modules, how long it is necessary (connection with ROI), for how long productivity improvements can be implemented with tangible results, and what resources are needed. Therefore, without such information, the promotion of the SBTP program is not very impactful. It is important to establish a detailed system for measuring losses and waste (see Tables 3.1–3.3) so that the results of improved productivity can be used effectively in concrete forms. The continuous awareness by top managers of the possible preventable CLW level is very important.

- *Improving productivity mind:* The management team must constantly strive to raise awareness among all people in the manufacturing plant and beyond to make improvements to CCLWs, provide everyone with the know-how to make improvements, and support everyone's efforts in this regard. An idea for improvement that comes up without knowing the know-how of improvement may sooner or later run out of results. In this context, the top management cannot expect an approach of continuous improvement of CLWs and implicitly of productivity. Therefore, it is desirable to continuously promote activities for measuring and improving CLWs and implicitly productivity, especially by top managers. Improving productivity mind is the essence of *KAIZENSHIRO culture* presented in the next section.

- *Top-down and bottom-up activities:* This approach refers to the responsibility of the top managers for the implementation of the measures to reach KAIZENSHIRO (top-down) and for the deep understanding of the feedbacks especially at the level of the shop floor (bottom-up). The choice of the most effective and efficient improvements and solutions to problems is made with the help of a catchball process until the requests from top managers can be met.

- *Correct and complete implementation of improvements:* One of the main desired effects of the previous success factors is the effective and efficient implementation of predictable CCLW improvement projects, with visibility in the annual and especially multiannual KAIZENSHIRO fulfillment. The members of the improvement project teams must clearly understand the necessary impact of the improvements in the expected performance. The proper implementation of the improvement projects is based on the correct understanding and application of improvement methodologies, tools and techniques, including PDCA and/or define, measure, analyze, improve, and control methodologies. The full implementation of improvements requires continuous synchronization between kaizen and/or kaikaku projects and company strategies. With the continuous measurement of the CLW level that can be avoided, at the level of each improvement project, the possible state in which the necessary resources are not allocated to the improvements at the right time is eliminated (this is one of the advantages of improvement budgets). In conclusion, only the correct (effective) and full (efficient) implementation of the improvements can contribute to supporting the use of SBTP to meet competitive challenges.

Therefore, these critical success factors of SBTP are found at all levels of a company, from top-down management to trenches, to support the effort to meet SBTP objectives.

5.6 KAIZENSHIRO CULTURE: IMPROVING PRODUCTIVITY MIND

The manufacturing plants have different types of losses and waste, different systems for determining costs and budgets, and different ways of approaching improvements and problems. However, it is important that losses and waste are eliminated, especially those that are expected to occur in the next period and especially those that can be addressed effectively and efficiently.

First of all, as presented in the previous section, it is important that for KAIZENSHIRO culture there is a clear commitment from top managers. But what is the KAIZENSHIRO culture? The KAIZENSHIRO culture refers to the beliefs and behaviors that determine how employees and the management of a company interact and address the goal of annual and multiannual reduction of predictable CCLWs. Often, the KAIZENSHIRO culture develops organically over time through improving productivity mind continuously supported by the team of managers. The KAIZENSHIRO culture is the culture of productivity improvements in which the target is always clearly defined and distributed at the level of each module or structure in the company, so that each person regardless of hierarchical level knows continuously his role for the fulfillment of the annual and multiannual KAIZENSHIRO (fulfillment of CCLW targets). KAIZENSHIRO culture will be reflected in the daily activities of all the people in the company in terms of their struggle with the targets set for CCLWs at the level of each module (see Figure 5.7).

FIGURE 5.7
KAIZENSHIRO culture for planning and developing synchronous profitable operations.

The elements in Figure 5.7 were discussed in detail in the previous sections, except for the concept of improving productivity mind. It is based on effective leadership and involves:

- visibility of real facts and data;
- continuously providing direction and providing everyone with the know-how to make improvements and problem-solving on CLWs;
- continuous stimulation of people's creativity by offering examples and helpful best practices;
- clear and visible planning of what is to be done (CLW/CCLW targets at the level of manufacturing plant and at the level of modules; expectations, strategies and managerial suggestions; allocated resources), of what has been done (the degree of achievement of the related targets KPIs of CLW; challenges) and of what remains to be done (with the specification of the deadline);
- expressing the need for help for fulfilling the CCLW targets and implicitly the annual KAIZENSHIRO; and
- searching for ideas in work groups through real involvement and active participation.

In this context, with the help of KAIZENSHIRO culture, the continuous direction toward obtaining the state of synchronous profitable operations becomes a way of life and an ethos with a high level of motivation for the continuous fulfillment of KAIZENSHIRO at all hierarchical levels.

5.7 CONCLUSION: THE PRODUCTION MANAGEMENT MUST LEAD THE SYNCHRONOUS PROFITABLE OPERATIONS

Therefore, for the SBTP approach, a three-phase control is required, starting with production planning and scheduling in order to visibly improve productivity and continuing with *concurrent controls* or CLW's daily management and with *feedback controls* or total synchronous profitable operations control.

The importance of day-to-day activities on mastering CLW has become necessary for the survival of manufacturing companies in a competitive

284 • *Speed-Based Target Profit*

world. The review of the role of manufacturing operators, supervisors, and managers and the control of the CLW level has become necessary. The establishment of leadership tasks, instruments, and behaviors is necessary to continuously support the KAIZENSHIRO culture.

In conclusion, in order to have a consistent approach to SBTP, a total involvement of production management is needed, which must lead the synchronous profitable operations. Establishing, sustaining, and continuously developing the skills needed to make a positive contribution to the company's expected results are essential. The continuous improvement of both people's knowledge and skills creates the premises for a learning organization. The implementation of SBTP must be done in a structured way based on a master plan adapted to the specifics of each company. Create safe and enjoyable work environments in which you involve the entire workforce in the ideal CLW (zero CLW) plan to support the KAIZENSHIRO culture.

Use SBTP to generate the expected profit because SBTP completes the production management function of each company, in particular the production planning and scheduling, continuous improvement and cost management functions, and it is compatible with any production system of any manufacturing company to transform the operations of the organization so that they concurrently and continuously meet the expectations of customers and those of long-term profit.

6

Speed-Based Target Profit Case Studies

This chapter presents the implementation of two real case studies on planning and developing synchronous profitable operations using the speed-based target profit (SBTP) mechanism more precisely.

- Case Study 1 at "AA Plant": SBTP for sales increase scenario (with an emphasis on maximizing outputs)
- Case Study 2 at "BB Plant": SBTP for sales decrease scenario (with an emphasis on minimizing inputs)

For each of the two case studies, the control trilogy for KAIZENSHIRO will be presented. The following will be discussed:

1. How to plan strategic improvements (*feedforward-driven control*; real systematic – kaizen and/or systemic – kaikaku) improvement projects;
2. How to implement the improvements and address the day-to-day issues of costs of losses and waste (CLWs) (*concurrent-driven control*; using the A3 technique); and
3. Verification of the production and improvements results (*feedback-driven control*) in order to be able to make decisions on the resumption of the trilogy for KAIZENSHIRO control cycle by developing feedforward-driven control for the next period.

6.1 CASE STUDY 1 AT "AA PLANT": SPEED-BASED TARGET PROFIT FOR SALES INCREASE SCENARIO

The main objectives of this application are to highlight the main actions and activities necessary for a harmonious transformation of the production flow through planning and developing synchronous profitable operations using SBTP in the scenario of predictable sales growth for the next period or, in other words, in the scenario of maximizing outputs mainly (by increasing equipment effectiveness to ensure external manufacturing target profit).

Therefore, this section presents a real application of SBTP to a manufacturing company (continuation of the example from "AA Plant" in Chapters 1–3).

The plant manager from AA Plant explained his need for SBTP approximately as follows:

> The capacity bottleneck process in our factory is the assembly line. To meet customer demand for small batch production (for different types of products), for optimal equipment loading and on-time delivery, the production line is functional with two day shifts and one night shift. Overtime and work during holidays are used to avoid delays in delivery to customers. Working hours are 8 hours per shift (60 minutes × 8 = 480 minutes) and one hour is allocated to the lunch break, leaving 7 hours of work. Approximately 30 minutes a day are allocated for meetings at the beginning and end of the program, cleaning, lubrication, and equipment inspection, absenteeism and holidays, etc. Therefore, the *actual loading time* is 390 minutes. Taking into account that the *standard cycle time* per product unit of 6.57 minutes, the theoretical production could be 60 units of product/shift/line (dividing 390 minutes by 6.57 minutes; 60 products). However, in reality, taking into account the *net standard operating time or net capacity* the average production records only 44 units/line during normal operating time. This means 74% of the amount of theoretical production. In order to achieve the annual and multi-annual profit plan and to meet customer demands, a minimum of 50 units per shift/line should be produced. Furthermore, he added: (1) the cost reduction has become a key issue for the company's survival and development lately as sales prices tend to fall and a cost reduction of at least 6% per year is needed in the next 5 years, and for some products the decrease should be higher to meet the expected profit target, (2) the cost of new equipment is becoming more expensive and we have problems keeping up with the latest production technologies (for example,

Industry 4.0), (3) even if we master the efficiency of labor, raw material and auxiliary material costs tend to increase, so as do the utilities, (4) the need to increase flexibility through minimal changeover times is increasingly pressing, (5) customer demands are fluctuating and there are situations of unforeseen change in production scheduling. In this context, as there is a need to increase the level of synchronization of the entire manufacturing flow to the needs of the market at the same time as increasing profitability, I am considering using SBTP to address these challenges.

6.1.1 Company Characteristics and Manufacturing System

Therefore, the information about AA Plant is as follows:

- It is a manufacturing company in the field of the automotive components;
- The manufacturing regime is the manufacturing and assembly industry – repeated lot;
- The main manufacturing modules are four in number;
- The bottleneck capacity module is the assembly line;
- There is only one family of products; and
- It already uses the manufacturing cost policy deployment (MCPD) system.

Until the use of SBTP at AA Plant, top management was mainly concerned with the following issues:

- reduction of production delivery time;
- cost reduction;
- reaching the target production volume;
- on-time delivery;
- availability of equipment and their optimal loading; and
- development of new unique and profitable products.

6.1.2 Requests from Headquarters and Top Managers for Implementing the SBTP Mechanism

The request for the introduction of SBTP was to create a production system through production planning, scheduling, and control to concurrently achieve the following two requirements:

- Mitigation and elimination of capacity gaps in each production module and continuous synchronization of modules to customer requirements; and
- Continuous synchronization of production to the need to fulfill the annual and multiannual profit plan.

Guided by the need to meet the annual and multiannual ROI targets, the request from headquarters was to reduce: (1) total plant lead time; (2) all categories of stocks; and (3) unit product costs.

The request from the top managers was to build a system that could accurately predict, maintain, and control the profitability and delivery time of an order from the moment of receiving the order from a customer and to be able to plan systematic and systemic improvements so as to prevent as much as possible the non-acceptance of orders due to lack of capacity and profitability. At the same time, the reduction of stocks, the reduction of the total plant lead time, the increase of the synchronization between plant lead time and delivery lead time, and the increase of the synchronization between operations were the requests of the top managers.

6.1.3 Problems Prior to Introducing SBTP

Following the review of the current state of the production system and the levels of productivity and profitability, the following problems were identified:

- Manufacturing lead time depended on the ability of the production department and had fluctuations; manufacturing lead time does not continuously synchronize with delivery lead time; there were fluctuations in the distances at the layout level; transfer times fluctuated – especially manual ones; the standard setup time was sometimes significantly exceeded; the time cycles had large fluctuations for certain products/in certain operations, etc.
- Production planning and scheduling sometimes accepted a larger volume of orders than the actual capacity in the bottleneck capacity module – assembly line; stocks of all kinds were larger than what was needed at a given time; some types of raw materials and auxiliary materials were at a much higher level than necessary; the actual stock was not known at all times.

- The synchronization between the assembly line and the upstream (or parallel) equipment was often deficient, which sometimes generated the lack of materials at the assembly line.
- The achievement of the profit was not reflected in the delivery term of the production for profitable products; production planning and scheduling was almost exclusively for customers and less for the company's profitability; standard cost levels were often exceeded, especially for special orders with small volumes; the acceptance of an order depended more on the production capacity and the possibility of timely delivery of the order and less on the real profitability in that period of the year of that order.
- The delivery time to customers was not synchronized with the delivery time of the assembly line (the last module in the manufacturing phase).
- The supply of the modules had fluctuations and was sometimes done with significant delays; the level of near to line inventory was fluctuating (sometimes it was too high and sometimes there were no landmarks).
- Work in progress (WIP) was often fluctuating and did not take into account the planned setup activities.
- Often production takt time was not synchronized with the activity of raw materials supply from the external suppliers.
- Sometimes the order of the orders from the assembly line was not the same as in the processing phase (based on the analysis of the daily load of the assembly line and based on the analysis of the daily tasks of the processing phase and the assembly phase).
- Sometimes the production continued outside the production plan.
- Sometimes the production continued even if defects were made.
- Sometimes the planning of setup activities was not observed and some setup activities for certain products did not meet the time standards.
- The production planners had in mind when planning the production the maximum speed previously obtained.
- Not all time was allocated in production planning for nonproductive hours (NOT engaged on production; engaged on production, but non-producing; see Figure 2.9).
- Planned and autonomous maintenance activities required standardization or re-standardization.

- There was no correlation between planning and results obtained.
- Sometimes the materials were already paid to the suppliers when they reached the assembly phase.

These problems were identified following the manufacturing lead time analysis (see Figure 6.1).

In addition to the observations and analyses by the consultants in SBTP, the intra-group benchmarking analyses and those related to the main competitors helped to identify the above problems. At the same time, in this first stage of the implementation of SBTP (phase one of SBTP: establishment – one month) the following activities were also carried out: establishing the SBTP team; promoting SBTP; introductory training in SBTP; establishing SBTP policy and goals; draft a master plan for implementation of SBTP; the KAIZENSHIRO level for the next period – request from top managers.

6.1.4 Defining Systemic Measures

Following the analysis of major problems at the level of the production system, regardless of the probable evolution of sales, increasing or decreasing, the following 11 measures to transform the manufacturing flow were defined. These measures underlie the subsequent, annual, and multiannual systematic (kaizen) and systemic (kaikaku) improvements in order to fulfill KAIZENSHIRO:

1. clear delimitation of areas of responsibility at the level of manufacturing flow;
2. understanding the current way of working at the level of physical areas (modules) and departmental; the behavior and constituent elements of each module (especially those aimed at involving several departments) were strictly observed;
3. innovative standardization of the working method for each module;
4. centralization of planning, scheduling, and control of production profitability and synchronization with customer requests;
5. re-standardization of the transport of raw materials, materials, and components for each module;
6. defining profitable target products and identifying their routes;
7. continuous measurement of the level of non-productivity by implementing KPIs related to losses and waste specific to AA Plant;

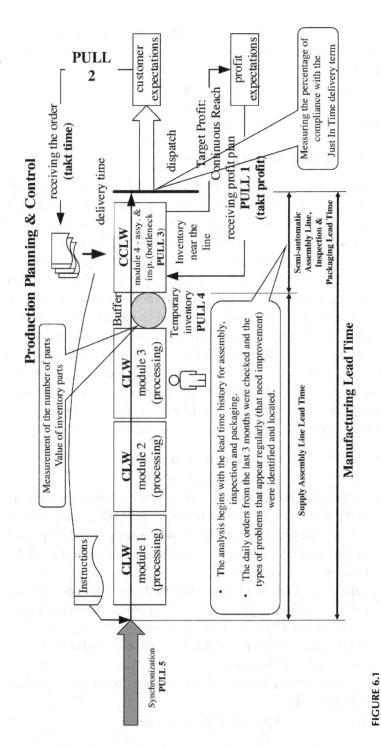

FIGURE 6.1
Manufacturing lead time at "AA Plant".

8. continuous measurement of the CLW level; the assembly line was both bottleneck capacity module and bottleneck profit module (in this phase the unique rate method was used);
9. making the waste deployment maps;
10. KAIZENSHIRO budgeting development; and
11. implementation of CLW's daily management.

6.1.5 Annual KAIZENSHIRO Design

As the increase in profit by increasing outputs [effectiveness, from 74% overall equipment effectiveness (OEE) to 85% OEE] is not enough to achieve the annual and multiannual target profit, it was also necessary to achieve increased manufacturing cost improvement (efficiency).

After understanding the profit need and customer requirements, AA Plant establishes the three target product groups ("A", "B", and "C"). All these types of products go through the four modules (three processing and one assembly and inspection – bottleneck capacity module same as bottleneck profit module; see Figure 1.3; some components are purchased from suppliers, others are made in AA Plant in parallel with the analyzed manufacturing flow). During the SBTP mechanism development meetings, in order to fulfill the annual profit plan in accordance with the multiannual profit plan, two phases are discussed mainly (the current state – A and the future state – B; see Section 2.2 of this book).

1. The current state of the previous period, such as:
   a. Profit per product in last period: $138;
   b. Takt profit established in the last period (in bottleneck capacity/profit module; the pace of profit demand): $138/6.57 minutes/unit;
      Note: Every 6.57 minutes of net processing production per unit in bottleneck capacity/profit module must generate a contribution profit per unit of $138.
   c. Takt time established in the last period (per month on a shift; in bottleneck capacity/profit module; the pace of customer demand): 10,798 minutes/1,643.5 units = 6.57 minutes (394 seconds)
      Takt time (daily on a shift) = 360 minutes/54.78 units = 6.57 minutes (394 seconds)
      Takt time (per hour) = 45 minutes/6.84 units = 6.57 minutes (394 seconds);
   d. The SBTP in last period: $ 20.99/minute;

2. Future state of the this period, such as:
   a. Profit per product in this period (see Figures 1.7, 1.8, 1.10, 1.12): $150;
   b. Setting the takt profit for this period (in bottleneck capacity/ profit module; the pace of profit demand): $150/5.33 minutes/ unit);

      Note: Every 5.33 minutes of net processing production per unit in bottleneck capacity/profit module must generate a contribution margin per unit of $150.
   c. Takt time established for this period (per month on a shift; in bottleneck capacity/profit module): 11,673 minutes/2,190 units = 5.33 minutes (320 seconds);

      Takt time (daily on a shift) = 389 minutes/73 units = 5.33 minutes (320 seconds)

      Takt time (per hour) = 48.6 minutes/9 units = 5.33 minutes (320 seconds)
   d. The SBTP for this period (next period): $28.14/minute

In order to achieve SBTP (takt profit and takt time), as sales trend is expected to increase as planned, ten improvement projects have been set up that will focus in particular on achieving the target for net processing production in bottleneck operation (to increase the average OEE for the next 12 months from 74% to 80%; including reducing cycle time from 394 seconds/unit to 320 seconds/unit by running a methods design concept (MDC) project for bottleneck operation; the rest of the OEE increase to 85% of current equipment is the target for next year), but also on the CLW.

Unit annual reduction target for CLW is $35 (see Figure 2.17). The estimated production volume for the next period is 78,840 units. KAIZENSHIRO for the next period is $2.759.400 ($35 × 78,840 units). For this, KAIZENSHIRO budgeting was developed for the next period (see Figure 3.27 as an example).

6.1.6 Countermeasures Using SBTP for Performing Synchronous Profitable Operations

In order to fulfill the profit plan for the next year, both by increasing sales and by fulfilling the annual KAIZENSHIRO, as the basis of the ten improvement projects, the following countermeasures were established for the following year (for setting improvement priorities please see Figures 2.14 and 2.15, at the same time the feasibility analysis of the chosen improvements was made):

a. reducing the time cycle of operations considered bottleneck of the assembly line (cost of line performance losses) – Kaizen project presented in the next section;
b. synchronization between the assembly line and a plastic parts painting equipment – the Kaizen project presented in the next section;
c. increase capacity by purchasing equipment – the Kaikaku project presented in the next section;
d. time reduction setup (cost of setup losses and costs of WIP from setup waste);
e. reduction of line transfer time (costs of WIP from transfer waste);
f. reduction of man × hour by product (cost of assembly line – human work losses);
g. reduction of maintenance costs and spare parts costs (cost of maintenance losses; cost of obsolete spare parts losses); and
h. reduction of costs for auxiliary materials and raw materials (cost of auxiliary consumables losses; and cost of material yield losses).

As the sales scenario is growing for the next period, to support the need to maximize outputs, the priorities for improvement will focus on points "a", "b", "c", and "d". The pursued objectives are: reduction of the lead time of the assembly line, increase in the OEE level of the assembly line, and reduction of the manufacturing lead time. These countermeasures, on the basis of which the improvements are chosen, are part of the *feedforward-driven control* – activity within the profitable production planning through SBTP.

6.1.7 Implementing Improvements and Solving Problems

Concurrently with the production, specific activities of *concurrent-driven control* are carried out – implementing improvements and solving problems. To support sales growth, out of the ten annual strategic improvement projects (for KAIZENSHIRO's $2,759,400 annual fulfillment, for production plan and profit plan fulfillment), we will present two systematic (kaizen) improvement projects and one systemic (kaikaku) improvement project. At the same time, we will present a project to solve CLW problems.

6.1.7.1 Improvement Project 1: Systematic Improvement (Kaizen) by Cycle Time Reduction at an Assembly Line

Therefore, the first Kaizen project refers to cycle time reduction at an assembly line. Of KAIZENSHIRO's total annual value of $2,759,400, this project will contribute 25%, respectively $690,000 [representing critical costs of losses and waste (CCLWs) throughout the flow; these CCLWs can be prevented from occurring in the next period]. After reaching the managers' consensus on the priorities in approaching the CCLWs, after a first brainstorming session to make a draft improvement plan, the kaizen project approach had four phase: (1) theme; (2) plan – targets; (3) action; and (4) results – effects.

1. *Theme:* Reduction of cycle time at an assembly line (bottleneck capacity/profit module) to meet 25% of the annual KAIZENSHIRO and to meet the need to support sales increase.

2. *Plan/Targets:* From the current data (already presented: current daily production capacity, current takt profit, current SBTP) and from the establishment of the necessary SBTP (already presented: daily production capacity required, required takt profit, required SBTP), the following information is known:
   • Current takt time: 394 seconds; and
   • Required takt time: 320 seconds.

   The duration of the project was set to be ten weeks to reduce the current cycle time of the bottleneck operations of the bottleneck capacity/profit module.

   The layout analysis of the assembly line was performed before the improvement. The cycle times of the 14 workstations were analyzed. All cycle times were identified and measured for transfers and machinery/robots. Following the preliminary measurements, four cycle times were identified (operations from 9 to 12; final test area) that needed improvement to achieve takt time and takt profit at the same time (see Figures 6.2 and 6.3).

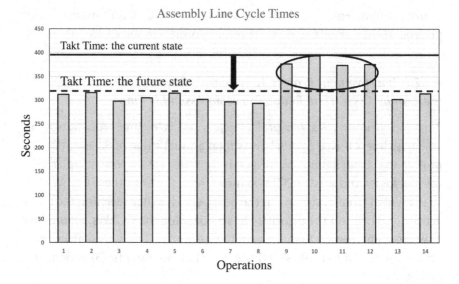

FIGURE 6.2

Identification of time cycles that need improvement for bottleneck capacity/profit module (semi-automatic assembly line) at AA Plant.

The annual KAIZENSHIRO budget was checked to see the impact of CCLW improvement through this kaizen project. The following activities were performed:

- The cost-benefit analysis was carried out in advance; the cost associated with the improvement was insignificant; the costs of improvement were mainly associated with the kaizen team hourly cost.
- The profitability of the lost opportunity to achieve production was assessed – the equivalence of the pieces for line cycle time reduction for bottleneck operations.
- The SBTP project team has carefully followed the KAIZENSHIRO budgeting cycle (the six steps described in Figure 3.28; see Figures 3.27 and 3.29).

The main tasks of the team were:

- to carry out an assessment of the current status of the assembly line;
- to check the current status of the CLW associated to cycle time at an assembly line (bottleneck capacity/profit module for the

Line name: 1
Date of measurement:
Process: Operation 9 - loading for functional testing (transfer time)

TIME

No.	Operating Procedure (work elements - order of movements)	Standard time	Actual time	Dif.
1	Moving carousel "x"	151	151	
2	Waiting	19	19	19
3	Connecting "y"	56	56	
4	Lifting "z"	38	38	
5	Product transfer	19	19	
6	Download "a"	56	56	
7	Withdrawal "b"	38	38	

Cycle Time (seconds) — Time Study axis: 150, 151, 152, ..., 170, 171, 172, ..., 225, 255, 256, 257, ..., 293, 294, 295, ..., 313, 314, 315, ..., 367, 368, 369, 370, ..., 377

Directions for improvement

No.	Elimination (E)	Combination (C)	Rearrangement (R)	Simplification (S)	Automation (A)	Digitization (D)	Motion	Walking	Release workload	Hand holding	Inspection	Waiting	Component	Instruments	Assembled piece	Conveyor	Opportunity	Action required	Effects (time – sec.)
1	X			X	X												o1	a1	20
2												X					o2	a2	19
3			X	X	X												o3	a3	17
4																			
5																			
6																			
7						X	X										o7	a7	15

FIGURE 6.3
Establish opportunities to improve CCLW for operation 9 (lift loading for functional testing – transfer cycle time) at the assembly line.

entire manufacturing flow analyzed) for operations identified as bottleneck;

- to prepare a plan of consistent measures to eliminate costs of line cycle time losses;
- to propose countermeasures for problems identified at the line cycle time level;
- to define new standards of work – new standard operating procedure (SOP); and
- to extend validated solutions to other similar conditions (if applicable).

3. *Action:* The four cycle times were marked on the line layout as follows:

- Operation 9: loading for the functional test (transfer cycle time); actions: study the times and movements for 377 seconds and identify the times that can be improved (see Figure 6.3);
- Operation 10: functional tests of the product (machinery cycle time); actions: following the study of times and movements for the 394 seconds, opportunities for improvement of only 34 seconds were identified; whereas the 320-second target was not met, it was decided to carry out an MDC project to redesign the method (establishing an innovative working method model; no investments); the activities were completed: establishing a model of the working method – defining inputs and outputs; defining the functions of all work contents – basic functions (BF) and auxiliary functions (AF); setting the design target as the value of improvement – KAIZENSHIRO at the micro level at the minimum level of 40 seconds; searching/creating ideas for improvement – extreme brainstorming; modifying and summarizing ideas as a concrete new method and implementing new methods as a new model. The MDC project was a complete success. Elements associated with auxiliary functions (AF) were identified in 33% of the 394 seconds (130 seconds). 60 seconds were chosen to be reduced, which were considered accessible and without investment. The implementation of the solutions was done on time and aimed at eliminating and combining the times of the new work elements related to the new product testing method;

- Operation 11: download from the functional test (transfer cycle time); actions: following the study of times and movements for the 374 seconds, improvement opportunities were identified for speed variators on the roller conveyor and the unloading time from the tester was reduced by reducing the lift ascent and descent time;
- Operation 12: transfer to the rotary table (transfer cycle time); actions: following the study of times and movements for the 376 seconds, opportunities for improvement were identified for variable speed drive on the conveyor chain and for variable speed drive on the roller table.

4. *Result:* Following the implementation of the solutions identified for reducing the cycle time of operations from 9 to 12 (final test area), both the required takt time of 320 seconds (see Figure 6.4) and the KAIZENSHIRO level of $690,000 related to this improvement were met. Output capacity was increased to 219 units (3 shifts × 73 units per shift) per day.

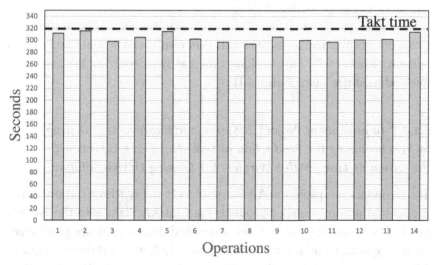

FIGURE 6.4
Operational results of improving the cycle time of the bottleneck capacity module (assembly line) at AA Plant.

The project team has performed the performance analysis of manufacturing improvement budgets targets and actual manufacturing budgets. The targets have been met. The team has performed the analysis of the performance of the cash flow improvement budgets targets and actual cash budgets. The targets have been met. Therefore, the cost of the improvements was not significant as they did not involve investments (the cost-benefit analysis was performed in advance; the cost associated with the improvement was insignificant; no material purchases were needed to make the improvements; the cost of the improvement was associated with the *kaizen* team hourly cost). The improvements were based on the innovative ideas of the project participants. The sponsor of the project was the engineering manager. The project team consisted of seven people (industrial engineering specialists, maintenance specialists, and operators; a project leader – industrial engineering specialist).

The project team carried out the evaluation of the line losses and waste performance indicators after implementing CCLW improvements (after 30 days, through specific activities of concurrent control – CLW's daily management and feedback control – total synchronous profitable operations control). The team leader of this project has conducted an evaluation of the degree of involvement of team members to achieve the CCLW improvement target of this project.

The default project duration of ten weeks was met (including implementation of improvement ideas, verification of results and benefits, and development of new SOP). Future plans aimed at synchronizing the assembly line and modules 3 (see Figure 6.1).

6.1.7.2 Improvement Project 2: Systematic Improvement (Kaizen) by Synchronizing the Production of Semi-Finished Products with the Assembly Line (With a Wireless IoT Sensing Device Solution)

The second kaizen project at AA Plant refers to the synchronization of the production of semi-finished products made at AA Plant with the assembly line in Figure 6.1 (some of the assembled components are purchased from suppliers, some are made in modules 1, 2, and 3 shown in Figure 6.1, and some parts are made in other areas of AA Plant). Therefore, this kaizen project of profitable synchronization refers to the synchronization between the components made in other areas of AA Plant and are assembled in the line shown in Figure 6.1 (the effects are visible at the level of cost of downtime losses).

Of KAIZENSHIRO's total annual value of $2,759,400, this project will contribute 18.5%, respectively $510,000 (representing CCLWs throughout the flow). The approach of the kaizen project will have four phases like the previous project: (1) theme; (2) plan – targets; (3) action; and (4) results – effects.

1. *Theme:* In the last 12 months, deficiencies of components claimed at the assembly line have been identified. In proportion of 85% are components made in own production – painted plastic parts. This delay resulted in 3,700 minutes of downtime at the assembly line. Of the total losses of the assembly line, these minutes represent 11.7% (76 events of finding deficiencies; four types of components represented 92% of the total deficiencies; these losses are included in non-productive hours – engaged on production, but non-producing; losses not included in the calculation of OEE; see Figure 2.9).

2. *Plan/Targets:* Elimination of all deficiencies (complaints) in the assembly lines caused by the lack of painted plastic parts made in own production (see Figure 6.5). The duration of the project was set to be 12 weeks. The project team consisted of seven people (specialists

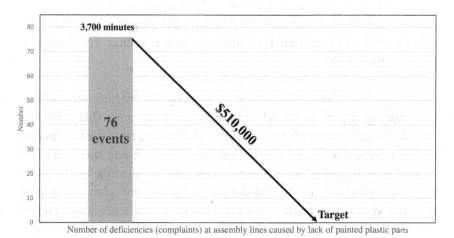

Number of deficiencies (complaints) at assembly lines caused by lack of painted plastic parts

FIGURE 6.5

Setting annual CCLW target for eliminating number of deficiencies (complaints) at assembly lines caused by lack of painted plastic parts (in the last 12 months).

in industrial engineering, maintenance specialists and operators in the areas of plastic injection and painting; a project leader – specialist in industrial engineering).

Again the team checked the annual KAIZENSHIRO budget to see the impact of CCLW improvement through this kaizen project. The following activities were performed:

- The cost-benefit analysis was carried out in advance.
- The profitability of the lost opportunity to achieve production target was assessed – the equivalent of the number of parts associated with the number of 3,700 minutes of inactivity at the assembly line.
- The project team has carefully followed the KAIZENSHIRO budgeting cycle.

The main tasks of the team were:

- to carry out an assessment of the current status of the assembly line and plastic injection and painting areas;
- to check the current status of the CLW associated with waiting for materials at an assembly line;
- to prepare a plan of consistent measures to eliminate costs of waiting for material losses;
- to propose countermeasures for problems identified at the assembly line and plastic injection and painting level areas;
- to define new standards of work in the painting area – new SOP; and
- to extend validated solutions to other similar conditions (if applicable).

3. *Action:* The flow of information regarding the distribution and processing of production scheduling for the equipment that made the painted plastic products was analyzed. Starting from the production planning that aimed at fulfilling both takt time and takt profit, the plastics injection department received every morning by email the daily production plan (the daily plastics injection plan was part of the weekly plan made in the previous week), the stock was prepared manually for each day at the beginning of each shift, and the orders were executed in the order established by production scheduling. At the same time, the plastic parts painting department received every morning by email the daily painting plan in correlation with

the plastics injection department. The WIP level between the plastic marking injection phase and the plastic marking painting phase was 12 hours. The WIP level between the plastic parts painting phase and the assembly line was 8 hours. At the end of each day, the production was reported. After analyzing the layout, the process parameters and the WIP in dynamics, it was concluded that the plastic parts painting department was the problem. The working method of the painting equipment was analyzed in detail with the help of the flow chart for the painted parts (conveyor length, painting installation sequences, speed, total cycle time, useful cycle time – of basic functions, types of painting, types of painted parts, types of scrap, types of rework) and the following losses have been identified:

- losses caused by the lack of clear evidence of the inventory of painted parts (physically and from the system): (1) in real time; and (2) at the time of transfer to the assembly line; and
- losses due to lack of real-time assembly line information: downtime (including setup time), scrap level, and rework level.

After identifying these losses, their detailed analysis was made in order to reach the root causes regarding the lack of parts caused by the lack of synchronization between the parts coming from the painting department and the assembly line. In this sense, a series of questions arose: Why were there those shortcomings at the assembly line? Why weren't the painted parts delivered to the assembly line on time? Why weren't the landmarks completed on time? Why weren't they planned to be done? Why does it take so long to find them in stock? Why didn't the scrap landmarks from the assembly line generate the adjustment of the work plan to the painting department? The conclusions of these causal analyses were: increasing the level of control of the painting and assembly line operations (concurrent-driven control) and the need to develop a real-time production tracking system (planned vs. performed; concurrent-driven control). The solutions chosen to be implemented were: real-time inventory control in the production management system (real-time control of inventory inputs and outputs); hourly control of the assembly line order and the painting inventory (hourly planning of the parts to be painted); real-time visibility of order prioritization, order scheduling, and assembly line scrap and rework level.

4. *Result:* The level of stocks between the painting department and the assembly line decreased from 8 hours to 0.5 hours (accepted as a required standard); real-time electronic stock control has been implemented for the minimum/maximum level for WIP; production scheduling is done automatically – based on the implementation of a wireless communication device with sensors between the assembly line and production scheduling in the painting area (KAIZENSHIRO's $510,000 target was met in the 12 weeks of the project by eliminating the 3,700 minutes of downtime at the assembly line caused by a lack of painted parts. The cost of the improvements was approved by management. The targets in the annual improvement budgets were met (the cost-benefit analysis was performed in advance). New SOPs were developed and training sessions on the new SOPs were planned and conducted.

The top management has decided to expand the use of wireless IoT sensing devices in order to track real-time product making, WIP level throughout manufacturing lead time, and continuously collect the level of losses and waste and to continuously know the level of CLWs and CCLWs.

The project team has performed the performance analysis of manufacturing improvement budgets targets and actual manufacturing budgets. The targets have been met. The team has performed the analysis of the performance of the cash flow improvement budgets targets and actual cash budgets. The targets have been met.

The project team carried out the evaluation of the line losses and waste performance indicators after implementing CCLW improvements (after 30 days, through specific activities of concurrent control – CLW's daily management and feedback control – total synchronous profitable operations control). The team leader of this project has conducted an evaluation of the degree of involvement of team members to achieve the CCLW improvement target of this project.

6.1.7.3 Improvement Project 3: Systemic Improvement (Kaikaku) by Increasing Capacity through the Purchase of New Equipment

This kaikaku project at AA Plant refers to the increase of production capacity in processing module 1 (see Figure 6.1). The effects were visible at the cost of downtime losses in modules 2 and 3 and in the assembly line.

Of KAIZENSHIRO's total annual value of $2,759,400, this project will contribute 8.5%, respectively $234,500 (representing CCLWs throughout the flow). The kaikaku project approach will also have four phases like the previous kaizen projects: (1) theme; (2) plan – targets; (3) action; and (4) results – effects.

1. *Theme:* Taking into account the planned increase in production volume, the cutting capacity of module 1 can no longer be ensured through systematic (kaizen) improvements. It is necessary to change the cutting equipment with a new one. The new equipment must cover the capacity of modules 2 and 3 and the released capacity of the assembly line through the two previous kaizen projects, be more flexible (a shorter setup time) and fit into the layout of the module 1 area.

2. *Plan/Targets:* A project team of eight people was formed (an industrial engineering specialist, two maintenance specialists, an operator, a procurement specialist, a cost specialist, and a project leader – industrial engineering specialist). All the targets necessary to be met by the new equipment have been set, namely: cycle time, OEE, setup, labor, scrap, investment cost, and time to production (time to start production).

   The team checked again the annual KAIZENSHIRO budget to see the impact of CCLW improvement through this kaizen project. The following activities were performed:
   - The cost-benefit analysis was carried out in advance.
   - The profitability of the lost opportunity to achieve production target was assessed.
   - The project team has carefully followed the KAIZENSHIRO budgeting cycle – the degree of equipment load and feasibility of the investment (see Figure 2.20).

   The main tasks of the team were:
   - to carry out an assessment of the current status of the cutting equipment;
   - to check the current status of the CLWs associated with obsolute equipment loss (see Table 3.3); and
   - to prepare a plan for removing the old equipment and introducing the new one – minimum lead time as a goal (or minimum time to production).

3. *Action:* Three offers from suppliers were analyzed. The supplier selection criteria were: production capacity, operating costs after installation and purchase cost (life cycle cost), flexibility (setup time), ease of maintenance, operational safety, installation time, etc. The best supplier was chosen.

4. *Result:* The $234,500 KAIZENSHIRO target was met in 16 weeks of the project. The cost of the improvements was approved by the management. The targets in the annual improvement budgets were met (the cost-benefit analysis was performed in advance). New SOPs were developed for the new equipment and training sessions on the new SOPs were planned and conducted.

The project team has performed the performance analysis of manufacturing improvement budgets targets and actual manufacturing budgets. The targets have been met. The team has performed the analysis of the performance of the cash flow improvement budgets targets and actual cash budgets. The targets have been met.

The project team carried out the evaluation of the new equipment losses and waste performance indicators after implementing CCLW improvements (CLW's daily management and feedback control). The team leader of this project has conducted an evaluation of the degree of involvement of team members to achieve the CCLW improvement target of this project.

6.1.7.4 Improvement Project 4: Problem-Solving Project for CLW (A3 for Elimination of Functional Testing Errors)

Concurrently with the development and implementation of solutions for kaizen and kaikaku projects (activities associated with *feedforward-driven control* – at the decision level, but carried out during production), projects are carried out to solve problems related to CLWs (activities assimilated to *concurrent-driven control*; by A3 technique).

Figure 6.6 shows an A3 project for the elimination of identification errors of "X" type products tested in the laboratory to reduce the functional testing time.

The elimination of human errors in the identification of defective products in the laboratory testing phase had positive effects in terms of

Problem Solving A3 for CLW improvement (results area: productivity and quality)

Author:	Project leader: AAP, members: SP and AP	President:
Dept:	Quality	Vice President:
Date:	April 15th – May 22nd	Manager: EAP

Theme: Elimination of identification errors of "X" type products tested in the laboratory to reduce the functional testing time

Problem Situation:

Background: Functional testing of "X" products in the test lab takes a long time. Within the daily monitoring report of the tested products in the test laboratory (visible at the activity panel module - assembly line; at the activity of the functional test laboratory module and in shift handover report of CLW / CCLW) the series of products and basic performances are continuously recorded of them.

Standard: The operator manually notes the series of products in a register and then transfers them to the database on the computer.

Current Situation: Sometimes there are errors in registering the tested products in the test laboratory; the series of products from the laboratory database do not coincide with the series of products entered in the finished products warehouse (visible in the end-of-month report).

Discrepancy: Number of errors: 45 in March; 49 in April and 17 in May; average minutes lost per month 450 minutes; cost of quality testing losses (CCLW) is $ 28,500 per month; (CCLW is $ 342,000 per year;

Extent: Elimination of identification errors of tested products;

Rationale: Zeroing down the identification errors of the tested products

Target:

Do What: Review the testing process
To What: Identification of all types of errors and solutions to eliminate them
How Much: Zero identification errors of the tested products
By When: April 15th year "N"

Cause Analysis:

Potential Causes:	How What Checked:	Results:
1) the operator does not correctly associate the product series with the test station number	1) identifying the series of products that did not enter the warehouse of finished products from the end of the month report	1) Differences in SAP
2) the series is misspelled;		

Problem:
Discrepancies in the identification of tested products and the stock of finished products at the end of the month.

Root cause:
1) Human errors in identifying tested products

Countermeasures:

Short Term: Strengthening the control of the identification of the tested products

Long Term: Use of magnet cards on which a barcode with the test station number is printed.

Why Recommended: Purchase a fixed scanner for barcode scanning (product series / card series).

Implementation:

WHAT	WHO	WHEN	ACTUAL	REASON
1.) Making cards with test station numbers (in your own workshop)	Head of workshop	April 25 year "N"	done	
2.) Barcode printing	Production team leader	May 10 year "N"	done	
3.) Panel making for magnetic cards	Head of workshop	May 10 year "N"	done	
4.) Purchase a fixed barcode scanner	Procurement team leader	May 10 year "N"	done	
5.) Operator training was conducted on how to use the scanning devices	Production team leader	May 20 year "N"	done	
6.) -				
7.) -				

Follow-up:

How / When Check:
1.) 30-day verification of the effectiveness of the scanning system

Recommendations:
1.) Development of standard maintenance of the scanning system

actual (45 events per month - average)

50	
45	
40	
35	
30	
25	
20	
0	March — June

target

FIGURE 6.6

Elimination of identification errors of "X" type products tested in the laboratory to reduce the functional testing time.

reducing lead time for laboratory testing and in terms of reducing stocks of finished products in the warehouse.

6.1.8 The Main Challenges of Implementing the SBTP Mechanism

For AA Plant, defining sales scenarios for each product, increasing or decreasing – to ensure the target profitability level based on productivity, modifying conventional cost and budget approach, more precisely identifying the CLWs and building budgets to present CLWs in their structure at the level of each modules and product, articulation of company's KPIs with SBTP specific KPIs (KPIs of losses and waste) is the relatively simple part of the restructuring. Changing the attitudes of all people and achieving their commitment – especially top managers, reducing their resilience to presenting CLWs and the correct, complete, and timely implementation of profitable kaizen and kaikaku projects to achieve annual KAZIENSHIRO goal is much more difficult to achieve. However, without the involvement and trust of all employees in all departments and beyond, setting targets and means for CLWs at the level of each module (especially for bottleneck capacity/profit module – assembly line) to achieving annual and especially multiannual KAZIENSHIRO targets and the means associated with achieving these targets is practically impossible to achieve. What measures have managers taken to achieve real employee engagement? AA Plant have succeeded in successfully implementing the SBTP mechanism due to the fact that managers have gone over autocratic barriers and have replaced them with a system of total involvement of all the people in the company and beyond, and have emphasized this way on the manufacturing flow and on CLW. First, the plant managers fully supported the SBTP program. Second, under the guidance of the SBTP consultant, interdepartmental teams were formed to determine the annual and multiannual KAZIENSHIRO and targets for KPIs of losses and waste were cascaded down to individual modules, departments, operations, and every employee was familiar with them, to consistently address the bottleneck capacity/profit module analysis to determine the behavior of losses and waste, associated CLWs and CCLWs at the level of modules in order to direct the scientific setting of targets and means for KAIZENSHIRO, to address the cost reduction at budget and balance sheet levels by using multiannual and annual manufacturing improvement budgets, to present the way of monitoring and continuously improving the

SBTP mechanism using the control trilogy for KAIZENSHIRO. Third, managers immediately applied annual KAZIENSHIRO means based on an effective catchball process. Finally, all employees actively participated in the correct, complete, and timely implementation of profitable kaizen and kaikaku projects to achieve the annual KAZIENSHIRO. The last two elements, the real involvement of managers and the active participation of all employees in the company, and of all entities and individuals beyond the company often convinced the staff that management was fully committed and that their suggestions for annual means targets are of great importance.

6.1.9 Conclusion

Often, managers are making the following statements: "We have reduced our costs to the most in the previous years and costs can no longer be reduced" or "Show me the money earned from kaizen projects and real cost reduction at budget and balance sheet level". Therefore, the reasons for joining SBTP mechanism are mainly related to the need to move from a conventional cost and budget approach and from an improvement approach based mainly on time and quality, to improving the way of consistently reducing unit manufacturing costs and increasing the use of current and future production capacities to ensure annual and, above all, multiannual target manufacturing profit, regardless of the sales volume.

6.2 CASE STUDY 2 FROM "BB PLANT": SPEED-BASED TARGET PROFIT FOR SALES DECREASE SCENARIO

The main objectives of this application are to highlight the main actions and activities necessary for a harmonious transformation of the production flow through planning and developing synchronous profitable operations using SBTP in the scenario of foreseeable decrease in sales for the next period or, in other words, in the scenario of minimizing inputs in principal (by reducing the CLW for production costs and CLW for production control, see Figure 1.15 and Tables 3.2 and 3.3, to ensure internal manufacturing target profit).

Therefore, this section presents a real application of SBTP in the first year at BB Plant for a pilot area (zone "A" with two production lines).

BB Plant is a manufacturing company that is processing in the food field, with a continuous manufacturing regime, and whose main goals are to extend the number of days of continuous manufacturing, improve shutdown efficiency, and save energy and improve profitability.

6.2.1 Background to Developing SBTP

The plant manager from BB Plant explained his need for SBTP approximately as follows:

> We have two identical production lines in area "A" with two day shifts and one night shift. Our bottleneck process for these two lines is the "G" process, and maintenance is what creates the most problems. Now sales are declining and the emphasis is on preventive maintenance to move production to just one line. But, unfortunately, it is difficult to eliminate the sporadic fall of the line. In our factory we have made a rule to record downtime on the line and equipment falls in the production hall of more than 10 minutes due to sporadic falls. If we look at the historical records, the sporadic falls in the "G" process on both lines is on average 30 minutes/shift/line during normal working hours. In addition to the sporadic falls, there are also line stops for setups and adjustments. The working hours are 8 hours per shift (60 minutes × 8 = 480 minutes) and 45 minutes are allocated to the lunch break, leaving 435 minutes of work. Approximately 35 minutes a day are allocated for meetings at the beginning and end of the program, cleaning, lubrication, and equipment inspection, absenteeism and holidays, etc. Therefore, the *actual loading time* is 400 minutes. Although the *standard cycle time* to produce a product is 0.3 minutes, the *actual measured cycle time* is 0.4 minutes. This means that if the 400 minutes of loading time were fully used, the production of 1,000 units of products/shift/line could be possible. The daily production could be 3000 units per day (cumulated in the 3 shifts). However, our production is only 1,650 units per day (cumulated in the 3 shifts; 550 units per shift for each line).

Then the maintenance manager expressed his point of view as follows:

> Even if 60 minutes were caused by downtime due to falls or setups and adjustments, the production could be considered 850 units product/shift (400 minutes − 60 minutes = 340 minutes; 340 minutes/0.4 minutes per product = 850). However, our production which is only 550 units per shift tends to decrease even more, but we still use two production lines. I think

there are many minor stops and many other causes of declining sales volume. Our forecast of capacity needs for the products made by the two lines in zone "A", according to the sales forecasts, are 400 products per shift/line. If we could keep the *standard cycle time* and eliminate many of the other losses, then we could make this production with only one line. The second line, with some small transformations that do not require major investments, could make "V" type products for which there is demand from customers and they are profitable.

Therefore, the challenge for BB Plant is to move the planned production to two production lines on one and to increase the profitability of the products made on the remaining line.

6.2.2 Establishment of Continuous Measurement Indicators for CLW and KAIZENSHIRO Design

The types of losses and waste specific to the two lines at BB Plant and for each of the six modules of the lines were discussed and agreed. Losses and waste were monitored for a period of three months. In parallel, the cost calculation and budgeting system was analyzed to establish the connections between losses and waste, modules and processes.

Following the CLW, measurement for each module were identified: module "G" is bottleneck capacity module (BCM) and module "B" is bottleneck profit module (BPM; mainly material loss costs and depreciation cost of machinery are much larger than in the other modules).

The main phenomena causing CLWs were determined as follows:

- The sales plan used target sales values while the manufacturing plan was coordinated by the past results of the main product categories; many stock issues stemmed from this.
- Production load and production capacity were not fully coordinated, which generated an excess of capacity in production scheduling (not all products scheduled to be made were possible to make); moreover, the scheduling of the batches was deficient because in the production scheduling only the total production volumes were known – which determines a difficulty in planning the setup activities (some batches were too big) and frequent changes of the production plan; at the same time, there were frequent delays in delivering orders to customers and the impossibility of complying with the standard level of stocks.

- Poor control of warehouse inventory (products and row material) leads to uncertainty regarding inventory allocations for production orders and deliveries of finished products; not all stocks were needed for a foreseeable period of time.
- Supply lead time often had delays which determines downtime for the two lines.

Following the analysis of losses and waste and the CLW, the following feasible opportunities emerged:

- The need to decrease material stock days;
- The need to decrease WIP;
- The need to decrease material handling;
- The need to decrease rework;
- The need to decrease production cost – especially direct material cost and direct labor cost;
- The need to decrease breakdown and setup times; and
- The need to decrease man × hour by product – manual processes cycle time.

Following the measurement of CLWs for each module, CCLWs were defined to contribute to the annual fulfillment of KAIZENSHIRO of $1,850,000 for the two lines. Eight kaizen projects were chosen to increase the capacity of line 1 (to support the relocation of the entire production from line 2 to line 1). In order to address the opportunities identified by measurements and to reach the annual KAIZENSHIRO for the two lines, it was decided to implement SBTP to support the achievement of synchronous profitable operations (takt time and takt profit concurrently).

6.2.3 Promotional Organization for Introducing Speed-Based Target Profit

The top managers of BB Plant agreed with the following four main activities regarding the promotional organization of SBTP:

- *Top managers to be considered project leaders*: Top managers have fully understood that their full involvement is essential to the success of the SBTP project – at least in the pilot project phase. In addition to the day-to-day management of operations, managers went on to support the SBTP project by planning project activities on time, in accordance with company policy, by ensuring the necessary time for employees to participate in improvements, by providing all material and informational resources needed for improvements, etc. By involving the team of top managers, it seeks to provide an understanding of the needs for change and the changes themselves by everyone in the company and beyond, to eliminate suspicions and to provide confidence in the direction and objectives of change (purpose is to reduce and eliminate CLWs and not a struggle with people), to eliminate anxiety, and to encourage proactive action and the courage to think differently about how to work. After the 12-month pilot project period, it was decided to appoint a project leader.

The tasks of *project leaders* mainly include:
- operational and budgetary planning;
- planning and collecting CLWs;
- establishing the annual KAIZENSHIRO;
- planning and continuous development of the control trilogy for KAIZENSHIRO;
- verifying CCLWs and planning convergent improvement projects toward the fulfillment of KAIZENSHIRO and other annual and multiannual objectives (BB Plant used the causality method to establish CCLWs);
- acting as project supervisors;
- ensuring the control, monitoring, evaluation, and reporting of the KAIZENSHIRO budget;
- ensuring the control, monitoring, evaluation, and reporting of CLW's daily management;
- collaboration with all people in the company and other entities outside the company; and
- ensuring that project team members work effectively and efficiently internally and externally.

- *Project team members*: During the pilot project, project members will carry out promotion and improvement activities in addition to their basic daily activities. Subsequently, the members of the project team will be appointed to deal exclusively with the project activities.

Therefore, project members must have expertise in the area of improvements. They must have a great capacity for analysis and innovative thinking. Smaller teams have been designated to address specific products and the bottleneck capacity module and bottleneck profit module.

- *Top-down and bottom-up activities*: The implementation of productivity growth measures for the continuous support of KAIZENSHIRO and other objects of the company is the responsibility of top managers. The top managers need to provide strong leadership in setting goals for improving CLWs, studying proposals for improving CCLWs, and providing support in implementing the proposed solutions. The management consultants can provide a clearer direction of project activities. The meetings of top managers (top-down) and the meetings for the implementation of SBTP (bottom-up; including those on improvement projects) are held every month. The results of the discussions are made public at the CLW information center and module activity panel level. Between the two meetings, a *catchball process* is created that must reach a uniformity of decisions and actions. The top managers will not go into all the details of the proposed topics. The decisions made by senior management do not have to be concerned with all the details.

- Development of SBTP master plan: The top managers from BB Plant (project leaders in the first 12 months) together with the members of the project team, under the guidance of a management consultant, developed the SBTP master plan for the next three years. This master plan aimed to establish the activities for each module in the company to support the fulfillment of synchronous profitable operations.

6.2.4 Choosing and Implementing Improvements

Concurrently with the production, specific activities of *concurrent-driven control* are carried out: implementing improvements and solving problems. As I said before, the challenge for BB Plant is to move the already planned production on two production lines to one and to increase the profitability level of the products made on the remaining line. For this and for sustaining the target profit level in conditions of decreasing sales, eight annual strategic improvement projects were identified (for the annual fulfillment of KAIZENSHIRO of $1,850,000 for the two lines, of the production plan and of the profit plan). We will present two systematic improvement projects (kaizen) and a systemic improvement project (kaikaku) - out of the eight improvement projects (implementation of feedforward-driven control). At the same time, we will present a project to solve the problems regarding CLWs (concurrent-driven control).

6.2.4.1 Improvement Project 1: Systematic Improvement (Kaizen) by Eliminating Idling and Minor Stoppages

This kaizen project from BB Plant refers to the elimination of small stops of line 1 (the line on which production moves from line 2). These small stops are in proportion of 7% in the OEE calculation of line 1 and of the total annual value of KAIZENSHIRO of $1,850,000 for the two lines; this project will contribute 14.6% and, respectively $270,000 (representing CCLWs along the entire flow at the level of 12 months). The approach of the kaizen project will have four phases: (1) theme; (2) plan – targets; (3) action; and (4) results – effects.

1. *Theme:* Reduction of idling and minor stoppages of the movement and guidance of the packaging operations of the products of line 1 to meet 14.6% of the annual KAIZENSHIRO and to facilitate the relocation of production from line 2 to line 1 amid declining sales volumes. The packaging module was considered a bottleneck capacity module.

2. *Plan/Targets:* From the current data (current daily production capacity, maximum load capacity, current takt profit, current SBTP) and from the establishment of the necessary SBTP (daily production capacity required, required takt profit, required SBTP) the following information is known (see Figure 6.7):
   - The number of idling and minor stoppages cumulated for February and March were 270 events (153 events in February; 117 events in March) with a total of 2,600 minutes accumulated (in February a number of 1,560 minutes was accumulated; in March a number of 1,040 minutes were accumulated); number of idling and minor stoppages were measured daily and mean time between failures (MTBF) and mean time to repair (MTTR)

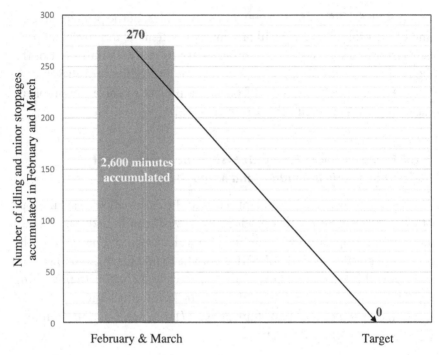

FIGURE 6.7
The number of idling and minor stoppages of the packing area.

were also established; for each intervention two operators were needed; the average duration of an intervention was ≈ 10 minutes.

• A lost opportunity to achieve production of 6,500 products (2,600 minutes/0.4 minutes on a current time cycle).

The duration of the project was set to be five weeks for the identification of solutions (most of the time was allocated to problem definition and process analysis) and another six weeks for the implementation of solutions. A team of five people was formed (mostly operators) a project leader and was named. The food packaging process is driven and guided by a translational movement by means of a ratchet chain consisting of: (1) drive mechanism; and (2) guide mechanism (fork). Stopping the packaging process in predefined places is done by means of stoppers positioned on the track. The project team analyzed the maximum load of the packaging process, the positioning of the guideway rollers, the speed of the line, the capacity of the electric motor, the causes of overloads on the ratchet chain, the triggering elements of the electric motor stop, the drive mechanism (the bolt that drives the ratchets on the chain), etc. The map with the locations of the stoppers was made – default of small stops. The main concern of the team was the problems of faulty guidance of the articulated arms of the stepper that ensured the actuation of the drive bolt in the chain (large variations in the joints).

The annual KAIZENSHIRO budget was checked to see the impact of CCLW improvement through this kaizen project.

So, the main tasks of the team were:

- to carry out an assessment of the current status of the assembly line in the packaging module;
- to check the current status of the CLWs associated to idling and minor stoppages in assembly line (bottleneck capacity module);
- to prepare a plan of consistent measures to eliminate costs of line idling and minor stoppages losses; and
- to propose countermeasures for problems identified.

3. *Action:* The analysis of the problem began with the analysis of the drive mechanism. It has been identified that a screw is unscrewed due to tamponade, which causes continuous contact between the bolt and the chain. In order to eliminate the random fluctuations of the stopper, a solution was sought to change the way the bolt is attached to the drive chain. The final solution was to build a new stopper in the plant's own workshop. For the development of the new stopper, all the elements necessary to establish the standard loading level and the line speed in the packing module were analyzed.

4. *Result:* Following the implementation of the solution of using a new stopper, the KAIZENSHIRO level of $270,000 related to this improvement was met because the number of idling and minor stoppages reached zero. The cost of the improvements was not significant as no large investments were involved (the cost-benefit analysis was performed in advance).

The project team carried out the evaluation of the line losses and waste performance indicators after implementing CCLW improvements (after 30 days, through specific activities of concurrent control – CLW's daily management and feedback control – total synchronous profitable operations control). The team leader of this project has conducted an evaluation of the degree of involvement of team members to achieve the CCLW improvement target of this project. The total duration of the project was 11 weeks.

Note: Four other improvement projects aimed to increase line effectiveness to support the transition of entire production from line 2 to line 1.

6.2.4.2 Improvement Project 2: Systematic Improvement (Kaizen) by Reducing Raw Material Leaks

This Kaizen project from BB Plant refers to the reduction of the consumption of raw material "X" in the area of the bottleneck profit module (module "Y") of line 1 (the line on which the production moves from line 2). This project was chosen to support the reduction of unit costs and, implicitly, the possibilities of price reduction without affecting the level of the annual target profit, but on the contrary. Of KAIZENSHIRO's total annual value of $1,850,000 for the two lines, these unnecessary consumption of raw materials, cost of material yield losses, will contribute $75,000 (at the level of 12 months). The approach of the kaizen project will have four phases: (1) theme; (2) plan – targets; (3) action; and (4) results – effects.

1. *Theme:* Four points were identified in which the unnecessary consumption of raw material was made. The theme of the improvement was reducing the consumption of raw material "X" in the area of the "Y" mode.
2. *Plan/Targets:* From the current data (current daily production capacity, maximum load capacity, current takt profit, current SBTP) and from the establishment of the necessary SBTP (daily production capacity required, required takt profit, required SBTP) it has reached the need to decrease from 1.5 kg (weighing done during three shifts) to 0.8 kg per 100 kg of processed raw material. In addition to reaching KAIZENSHIRO, the effects of this reduction would be: shortening the "A" raw material leakage removal time and increasing the quality level by reducing or eliminating "A" raw material in products that do not contain "A" raw material in their recipes.

   The duration of the project was set to be three weeks for the identification of solutions (most time was allocated for the analysis and establishment of solutions) and another four weeks for the implementation and verification of solutions. A team of four people (mostly operators) was formed and a project leader was appointed.

The annual KAIZENSHIRO budget was checked to see the impact of CCLW improvement through this kaizen project.

So, the main tasks of the team were:

- to carry out an assessment of the current status of the assembly line in the "Y" mode area (bottleneck profit module);
- to check the current status of the CLWs associated to cost of material yield losses;
- to prepare a plan of consistent measures to eliminate cost of material yield losses; and
- to propose countermeasures for problems identified.

3. *Action:* The 4 points ("a", "b", "c", and "d") were analyzed in which the raw material leaks "X" are manifested in order to identify the causes and the landmarks/subassemblies of the line in the area of the "X" mode which influences the leakage of raw material "X". The causes identified were:

- For point "a": a plastic flap that sometimes remained half-open;
- For point "b": a lid that sometimes was not completely closed by the operators;
- For point "c": the excess of raw material determines the intervention of the operator and implicitly a higher consumption of raw material "X"; and
- For point "d": the cleaning system of the equipment was not effective and sometimes there were traces of raw materials that did not allow the sealing of a container.

The team performed the elimination, combination, rearrangement, simplification (ECRS) analysis for value and non-value operations and solutions were sought to eliminate the causes of the four points of unnecessary consumption of raw material "X". The solutions chosen and implemented were:

- For point "a": redesign of the plastic flap;
- For point "b": operator training;

- For point "c": checking the process parameters with a higher frequency (SOP adjustment) and operator training; and
- For point "d": redesign of cleaning system and change of daily cleaning method (5S).

4. *Result:* Following the implementation of the four solutions, the KAIZENSHIRO level of $270,000 was reached and exceeded. The target for reducing unnecessary consumption has been exceeded and reached a level of 0.4 kg per 100 kg of processed raw material. The cost of the improvements was not significant as they did not involve large investments (the cost-benefit analysis was performed in advance).

The project team carried out the evaluation of the line losses and waste performance indicators after implementing CCLW improvements (after 30 days, through specific activities of concurrent control – CLW's daily management and feedback control). The team leader of this project has conducted an evaluation of the degree of involvement of team members to achieve the CCLW improvement target of this project. The total duration of the project was seven weeks.

6.2.4.3 Improvement Project 3: Systemic Improvement (Kaikaku) by Product Redesign

This kaikaku project from BB Plant refers to the reduction of unit costs of the product "P1" made on lines 1 and 2. Against the background of declining sales, at the request of the marketing department, the price of product "P" should be 34% lower to be competitive and to ensure target sales volumes. The need to increase sales and production volumes for the product "P1" determined the capacity analysis of line 1 (the line that will absorb the production volumes of line 2). Therefore, it has become necessary to redesign the product "P1" to reduce unit costs and also to identify opportunities to increase net capacity at line 1 (especially by reducing time cycles; see Figure 2.9).

The contribution of this improvement project to the annual KAIZENSHIRO of $1,850,000 for the two lines was $95,000 (at the level of 12 months), by optimizing the load of line 1, by increasing the net capacity at line 1, by reducing the unit costs of the product "P" and by reducing the CLWs of the current "P1" compared to the new "P1". The kaikaku project approach had four phases: (1) theme; (2) plan – targets; (3) action; and (4) results – effects.

1. *Theme:* Reduction of unit costs of the product "P1" by 35% (cost of ingredients and cost of processing) to ensure both the level of competitiveness required by the marketing department amid declining sales volumes and the optimal loading of line 1 with a low level of scrap.
2. *Plan/Targets:* Following the benchmarking analysis on the future market of the product "P1", it was concluded that the product "P1" will be the best-selling and most profitable product made on line 1 and, consequently, will ensure a 55% load of line 1 (other four products are made on line 1). Targets were analyzed and set for: target markets of the future product and potential sales volumes for each market, required level of raw material cost, required level of processing costs, required level of investment, time to market, required level of productivity (man × hour by product) and quality features. The current "P1" product was the reference for the new "P1" product.

   The duration of the project was set to be 12 weeks for the identification of solutions (most time was allocated for product implementation/trial planning). A team of six people was formed (from the departments: product development, marketing specialist, industrial engineering, quality control, team leader production line 1, cost specialist) and a project leader from the product development department was appointed.

   The annual KAIZENSHIRO budget was checked to see the impact of CCLW improvement through this kaikaku project.

   So, the main planned tasks of the team were:
   - performing the benchmarking analysis for the potential market of the "P1" product;
   - to carry out an assessment of the current status of the assembly line 1;
   - the needs for redesigning line 1 were analyzed (new line layout was established); and
   - to check the current status of the CLWs of the current product "P1" and which have a potential to manifest at the level of the new product "P1".

3. *Action:* The main activities of the project team were:

- defining the main competitors and defining the new product (low cost product for the purchasing power of future customers in the target markets);
- defining the new key characteristics of the future product to support the perceived value required by marketing (quality function deployment – QFD was performed);
- defining the costs of the basic and auxiliary functions of the new product (cost tables have been developed);
- estimating the selling price, cost and profit (target price – target profit = target cost);
- the feasibility study of the new product was performed (analysis of estimated volumes and profitability vs. the level of investment required);
- defining time to market for a new P1;
- defining the necessary solutions for redesigning three points of line 1 to reduce cycle time in order to increase the productivity of line 1 and reduce unit transformation costs (especially the cost of depreciating the line per unit of product);
- realization of first product design and product prototype P1 (execution, analysis, testing, and approval of managers). In the prototype analysis were simulated the target cost variants for the basic functions and especially the auxiliary ones of "P1" (at the level of the auxiliary functions were the most cost reduction simulations; the cost reduction solutions were identified for each type of raw material – without affecting the level of quality perceived by future consumers and respecting all legal norms; all ingredients used have been tested and corresponded from the point of view of an authorized independent laboratory); the achieved target cost was accepted by the marketing (within the target price) and by the managers (within the target unit profit and the potential sales and production volumes);
- presented for approval the three changes to line 1 (one for decreasing cycle time in the module considered bottleneck capacity module; MDC was used); the changes were approved by the managers (they were feasible); changes were made on time; no further modifications of the line were necessary after the launch of the new product "P1" in trials or after the start of production;

- established the new standard unit costs; bill of materials was introduced in the company's software for line 1;
- the new SOPs were developed; and
- the operators participated in the training to learn the new SOPs related to the new P1.

4. *Result:* The target of reducing unit costs by 35% has been met. The loading of line 1 with the new product "P1" has been completed (loading degree of approximately 55%). All initial targets were met: target markets for the future product and potential sales volumes for each market, the required level of raw material cost, the required level of investment, time to market, the required level of productivity and the quality characteristics. The $95,000 KAIZENSHIRO level was met and exceeded over time (CLWs on the new "P1" product decreased). The new "P1" product had the lowest price on the target markets compared to those of the competitors. Annual profitability has been met and sales have grown steadily.

The team leader of this project has conducted an evaluation of the degree of involvement of team members to achieve the improvement objectives for this project. The total target duration of 12 weeks of the project has been met.

6.2.4.4 Improvement Project 4: Problem-Solving Project for CLW (A3 – for Elimination of the Consumption of Stretch Wrap in Production Areas)

Concurrently with the development and implementation of solutions for kaizen and kaikaku projects (activities associated with *feedforward-driven control* – at the decision level, but carried out during production), projects are carried out to solve problems related to CLWs (activities assimilated with *concurrent-driven control*; using the A3 technique).

Figure 6.8 shows an A3 project for reducing of the consumption of stretch wrap in production modules.

The elimination of human errors in the packaging of semi-finished products has had positive effects in terms of reducing handling time and in terms of reducing scrap and rework.

Problem Solving A3 for CLW improvement (reduction of costs with auxiliary packaging materials in production modules)

Author: Project leader: AP; members: SAP and AAP   **Theme:**
Dept: Quality
Date: November 30th - January 15th

President:
Vice President:
Manager: EAP

Reducing of the Consumption of Stretch Wrap in Production Modules

Problem Situation:

Background: The packaging standard was defined for each type of packaging (in dimensions in millimeters - for length, width and depth; number of pieces / package; number of stocking levels and surface of a level; type of packaging - type of wooden pallet and type of stretch wrap; with photos and packing procedure).

Standard: Most food semi-finished products are stored on wooden pallets with cardboard sheets between them and wrapped with stretch wrap.

Current Situation: Packaging standards are not always respected by operators. There were sometimes small production delays and quality problems (scrap and rework of semi-finished products) - not measured.

Discrepancy: Stretch wrap consumption has increased by 25% in the last 3 months. The corresponding CLW is $12,500 per month.

Extent: Finding a way to pack and store the semi-finished products, so that stretch wrap is not used at all.

Rationale: The new semi-finished product storage solution ensures easy storage in the intermediate warehouse, can be easily handled and semi-finished products are protected from impurities.

Target:

Do What: review of all stretch wrap packaging processes in all production modules;
To What: identification of all types of stretch wrap and the types of packaging they were used for;
How Much: zero use of stretch wrap in the future;
By When: until January 15;

Cause Analysis:
Potential Causes:
1) human error
2) lack of time to comply with standard packaging
3) use stretch wrap for other activities
4) use of unnecessary high quality stretch wrap
Problems:
Discrepancies between physical and system stock;
Urgent stretch wrap orders;
Increasing the standard unit cost of products;
Difficulties in budgeting stretch wrap consumption;

How Checked:
1) the project team observations
2) the project team observations
3) the project team observations
4) the project team observations

Results:
1) Differences in the consumption standard of stretch wrap in SAP

Countermeasures:

Short Term: Increasing the supervision of stretch wrap packaging

Long Term: All semi-finished products A, B and C will be stored in gray plastic boxes of one type and size.

Why Recommended: The minimum and maximum levels of the boxes are defined. The cost of plastic boxes was considered feasible (annual benefits being $ 6000 /year- in addition to eliminating CLW). Both the plastic boxes and the packaging foil are reused, the losses being zero.

Implementation:

WHAT	WHO	WHEN	ACTUAL	REASON
1.) search 3 suppliers of plastic boxes	Procurement team leader	December 10th	done	
2.) choosing a supplier	Procurement team leader	December 10th	done	
3.) development of SOP for the new packaging standard	Production team leader	December 15th	done	
4.) operator training for the new packaging standard	Production team leader	December 20th	done	
5.) implementation of the new packaging standard in a pilot module	Production team leader	January 7th	done	
6.) checking the results of the new packaging in the pilot project	Production team leader	January 7th	done	
7.) SOP packaging extension to all modules in production	Production Manager	January 15th	done	

Follow-up:
How/ When Check:
1.) 30-day verification of the effectiveness of the new packaging method

Recommendations:
1.) Development of a standard for cleaning gray plastic boxes.

$12,500	actual CLW: $ 12,500 per month.
$10,000	
$7,500	
$5,000	
$2,500	
0	target
	December February

FIGURE 6.8

Elimination of the consumption of stretch wrap for the packaging of semi-finished products for all modules in production.

6.2.5 Tangible and Intangible Results of SBTP at BB Plant

For BB Plant, achieving their long-term goals by implementing SBTP through planning and developing synchronous profitable operations was a success, both in the period of decreasing sales and in the period of their increasing.

Among the positive effects of using SBTP are:

- establishing a synchronous and profitable production system that covered all activities from receiving orders to delivering finished products;
- synchronization between the sales plan and the manufacturing plan;
- change from monthly production planning to weekly scheduling in the week before the production one;
- reduction of lead time and working hours;
- performing a better management of WIP and production inventory;
- annual fulfillment of KAIZENSHIRO; and
- use of manufacturing improvement budgets.

In order to carry out improvement projects to meet KAIZENSHIRO, the management of BB Plant began to pursue a constantly profitable operating environment by continuously and scientifically identifying in the structure of manufacturing costs of 30–50% CLWs. The annual target for improving CLWs has been set at a minimum of 6% per year for the next five years. All overall management indicators were improvements (profitability, productivity, quality, cost, delivery, safety, and morale). In turn, all the people at BB Plant were involved in kaizen and kaikaku improvement projects (feedforward-driven control) and in problem-solving projects (concurrent-driven control). The real effects of the SBTP system became more evident after the first three years of sustained work to achieve the annual objectives of KAIZENSHIRO. The OEE level reached 85%. The continuous achievement of takt profit and takt time concurrently contributed to ensuring the state of consistent synchronous profitable operations.

In addition to the tangible effects of implementing SBTP at BB Plant, there were multiple positive intangible effects (which are not quantifiable and cannot be presented mathematically), such as:

- continuous and real involvement of top managers in making improvements to achieve KAIZENSHIRO (internal profit plan);
- teamwork has been improved among all employees (operators, specialists, office staff, and managers);

- employees became more motivated;
- job satisfaction increased due to the collaboration between all BB Plant employees;
- clear improvement tasks have led to people's confidence in the production system;
- people's general knowledge of their work area has increased;
- people's morale has risen in the face of solving the daily problems they face; and
- the visitors from PP Plant had good impressions about the changes made, etc.

6.2.6 Conclusion: Obstacles Encountered While Implementing SBTP

In order to reduce or eliminate the main obstacles to the implementation of SBTP at BB Plant, it was necessary to:

- obtaining collaboration between different departments and ensuring flexibility regarding CLW information center and module activity panel;
- increasing the level of self-discipline of all those involved in collecting data on losses and waste, their continuous transformation into CLWs, and then establishing CCLWs. Every new system has new rules. The adherence to these new rules is essential in maintaining and expanding the SBTP. The employees of BB Plant understood the role and the concurrent need to work in a synchronous way with the clients and a profitable way for the company. Their spirit of cooperation has been essential since the first weeks of the introduction of SBTP;
- the planning, development, and implementation of SBTP at BB Plant was considered as a part of their production system. Elimination of CLWs/CCLWs and making improvements to meet takt profit and takt time have become a way of life for all employees at BB Plant. An important part was that the experience of the consultants in SBTP was taken over with confidence by the top managers and then by all the people in the company and beyond.

By eliminating these three major obstacles from BB Plant, the premise was created to use the SBTP mechanism in order to have a manufacturing management system that ensures true synchronization and profitability.

6.3 CONCLUSION: WHEN JUST SYNCHRONOUS OPERATIONS ARE NO LONGER ENOUGH, THEN SPEED-BASED TARGET PROFIT ...

Requests and expectations from headquarters and top managers for implementing the SBTP mechanism are often successfully met. Plant managers often make statements like this: "Through SBTP we have built a more profitable production management system that facilitates directing our improvements to a goal clearly defined and understood by all of us: KAIZENSHIRO. Now we will be able to better respond to our customers' orders and we will be able to better plan the annual profit and especially the multiannual one".

The implementation of SBTP and implicitly a control trilogy for KAIZENSHIRO (feedforward-driven control, concurrent-driven control, and feedback-driven control) created the necessary conditions to achieve annual KAIZENSHIRO and implicitly a continuous increase of competitiveness.

In conclusion, it can be said that when the level of profitability is no longer sufficiently met by activities to synchronize operations to market needs (fulfillment of takt time), then the concurrent fulfillment of takt profit is needed.

Bibliography

Akao, Y., 1991. *Hoshin Kanri: Policy Deployment for Successful TQM* (Originally published as Hoshin Kanri Kaysuyo No Jissai, 1988). New York, NY: Productivity Press.

Altendorfer, K., 2013. *Capacity and Inventory Planning for Make-to-Order Production Systems: The Impact of a Customer Required Lead Time Distribution*, Springer International Publishing. American National Standards Institute, 1983. Industrial Engineering Terminology. Hoboken, NJ: Wiley-Interscience.

Ansari, S., Bell, J. and Okano, H., 2006. Target costing: Uncharted research territory. In: *Handbooks of Management Accounting Research*, vol. 2. Amsterdam: Elsevier, pp. 507–530.

Burnham, D. C., 1972. *Productivity Improvement*. New York, NY: Columbia University Press.

Burrows, G. and Chenhall, R. H., 2012. Target costing: First and second comings. *Accounting History Review*, 22(2), 127–142.

Chau, V. S. and Witcher, B. J., 2008. Dynamic capabilities for strategic team performance management: The case of Nissan. *Team Performance Management*, 14(3/4), pp. 179–191.

Chiarini, A. and Vagnoni, E., 2014. World-class manufacturing by Fiat. Comparison with Toyota production system from a strategic management, management accounting, operations management and performance measurement dimension. *International Journal of Production Research*, 53(2), pp. 590–606.

Choi, T. Y. and Liker, J. K., 1995. Bringing Japanese continuous improvement approaches to US manufacturing: The roles of process orientation and communications. *Decision Sciences*, 26(5), pp. 589–620.

Cooper, R., 1995. *When Lean Enterprises Collide: Competing Through Confrontation*. Boston, MA: Harvard Business Press.

Cooper, R., 1996. Costing techniques to support corporate strategy: Evidence from Japan. *Management Accounting Research*, 7(2), pp 219–246.

Cooper, R. and Slagmulder, R., 1999. Developing profitable new products with target costing. *Sloan Management Review*, 40(4), pp. 23–33.

Cooper, R. and Slagmulder, R., 2004. Interorganizational cost management and relational context. *Accounting, Organizations and Society*, 29(1), pp. 1–26.

Cua, K. O., McKone, K. E. and Schroeder, R. G., 2001. Relationships between implementation of TQM, JIT, and TPM and manufacturing performance. *Journal of Operations Management*, 19(6), pp 675–694.

Dahlgaard-Park, S. M., 2011. The quality movement: Where are you going? *Total Quality Management & Business Excellence*, 22(5), pp. 493–516.

Deming, W. E., 1986. Center for advanced engineering study. In: *Out of the Crisis*. Cambridge, MA: Massachusetts Institute of Technology.

Drucker, P. F., May 1963. Managing for Business Effectiveness. Boston, MA: *Harvard Business Review*, pp. 53–60.

Drucker, P. F., 2006. *The Practice of Management*. New York, NY: HarperCollins.

Feigenbaum, A. V., 1956. Total quality-control. *Harvard Business Review*, 34(6), pp. 93–101.

Gadiesh, O. and Gilbert, J. L., 1998. Profit Polls: A Fresh Look at Strategy. *Harvard Business Review*, May–June 1998.

Gåsvaer, D. and Axelson, von J., 2012. *Kaikaku-radical improvement in production.* In: *International Conference on Operations and Maintenance.* Singapore: World Academy of Science, Engineering and Technology, pp. 758–765.

Harrison, D. K. and Petty, D. J., 2002. *Systems for Planning and Control in Manufacturing,* Oxford: Elsevier Science.

Helmrich, K., 2003. *Productivity Process: Methods and Experiences of Measuring and Improving.* Stockholm: International MTM Directorate.

Hino, S., 2006. *Inside the Mind of Toyota: Management Principles for Enduring Growth.* New York, NY: Taylor & Francis Group.

Hirano, H., 2009. *JIT Implementation Manual – The Complete Guide to Just-in-Time Manufacturing.* New York, NY: CRC Press.

Hosomi, S., Scarbrough, P. and Ueno, S., 2017. Management accounting in Japan: *Current practices.* In: Lin, Z. (Ed.). *The Routledge Handbook of Accounting in Asia.* Abingdon: Routledge.

Imai, M., 1997. *Gemba Kaizen: A Commonsense Low—Cost Approach to Management.* New York, NY: McGraw-Hill.

Ishikawa, K., 1980. *QC Circle Koryo: General Principles of the QC Circle.* Tokyo: QC Circle Headquarters, Union of Japanese Scientists and Engineers.

Jackson, T. L., 2006. *Hoshin Kanri for the Lean Enterprise: Developing Competitive Capabilities and Managing Profit.* New York, NY: CRC Press.

Jacobs, F. R., Berry, W. L., Whybark, D. C. and Vollmann, T. E., 2011. *Manufacturing Planning and Control for Supply Chain Management.* New York, NY: McGraw-Hill Education.

Juran, J. M., 1995. *Managerial Breakthrough: The Classic Book on Improving Management Performance.* New York, NY: McGraw-Hill.

Kaplan, R. S., 1990. *Measure for Manufacturing Excellence.* Boston, MA: Harvard Business School Press.

Kato, Y., 1993. Target costing support systems: Lessons from leading Japanese companies. *Management Accounting Research,* 4(1), 33–47.

Lee, J. Y., Chen, I., Chen, R. C. and Chung, C. H., 2002. A target-costing based strategic decision support system. *Journal of Computer Information Systems,* 43(1), pp. 110–116

Lee, J. Y. and Monden, Y., 1996. Kaizen costing: Its structure and cost management functions. *Advances in Management Accounting,* 5, 27–40.

Liker, J., 2004. *The Toyota Way: 14 Management Principles from the World's Greatest Manufacturer.* New York, NY: McGraw-Hill Education.

Mather, H., 1986. *Competitive Manufacturing.* Upper Saddle River, NY: Prentice Hall.

Mitchell, F., Nørreklit, H. and Jakobsen, M., 2013. *The Routledge Companion to Cost Management.* New York, NY: Taylor & Francis.

Monden, Y., 1992. *Cost Management in the New Manufacturing Age: Innovations in the Japanese Automotive Industry.* New York, NY: Productivity Press.

Monden, Y., 2000. *Japanese Cost Management.* London: World Scientific, Imperial College Press.

Monden, Y., 2012. *Toyota Production System: An Integrated Approach to Just-in-Time.* Boca Raton, FL: CRC Press.

Monden, Y., Kosuga, M., Nagasaka, Y., Hiraoka, S. and Hoshi, N., 2007. *Japanese Management Accounting Today.* Singapore: World Scientific Publishing.

Nakajima, S., 1988. *Introduction to TPM: Total Productive Maintenance.* New York, NY: Productivity Press.

Ohno, T., 1978. *Toyota Production System–Aiming at an Off-Scale Management.* Tokyo: Diamond-Verlag.

Ohno, T., 1982. How the Toyota production system was created. *Japanese Economy,* 10(4), pp. 83–101.

Ohno, T., 1988. *Toyota Production System: Beyond Large-Scale Production.* New York, NY: Productivity Press.

Posteucă, A., 2011. Management branding (MB): Performance improvement through contextual managerial behavior development. *International Journal of Productivity and Performance Management,* 60(5), pp. 529–543.

Posteucă, A., 2013. Green Lean methodology: Enterprise energy management for industrial companies. *Academy of Romanian Scientists—"Productica" Scientific Session,* 5(1), pp. 17–30.

Posteucă, A., 2015. Manufacturing Cost Policy Deployment by Systematic and Systemic Improvement. PhD diss., University "Politehnica" Bucharest.

Posteucă, A., 2018. *Manufacturing Cost Policy Deployment (MCPD) Transformation: Uncovering Hidden Reserves of Profitability.* New York, NY: Productivity Press/Routledge – Taylor & Francis.

Posteucă, A., 2019. *Manufacturing Cost Policy Deployment (MCPD) Profitability Scenarios: Systematic and Systemic Improvement of Manufacturing Costs.* New York, NY: Productivity Press/Routledge – Taylor & Francis.

Posteucă, A. and Sakamoto, S., 2017. *Manufacturing Cost Policy Deployment (MCPD) and Methods Design Concept (MDC): The Path to Competitiveness.* New York, NY: Taylor & Francis.

Posteucă, A. and Zapciu, M., 2013. Quick changeover: Continuous improvement and production costs reduction for plastic-molding machines. *The 7th International Working Conference,* Belgrade, Serbia, 1(June 3–7), pp. 141–147.

Posteucă, A. and Zapciu, M., 2015a. Beyond target costing: Manufacturing cost policy deployment for new products. *Applied Mechanics and Materials,* 809–810, pp. 1480–1485. ISSN – 1662-7482.

Posteucă, A. and Zapciu, M., 2015b. Continuous improvement of the effectiveness of equipment driven by the dynamics of cost reduction. *Sustainable Design and Manufacturing, The Journal of Innovation Impact,* 8(2), pp. 59–173 Future Technology Press, KES International – Volume Editors.

Posteucă, A. and Zapciu, M., 2015c. Process innovation: Holistic scenarios to reduce total lead time. Academy of Romanian Scientists—"Productica" scientific session.

Posteucă, A. and Zapciu, M., 2015d. Setup time and cost reduction in conditions of low volume and overcapacity. *University "Politehnica" of Bucharest, UPB Scientific Bulletin, Series D,* 77 pp. 325–336.

Riggs, J. L., 1983. *Productivity by Objectives Results-Oriented Solutions to the Productivity Puzzle.* Englewood Cliff, NJ: Prentice-Hall.

Rother, M. and Shook, J., 2003. *Learning to See: Value Stream Mapping to Add Value and Eliminate Muda.* Boston, MA: Lean Enterprise Institute, Taylor & Francis.

Sakamoto, S., 1992. Design concept for methods engineering. In: *Maynard Industrial Engineering Handbook.* Hodson, W. K. (Ed.). New York, NY: McGraw-Hill.

Sakamoto, S., 2006. Methods design concept: An effective approach to profitability. *Journal of Philippine Industrial Engineering,* 3(2), pp. 1–11.

Sakamoto, S., 2009. Return to work measurement. *Industrial Engineering*, Norcross, GA: Institute of Industrial and Systems Engineers (IISE), 41, p. 24.

Sakamoto, S., 2010. *Beyond World-Class Productivity: Industrial Engineering Practice and Theory*. London: Springer.

Schonberger, R. J., 1986. *World-Class Manufacturing*. New York, NY: The Free Press.

Seeanner, F., 2013. *Multi-Stage Simultaneous Lot-Sizing and Scheduling: Planning of Flow Lines with Shifting Bottlenecks*. Wiesbaden: Springer Fachmedien Wiesbaden.

Sekine, K. and Arai, K., 1998. *TPM for the Lean Factory: Innovative Methods and Worksheets for Equipment Management*. New York, NY: Taylor & Francis.

Shingo, S., 1989. *Study of Toyota Production System from Industrial Viewpoint*. Tokyo: Japan Management Association.

Shirose, K., 1999. *TPM: Total Productive Maintenance: New Implementation Program in Fabrication and Assembly Industries*. Tokyo: JIPM.

Stamatis, D. H., 2010. *The OEE Primer: Understanding Overall Equipment Effectiveness, Reliability, and Maintainability*. Boca Raton, FL: CRC Press.

Suzuki, T., 1994. *TPM in Process Industries*. New York, NY: Productivity Press/CRC Press – Taylor & Francis Group.

Swedish Federation of Productivity Services, 1993. *SAM Training Program*. Stockholm: Swedish Federation of Productivity Services.

Tanaka, T., 1994. Kaizen budgeting: Toyota's cost-control system under TQC. *Journal of Cost Management for the Manufacturing Industry*, 3 (Fall), pp. 56–62.

Tapping, D., Luyster, T. and Shuker, T., 2002. *Value Stream Management: Eight Steps to Planning, Mapping, and Sustaining Lean Improvements*. New York, NY: Taylor & Francis Group.

Thomopoulos, N. T., 2013. *Assembly Line Planning and Control*. Cham: Springer International Publishing.

Winslow, T. F., 1911. *The Principles of Scientific Management*. New York, NY: Harper and Brothers.

Womack, J. P. and Jones, D. T., 1996. *Lean Thinking: Banish Waste and Create Wealth in Your Corporation*. New York, NY: Free Press.

Womack, J. P., Jones, D. T. and Roos, D., 1990. *The Machine That Changed the World: The Story of Lean Production—Toyota's Secret Weapon in the Global Car Wars That Is Now Revolutionizing World Industry*. New York, NY: Free Press.

Yamamoto, Y., 2013. *Kaikaku in production toward creating unique production systems*. PhD thesis, Department of Innovation, Design and Engineering, Mälardalen University, Eskilstuna, Sweden.

Yamashina, H. and Kubo, T., 2002. Manufacturing cost deployment. *International Journal of Production Research*, 40(16), pp. 4077–4091.

Zammori, F., Braglia, M. and Frosolini, M., 2011. Stochastic overall equipment effectiveness. *International Journal of Production Research*, 49(21), pp. 6469–6490.

Zandin, K. B., 1980. *MOST Work Measurement System*. New York, NY: Marcel Dekker.

Zawawi, N. H. M. and Hoque, Z., 2010. Research in management accounting innovations: An overview of its recent development. *Qualitative Research in Accounting & Management*, 7(4), pp. 505–568.

Zengin, Y. and Ada, E., 2010. Cost management through product design: Target costing approach. *International Journal of Production Research*, 48(19), pp. 5593–5611.

Zoysa, A. D. and Herath, S. K., 2007. Standard costing in Japanese firms: Reexamination of its significance in the new manufacturing environment. *Industrial Management & Data Systems*, 107(2), pp. 271–283.

Index

Printed in the United States
By Bookmasters